WRITING LIFE STORIES

HOW TO MAKE memories into MEMOIRS,

ideas into ESSAYS, and life into LITERATURE

FULLY REVISED SECOND EDITION

BILL ROORBACH

with Kristen Keckler, PhD

WRITER'S DIGEST BOOKS
Cincinnati, Ohio
www.writersdigest.com

For more fine books from F+W Publications, visit www.fwpublications.com.

22 21 20 19   21 20 19

Distributed in the U.K. and Europe by David & Charles, Brunel House, Newton Abbot, Devon, TQ12 4PU, England, Tel: (+44) 1626 323200, Fax: (+44) 1626 323319, E-mail: postmaster@davidandcharles.co.uk.

Visit Writersdigest.com for information on more resources for writers. To receive a free weekly e-mail newsletter delivering tips and updates about writing and about Writer's Digest products, register directly at http://newsletters.fwpublications.com.

Library of Congress Cataloging-in-Publication Data
Roorbach, Bill.

Writing life stories : how to make memories into memoirs, ideas into essays, and life into literature / by Bill Roorbach with Kristen Keckler. -- 10th anniversary ed.

   p. cm.

Includes index.
ISBN 978-1-58297-527-6 (pbk. : alk. paper)
1. Autobiography--Authorship. 2. Report writing. I. Keckler, Kristen. II. Title.
CT25.R66 2008
808'.06692--dc22

2008006395

EDITED BY LAUREN MOSKO
DESIGNED BY TERRI WOESNER
PRODUCTION COORDINATED BY MARK GRIFFIN
COVER IMAGE ©ISTOCKPHOTO.COM/PETER ZELEI

For Reba
July 17, 1926–April 16, 2006

ABOUT THE AUTHORS

Bill Roorbach writes fiction and nonfiction, and is the author of numerous books, including a novel, *The Smallest Color*, and a book of stories, *Big Bend*, which won the Flannery O'Connor Award for Short Fiction. The title story, "Big Bend," won an O. Henry Prize as well. *Temple Stream: a Rural Odyssey*, his most recent book, won the 2006 Maine Book Award in nonfiction and received a Furthermore Grant from the Kaplan Foundation. Other books are *Into Woods* (essays); *Summers With Juliet* (memoir); *A Place on Water* (essays, with Robert Kimber and Wesley McNair), *A Healing Touch* (essays, with Gerry Boyle, Wesley McNair, Richard Russo, Susan Sterling, and Monica Wood). Bill is also the editor of the Oxford anthology *Contemporary Creative Nonfiction: The Art of Truth*. His short work has appeared in *The Atlantic*, *Harper's*, *New York*, *The New York Times Magazine*, and many others. He has taught at the University of Maine at Farmington, Ohio State, and Colby College, and currently holds the William H.P. Jenks Chair in Contemporary American Letters at the College of the Holy Cross in Worcester, Massachusetts. He lives in Farmington, Maine, and is at work on a novel. For more information, updated biography, signed copies of books, news about readings and workshops, and to send queries and comments directly to the author, go to www.billroorbach.com.

Kristen Keckler is a teacher, writer, and editor whose PhD (University of North Texas) is in the field of creative nonfiction. She writes in all genres—nonfiction, fiction, and poetry—and her work has appeared in numerous magazines and journals, including *Ecotone*, *Sonora Review*, *The Dallas Morning News*, *cold-drill*, *Palo Alto Review*, and *Concho River Review*. She was editor-in-chief of *North Texas Review* and an editor of the Katherine Anne Porter Prize in Short Fiction, a national book contest co-sponsored by the UNT Press. On the way, she's worked as a clown, a cook, a librarian, and a group home counselor. She's just completing a memoir about life and work called *What Do You Do?*

TABLE OF
CONTENTS

PREFACE

So much has changed in the ten years since the first edition of *Writing Life Stories* was published. For writers, perhaps the biggest development has been the wholesale advent of the Internet, with its constant evolution, its endless opportunities for interaction, for instant research, for locating and speaking directly to readers via e-mail, blogs, and Web sites. Everyone's typing now. Continuing events like those of September 11, 2001, bring subtle changes in outlook around the world and underscore the need for freedom of expression everywhere. Cell phones, merely irritating in 1998, are everywhere, including my pocket.

In my own life, other shifts: my daughter, Elysia, was born in 2000; my mother, Reba, died in 2006. In between, both of my beloved dogs died, as well. I left a tenured position at Ohio State University to write full time, only to accept an endowed chair elsewhere when the opportunity arose. The new car I bought when this book first came out now has 150,000 miles on it. Time for change there, as well.

Memoir as a popular genre has moved past most of its early controversies, and enjoys new standing in the world of letters and in the university. But there's also brand-new hullabaloo, such as the James Frey scandal—an ex-addict makes stuff up, then lies about lying—or the Deborah Rodriguez dustup:

did all she said happened *really* happen at her beauty school in Kabul? And is this the end of the world? Of course it's not. That roar you hear comes from the explosive power of narrative as applied to real life. What is the role of memoir and the essay in the quest for truth? Or even Truth? You'll answer these questions over and over, always in your own way, with every paragraph you write.

To ensure breadth of outlook, I enlisted the help of a writer very different from me, Kristen Keckler, and together we have brought *Writing Life Stories* to a new century. Kristen adds a woman's point of view to what had been an excessively male enterprise, as well as a scholar's clear eye (her PhD is in the field of creative nonfiction). She's younger than I am, too, a whole generation younger, and she helped me see that cassette tapes were no longer the best way to record anything. And of course, that was just the beginning of her contribution.

We meant to just freshen these pages a little, but in the end, Kristen and I have wrought great changes. Old friends of *Writing Life Stories* will find plenty here to re-charge their batteries, lots of new ideas and fresh instruction. First-time readers will join those returning to find new exercises in every chapter, clearer explanations of difficult issues like the use of metaphor, more up-to-date information on publishing, examples from newer writers and more recent titles to complement the dozens of examples in the original edition, and a much more sophisticated look at the Internet. We've updated the very popular reading list with scores of new books in our field, every one of which challenges and ultimately changes the way we think of memoir, literary journalism, and the personal essay—those genres which together have come to be thought of and taught as creative nonfiction.

The new *Writing Life Stories* is still the perfect book for the independent writer trying to find her way into a whole lifetime of great material, but it's also much improved as a tool for the creative nonfiction or composition classroom.

Thanks for taking us home. Let us hear how you do!

INTRODUCTION

*In most books the I, or first person, is omitted; in this
it will be retained; that, in respect to egotism, is the
main difference. We commonly do not remember
that it is, after all, always the first person that is
speaking. I should not talk so much about myself
if there were anybody else whom I knew as well.
Unfortunately, I am confined to this theme by the
narrowness of my experience.*

—Henry David Thoreau

Gow Farris had a lifetime of stories and ideas. He surely had something to say.
Yet when he sat down at his keyboard to get it written, nothing came, or nothing he cared to show anyone, certainly nothing like the stories he'd always told
at family parties, the stories his kids said he'd better write down, the stories his
grandchildren were starting to ask for. The surprising thing was that Gow had
been a newswriter for forty-five years: forty-five years of writing other people's

stories; forty-five years of a confident professional approach to the facts; forty-five years of successful writing for a major newspaper.

Retirement brought this: silence.

Silence when he'd expected his life and humor and lessons to pour out whole, short memoir after short memoir, essay after essay, article after article, book after book. What was going wrong?

He needed a change of place, that's all. He kissed his wife good-bye (his third wife, truth to tell, quite a story there: death and heartbreak in the first marriage, betrayal and loneliness in the second), called a rental agent he knew on Cape Cod, hied himself for an amazingly inexpensive off-season ten days to Nantucket, where many writers had gone before him. Perfect. The surf pounded distantly, no phone to ring, no visitors, no pressures upon him, not even mail.

"My brother died when I was eighteen," he wrote. Always, he'd wanted to write a memoir of his brother. But nothing followed, just ten straight mornings of staring at his notebook. Guilty walks (longer each day), hourly snacks, resharpened pencils.

Occasionally he wrote lame sentences of description (his brother's great size, his brother's big teeth, his brother's favorite expression) that did nothing to bring his clear memories of the lost sibling to the page, nothing to shape those memories into something someone else might enjoy reading—a memoir—much less into anything resembling literature. Afternoons he roamed the October beach in writerly despair.

During the night before his last day on the island, he woke to a fit of inspiration, clicked on the bare bedside bulb, took notes for a different project, a memoir of his career. Next morning he didn't pause for breakfast, rushed to the kitchen table (he'd come to distrust the little desk his landlord had provided), wrote, "I was a newspaperman for forty-five years," and kept going, ten pages, a rush of words, great relief, something to show for his trip and the lonely days of his vigil.

Home the next night, he pulled out his pages and read. This didn't take long.

He read fast and with growing embarrassment. What he'd meant triumphantly to show his new wife, he tucked into his desk drawer beneath a stack of similar pages. The day's ferry ride and drive home had given him enough perspective to hear clearly how the opening of his journalist's memoir came off: pompous, puffy, wordy, nostalgic, nothing like what he'd envisioned in that moment of wakefulness, as far from the truth as Pluto from the sun. Gow was a reasonable, humble, reserved person; Gow was a precise and no-nonsense man. Why couldn't he get that on the page?

I know Gow's story because after a couple more months of false starts and increasing discouragement, he signed up for a summer class I happened to be teaching at the University of Vermont. First day of class he sat there glowering at me.

Gow Farris was pissed.

And Gow, of course, is not alone.

Janet Bellweather had taught writing for nine years to high-school kids, knew all the rules, knew what she liked when it came to student work, knew how to get even the most challenging kids to pull off their headphones and write. Her particular pride came in helping her young students see that what they had to say mattered, that their lives were important, that they could reach readers. She had wonderful exercises. The kids had a blast. She'd march around the room giving praise and advice, urging and scolding, reading passages aloud. Janet was a great teacher, funny and smart and eloquent, passionate and caring, maybe even a little eccentric.

She had no trouble turning out the pages. She wrote short memoirs of her youth, many poems, an essay a month, even a column for the school district's award-winning newsletter. Her writing was sometimes funny, but seldom eloquent or passionate, and never eccentric. She showed it to friends, but few said much of anything when they were finished reading. A wan smile here and there. But never the praise and approval she wanted, except from her mother, who didn't understand why *The New Yorker* didn't buy every word. Janet didn't expect miracles on that order, but she couldn't understand why smaller magazines didn't seem interested in her. She had a folder of rejections thick as the phone book in Manhattan, where she lived. In rare moments of clarity, Janet knew why the magazines didn't take her work: it just wasn't as good as she knew she could make it. What was the problem? Why couldn't she do for herself what she did for her students every day?

Janet turned up in a memoir class I taught for the Riverside Writers' Group in New York City and right away—first night's class—raised her hand to make a comment, and in the course of this comment (ostensibly about writing memoir), she made it clear that she, too, was a teacher, that she, too, had written plenty, and, finally, that she didn't really need a class or know what had possessed her to sign up. She knew all the rules, she'd read all the books, she certainly didn't need us. Her intensity was both charming and frightening. She was nearly shouting: "I only want this class so that I might have an audience." She had a truly great essay subject: being single and wanting to stay that way.

Okay, Janet, okay! You're in the right place!

As were a wonderful, long list of my college and graduate-school students over the years, with more compelling stories than time to write them all (a semester is a bureaucratic unit, not a creative one), though sometimes the barriers to expression were a little different: "How do I get an A?" and more seriously, "Why should anyone want to read my story? I'm only eighteen (or twenty, or twenty-four) years old."

Drama is drama—the young woman whose sister was murdered had an obvious story, but then again, so did the young man in the same class who wrote about a different sort of disaster: a B on a high-school math test when he'd expected an A.

The story's in the telling.

Mindy Mallow-Dalmation was a junior at Colby College, where I taught briefly as a visiting professor. She was one of the ninety percent of my students convinced she had no true story to tell. I mean, she'd barely had a life yet! And what was so interesting about her struggles to find love while wearing black from head to toe? Who gave a flying flirt about her semester in France? Her obsession with her weight, her looks? Her love of exotic cooking? Her parents' withholding of love and praise? Her goofy hyphenated name? Weren't these just the standard woes of self-absorbed American college kids everywhere?

Yes, Mindy.

And no.

Other writers who have turned up in my classes: an accomplished poet (four fine books published, multiple awards), struggling unexpectedly with the switch to nonfiction; a physician with an amazing story—not getting told—of an internship in the Amazon; a Holocaust survivor whose book on his teen days in Warsaw, then Auschwitz (including a miraculous escape), was crawling past nine-hundred pages with no end in sight; a technical writer who wanted to find escape from aircraft manuals to write about his love of flying, but who—in his clinically self-aware way—knew his writing was dull, flattened by years of mechanical sentence making; a college professor in bioethics who wanted to dramatize bioethical case studies for a lay audience, but who couldn't get characters to emerge from the extraordinary people he'd known; a former nun who wanted to write about her faith, how it was broken, how it lately had come to be restored; a wildly successful "chick-lit" novelist who was struggling to find the nerve required to tell her own (not very romantic and not very comical but scary-as-hell) love story; a high-school kid bubbling over with the charming story of a horse, a girlfriend, and a homemade steeplechase; a businessman who wanted to combine tales of his travels with advice about commerce in Asia; a college sports star with a potentially career-ending secret; the list goes on and on. Good people all of them (well, all but one or two), with wonderful ideas and compelling stories and fascinating lives not coming to the page quite as simply as they'd hoped.

Welcome, welcome.

You, too: welcome. You and your stories are in the right place.

All the arts depend upon telepathy to some degree, but I believe that writing offers the purest distillation. I didn't tell you. You didn't ask me. I never opened my mouth and you never opened yours. We're not even in the same year together, let alone the same room ... except we are together. We're close.

—Stephen King

A Note on the Exercises

I have designed this book to take you by way of exercises through a series of approaches to certain branches of the vast field that's come to be called creative nonfiction, and especially to the making of memoir. The usefulness of any one exercise may not seem apparent at first, but if you trust yourself and trust the exercise, if you do the work on a steady (preferably daily) basis, you'll soon find what you're looking for: access to memory, access to material, access to ideas, access to the unconscious, and, finally, access to meaning—some corner of understanding that is both satisfyingly personal and invitingly universal, something readers will care about and like.

John Gardner, the quirky teacher, novelist, controversial medievalist, and all-around literary luminary and daredevil (he died in a tragic motorcycle crash), thought exercises were valuable because of the low stakes. And it's true; it's easier to set out to make something small than something large (like, say, the story of your life). Then again, Norman Mailer said that exercises are worse than useless, even damaging, precisely because the stakes are so small. Why waste time on something that doesn't count? All writing should be out there at the edge or in close to the heart, vital and urgent and necessary. I'm in between these titans (and getting crushed by huge ankles). I do think drills, the memorization of rules, are a waste of time. But when exercises discover material or open the vaults of memory or give access to real emotion or offer points of entry into the massive story that is a human life and mind, the stakes are high, indeed, and what may seem at first mere practice turns out to be writing of the most urgent kind.

To be taught, one must be willing to learn. One must be willing to change, sometimes in fundamental ways, because to learn *is* to change. A writer who really wants to make the next step—to grow—must learn to have compassion for herself as both writer and learner (so difficult for Mindy Mallow-Dalmation), must give up the idea that she's already arrived (remember Janet Bellweather?), must give up the idea that he already knows what to do (think of Gow Farris).

Here's a Confucian aphorism: "If you don't know where you are going, get there by a way you don't know."

And here, Shunryu Suzuki's famous observation from his peaceful and important (and perhaps puzzling) book, *Zen Mind, Beginner's Mind*: "In the beginner's mind are many possibilities, in the expert's mind there are few."

I like Donald Hall's one and only exercise, which he recommends in his essay "On Ambition," and which I'll freely paraphrase here: Write something better than the best thing ever written. Take all the time you wish.

The exercises in this book are meant to discover mounds of juicy material for you, of course. They're meant to give you practice, for sure. They're also meant to help you develop and then further develop your critical eye. But quietly, they are meant to challenge the ways you already write, the ways you already find material, the ways you have settled into and that—if my own experience and the fact that you have read this far are any indication—are no longer producing satisfactory results, much less great results.

Nancy Kuhl, one of my graduate students back when I taught at Ohio State (and now a well-regarded professor and much-published poet and nonfiction writer), included a note when she offered the use of some of her writing for this book: "I was a little resistant doing these exercises. When I examined that resistance, I learned some very valuable things about my writing process. So, for me, part of what was important about these exercises was paying attention to my own response to the assignments and thinking about what my response revealed about me as a writer."

Yes!

We all want to get to the masterpieces of our writing lives by the shortest route possible. Trouble is, the shortest route possible is always the road ahead.

Honestly examining whatever resistance you find in yourself and overcoming it (just simply doing the exercises is probably the best way) is going to be a key step in your improvement as a writer. In fact, it's the surest shortcut. Most of my students, and by extension most of the readers of this book, and probably you, gentle reader, are already good writers. It's certainly hard to turn the clock back, be a beginner again, a learner. I'm glad you're willing to try.

YOUR FIRST MILLION WORDS

R.V. Cassill, in his classic book of instruction, *Writing Fiction*, says a writer's apprenticeship isn't over until his first million words have been written.

Time to get to work.

CHAPTER ONE
GETTING STARTED

I certainly don't [enjoy writing]. I get a fine warm feeling when I'm doing well, but that pleasure is pretty much negated by the pain of getting started each day. Let's face it, writing is hell.

—*William Styron*

Why is it so hard to sit down and write? Great expectations, for one thing. Our favorite high-school English teacher, Janet Bellweather, is infinitely patient and caring with her charges at P.S. 239, but from herself expected excellence (yes, *The New Yorker*) instantly.

Our friend Gow Farris thought he'd take on a new kind of writing and an entirely new subject (his own life) and get it perfect—prize winningly publishable—the first time he tried.

Mindy Mallow-Dalmation just didn't think her life would be of much interest to anyone but her therapist, and even her therapist fell asleep half the time (Mindy said, to much laughter, in our classroom there at Colby College). And something else—the stuff she really wanted to talk about? The hard stuff? The kind of icky stuff? She didn't really actually in fact want to talk about.

Ease and instant excellence are illusions, illusions that successful writing conjures up, illusions that make it hard—maybe impossible—for Janet Bellweather or Gow Farris (or perhaps you) to believe that their (or your) favorite writers have gone through anything like the struggles Janet pretended not to have or the unexpected battle that made Gow so furious. And the idea that we aren't interesting, that more than likely people are going to make fun of how boring we are (while at the same time hiding all the most important stuff out of shame or self-protection) leads to crippling self-doubt, the kind of self-doubt that Mindy pre-empted with a continual, always articulate but obfuscatory attack on American culture, and jokes, really funny jokes, lots of jokes, and a wry, sometimes furious refusal to delve past the ironic surface of things.

To compound the problem, partners and friends and parents (and certainly we ourselves) are caught up in the old myth of talent: you have it or you don't, and there's no sense in struggling along if your first efforts aren't Shakespeare (or, more to the point, since we're talking about memoir here), Annie Dillard, Mary Karr, Frank McCourt, or Augusten Burroughs.

So often what's missing is compassion: compassion for the poor soul who turns to writing after a long day of less satisfying work; compassion for the creative one, who can't rest till the story is made, even while those around him play; compassion for the learner, too, the person who at any age sits down to write thinking she already has what it takes, only to discover, as all good writers continually do, that there is still a lot to learn; compassion, in the end, for you, gentle writer, for you yourself.

EXERCISE ONE: *A Clean, Well-Lighted Place*

Of course the name of this exercise comes from an Ernest Hemingway story, but I can't help but think of Virginia Woolf when I give this assignment, which is about compassion, really, about having compassion for yourself as learner and seeing to the needs of that learner.

In her series of lectures and subsequent book *A Room of One's Own*, published in 1929, Virginia Woolf points out the unhappy fact that women often didn't (and don't) have a place where they might get some thinking and work of their own done, away from the duties of the mother, the wife, the housekeeper (and today, all of the above plus full-time employment, elder care, late-life graduate degrees, cell phone and e-mail accounts).

The idea here—male or female—is to set yourself up in a decent writing environment. Not too beautiful (lest you get distracted by the view), not too Spartan (lest you find it best avoided), but a place you can hope to be uninterrupted for the blocks of time available for writing.

In my house, I used to write in a small attic room (hot in summer, but that was okay) with a single window looking on grapevines and bird feeders, a spruce tree, a lilac, a tamarack, the porch roof, the clothes-line. That room is now my daughter's—Elysia, born in 2000. Which was the year I converted an old sugar shack into a studio. I like being out separate from the house, have a sense of walking to work in the morning, even if the walk is only a hundred feet or so. My desk is simply an old door set on two-drawer file cabinets. Add a good chair (my aching back), an old lamp, bookshelves along the walls, a maddening laptop, a long row of bubbled-glass windows. Also a lot of junk: seashells, coins, stacks of old manuscripts, canceled checks, piles of letters, CDs, maps, odd postcards and cookie fortunes and notes to myself, a sleeping bag for naps, a wood stove for winter heat, a calculator, scissors, blank note-books (empty and full). (The story of building that little haven can be found in my book *Temple Stream*, which among many other things in-cludes the story of the birth of my daughter.) And now even that refuge is more often than not superseded by a secondary desktop in my office at some new job, the arm of a couch in a hospital waiting room, or the coffee table at a new friend's house on the road, even a nice, flat rock in a goat's cozy crag.

If there's nowhere obvious to set yourself up, be like the great La-kota chief Crazy Horse, who said, "This is my lodge!" wherever he had to stay, even when finally imprisoned. (Since we're on the subject of writing nonfiction—and since in chapter five I'll quote from the book—I think it's appropriate to let you know that I learned about Crazy Horse in Ian Frazier's beautifully hybrid work of memoir, history, journalism, and geography, *Great Plains*.)

Say out loud: "This is my office!"

Don't get fancy; just give yourself some continuity.

I'm thinking of Mario Puzo, who, flush from the success of his novel *The Godfather*, decided to build himself a beautiful office off the back of his house, a large, bright room with two huge desks and everything a writer could possibly want. Trouble was, he couldn't write there, and before long he went back to the kitchen table, where, amid the bustle of his household and in the midst of the lives of his children, he got back to work.

Talent alone won't make you a success. Neither will being in the right place at the right time, unless you are ready. The most important question is: "Are you ready?"

—Johnny Carson

Memoir Is Memory's Truth

Let's try for a working definition of the word *memoir*: A memoir is a true story, a work of narrative built directly from the memory of its writer, with an added element of creative research. In memoir, the writer is also the protagonist—the person to whom the events of the story happen—or at least an observer closely involved with the protagonists. Memoir arises in and exists only because of the first-person singular: the *I* remembering.

When I say memoir, I don't mean one's memoirs (plural) in the sense of one's whole life presented as a historical artifact. That's for the famous—heads of state, Nobel Prize winners, heroes, celebrities—tomes not infrequently ghostwritten (and not infrequently written badly, come to think of it). I mean memoir (singular) in the sense the word is used by the editors of, say, *Harper's Magazine* or *The Sun* when they publish narratives of real lives. I mean memoir in the sense that Frank Conroy's publishers use when they characterize his classic story of youth, *Stop-Time*, and in the sense Jeannette Walls's publishers use when they talk about her harrowing book about her eccentric family, *The Glass Castle*.

Phillip Lopate (an important teacher of mine, whom I will certainly quote again) has wryly called such work "half-life memoirs," works created before much of the story can be known. But, of course, the ambition of memoir (as opposed to memoirs) isn't often historical but *literary*. Information is almost never the first goal of memoir; expression often is. Beauty—of form, of language, of meaning—always takes precedence over mere accuracy, truth over mere facts. The successful memoirist respects facts, uses them accurately, rigorously represses the human impulse to lie or embellish, but knows that truth is both different from facts and greater than facts, and not always their sum.

Memoir is a report to others from foreign territory: the territory of the writer, of the self, of an *I*. When I say memoir, I only mean memory put to the page (as if memory could be put to a page—that "putting" is an act of art, not transcription, a fact we quickly recognize when we go to try). I do mean a true story, unadorned, but always a true story laid down with the understanding that memory can be faulty, that images fade, that the *I* itself is a construction, a kind of fiction capable only of representing part of the writer at any given time.

Tobias Wolff said it well in the small acknowledgments paragraph preceding his first book-length memoir, *This Boy's Life*:

> I have been corrected on some points, mostly of chronology. Also my mother thinks that a dog I describe as ugly was actually quite handsome. I've allowed some of these points to stand, because this is a book of memory, and memory has its own story to tell. But I have done my best to make it tell a truthful story.

In fiction writing, the contract with the reader has to do with "that willing suspension of disbelief which constitutes poetic faith" (Samuel Taylor Coleridge's memorable and oft-quoted or paraphrased or just plain butchered line). The writer implicitly says, *I'm making this up, but please go ahead and pretend all of it really happened. Enjoy.* In memoir, the writer implicitly says, *Hey, this is factual. You can believe it. Enjoy.* Both fiction writer and memoirist, of course, may be fudging a little or a lot: the fiction may be based absolutely in fact; the memoirist may be, consciously or unconsciously, a liar. When it comes to ourselves, we all have blind spots, whole blind oceans. Dishonest or honest, the contract remains the same, and thus readerly enjoyment remains the same. Every writer of memoir has his own conscience to grapple with, his own ethical stance when it comes to matters such as invented dialogue, compound characters, telescoped time. What constitutes artistic license, and what constitutes lying? The border shifts writer to writer, story to story. But there *are* borders. Best is to go with your conscience, to write in good faith. Because even the best liars get caught sometimes, and the results can be unfortunate, even ugly.

Terry Gross asked David Sedaris (on her NPR program, *Fresh Air*) how true his poignant and often hilarious memoirs are. "True enough," Sedaris replied. Good answer.

Memoir is not journalism, though journalism relies more heavily than many journalists like to admit on the same faulty human memory—that subjective sieve—that memoir does. (Old Russian insult: "He lies like an eyewitness.") This is a fact you need not repeatedly apologize for. The vagaries of memory are a given, accepted by readers of memoir, and might be stated once and for all as follows: I'm going to have to fill in some of the details where memory or my photo albums or my journals don't help me; to get to the truth, I'm going to have to make up certain things or disagree with the memories of others.

Disclaimers can be helpful—just a note before a stretch of dialogue, something like, "We talked, and it went something like this." Or, "My first abusive boyfriend—let's call him Jackson Phist—charmed me at first." A disclaimer can amend the contract with the reader, and as long as she's been warned what she's getting, she's got little reason to complain. Maxine Hong Kingston uses fiction in the service of nonfiction in her great book *China Men*. She announces that her father won't talk about his past, particularly not about the route of his emigration from China to the U.S., and then tells us that she's just going to have to make his story up. She does this in a sophisticated way, using extensive research to learn the four ways Chinese men her father's age could have come to the U.S., then creating a detailed story for each way, each story starring her silent father. The result is a much bigger story than her father's alone, and it carries a conviction that, despite the use of fiction and despite his silence, his story is getting told.

Then there's the blanket disclaimer. On the copyright page at the beginning of his book *Dry* (about trying to heal from serious alcohol and other addictions), Augusten Burroughs includes a nicely boxed "author's note":

> This memoir is based on my experiences over a ten-year period. Names have been changed, characters combined, and events compressed. Certain episodes are imaginative re-creation, and those episodes are not intended to portray actual events.

There are a lot of good reasons to change names, to combine characters, to compress time in a dark memoir, even good reasons to create episodes—we'll get to these reasons in future chapters.

But a readerly indulgence of your making things up in specific instances doesn't mean you'll get indulgence for lying in big ways. Approximating the words from a lecture you attended long ago at your modest college is something quite different from saying you studied under Robert Lowell at Oxford. A forgettable night in jail that turns into hard prison time is certainly stretching things too far. (But then again, so is a month of media attention on James Frey when much bigger and far more dangerous liars were and will always be afoot.)

Truth can be slippery, but one thing I know for sure: fiction is fiction, fact is fact. If you have half a conscience, you'll know where the line is, always, and always you'll earn for your work the name *nonfiction*, take honest part in what John McPhee has called "the literature of fact."

Even the Truth Can Be Hard to Believe

Facts or no, if your reader doesn't believe you, you're sunk as a memoirist. Much of the advice in this book is, in effect, advice about making the truth believable, with all the artistic tools at our disposal.

Weirdly, sometimes it's easier to capture a certain species of readerly belief when you're consciously making fiction. When I give readings, people will often come up to me after a short story or novel excerpt—pure fiction— and say confidently, "I *know* that was you." I can't tell you how many people believe I have teenage children, all because one of my characters in a short story did. People believe I have driven a truck for a living, that I have worked selling antiques, that I have crashed a Subaru station wagon through a hardware store.

I *wish*!

And after a reading of true stuff—plain facts of my life, verifiable, written in stone—at some bookstore or college podium, a certain sly kind of older woman or a certain kind of trench-coat guy will sidle up and say, "I *know* you made that up."

Can't win.

Here's a sort of corollary: When I ask students in fiction classes for more drama in a given scene, they will often say, "But that's the way it really happened!" Conversely, students in nonfiction classes: "But that's not the way it happened!"

To me, the first goal, the first excellence, is artistic. The needs of other excellences, such as mere accuracy, must follow the needs of drama in a kind of hierarchy that helps me make decisions as I write. And if that isn't enough, there's always the fear of Oprah's wrath, and the wrath of all her viewers, and the wrath of all the pundits in the land.

But I'm Boring!

When you announce that you are working on a memoir, the unknowing (perhaps a voice in your own head, perhaps Mindy Mallow-Dalmation's) will smirk and ask what makes you think anyone would be interested in *your* life.

But of course, your life is only a starting point, a cliff from which to leap into the great sea of human experience, or fly over it with new wings. "The chief danger memoirists face is starring in their own stories, and becoming fascinated," as Annie Dillard writes in her introduction to the anthology *Modern American Memoirs*. She's making the point that most good memoir turns out not to be about the memoirist at all. *Survival in Auschwitz* cannot be said to be primarily about Primo Levi, though it is his memory and experience that brings light to dark days. Isak Dinesen's *Out of Africa* is certainly more about colonialism than about Dinesen. *My Father and Myself*, by J.R. Ackerley, has a lot more *father* than *myself*. Lucy Grealy's *Autobiography of a Face* is about her personal struggle with cancer and multiple reconstructive surgeries, but it is just as much, or more, about the intertwined natures of truth, beauty, suffering, and art. Some memoir is more about place than person; think of *Desert Solitaire*, by Edward Abbey. Then there are the hard cases: is *A Moveable Feast* more about Hemingway or the people he dishes?

But always, the reader becomes a stand-in for the *I*, and the life of the *I* becomes the life of the reader, so no matter who is speaking, the successful true story is always the reader's story on some level.

Much more on this as we go along.

Autobiography Needs an *I*

When I think of autobiography, I think of big, staid, honorable tomes, like Henry James's autobiography, which he called *Autobiography*, as if it were the last word on the subject forever. In truth, of course, the word just means self-biography and covers a lot of ground. I use it primarily as a generic term to mean any writing in which the writer's self and history take on importance.

In the introduction to a special all-autobiography issue of *Witness* (a quality quarterly literary magazine formerly out of Farmington Hills, Michigan, and now out of the Black Mountain Institute at the University of Nevada, Las Vegas), former editor Peter Stine quotes the letter Rick Bass sent with his submission: "I don't know if this is autobiographical, but there's an *I* narrator and it's true."

"I was grateful," Stine says, "for a definition of the genre that might encompass [a] wide range of writings: private journals, meditations on nature, anecdotal reminiscences, acts of moral witness."

That *I* narrator is at the heart of things—one person, remembering. And this *I* appears two ways: as a lead character in a true story and as that ineffable quality called *voice* in narrative. With voice there is the sense of someone speaking to us, perhaps intimately, as over a candlelit dinner; perhaps jovially, as at a loud cocktail party; perhaps pontificating, as if at a state banquet; perhaps sharp and nasty and funny, as at a roast. But voice doesn't come easily in a culture that assiduously teaches its young not to have voices. Think of all the years American schoolteachers forbade the use of the first-person singular in any writing, ever.

Times change. The first person is not only acceptable but preferable in many writing situations. It can wear jeans and a T-shirt; it can wear a tux. It can shred the half-pipe on a snowboard; it can judge the snowboard competition, too. In fact, for writers the first person's been in vogue since ancient Roman times. To have a voice is to have a self, and to have a self is powerful. No wonder so many people, from teachers to critics to politicians, are threatened.

The Role of Memoir in the Personal Essay

When I use the term *personal essay*, I mean an informal essay, a discursive essay, a wandering self in words. The personal essay is an old form, elegantly defined by Phillip Lopate in his introduction to and selections for the anthology *The Art of the Personal Essay*, an essential book for the autobiographer of any stripe. The personal essay is an old form, yet no form, since under its rubric writers have ranged over huge territory for centuries. The starting place, once again, is the self. But the personal essay strides past storytelling, past simpler memoir, to offer counterpoint in exposition, quotes from other writers, arcane knowledge (How many rivets in the skin of a Boeing 767? What is the hometown of Kanye West? How do blue crabs shed their skins?), odd comparisons, grand metaphors—in short, whatever's in the writer's head, whatever's in his library, whatever's relevant in the world. From these juxtapositions of the funds from the writer's "well-stocked mind" (as Elizabeth Hardwick called it in a class I once took) comes *meaning*.

Part of what's in your head is going to be stories, and when you start telling stories from your life, your life itself becomes evidence. The personal essayist examines the evidence until it's plain to both reader and writer just what's evident. Abandon the outline, all ye who enter here! Discovery is the thing. Too firm a plan, and you miss the digression that takes you where you didn't know you wanted to go.

Essays written from outlines can succeed, of course, but there's nothing particularly inspired or adventurous or risky about arriving exactly where you planned. And inspiration, adventure, and risk are some of the things readers of the personal essay, in all its shape-shifting forms, crave.

More on this subject anon (in chapter four, to be exact).

Remember Socrates: "The unexamined life is not worth living."

EXERCISE TWO: *Reading and Writing*

After diligent study and many conversations and any number of trendy cocktails with a lot of smart people, I've come to the following observation: there are two things good writers always have in common.

1. Writers write.
2. Writers read.

And two things all good writers know:

1. Writing is reading.
2. Reading is writing.

A couple of decades ago, I came to the realization that I needed to schedule special time for hard reading. I couldn't count on clear blocks of quality time, time I wasn't half asleep or entertaining company or mired in life's poignant details. So I claimed the first hour of the day for reading. Magazines didn't usually count for this hour (they were for relaxing later in the day), "fun" reading didn't count, books read for book reviews didn't count (nowadays Internet reading wouldn't count—all those addictive blogs!). For the reading hour—just after breakfast, just after a walk—I carefully selected one difficult book or series of books, day by day, week by week, month by month. It still amazes me what I got done. I tried to choose harder stuff, authors I'd missed in college, books I'd been meaning to get to for years, whole areas of literature I'd managed to ignore, great discoveries all along the way, deep resources for later thinking and writing. And doing that work didn't mean I didn't do my usual obsessive reading at other times of the day (always I had several books and ten magazine articles going, several manuscripts by friends, piles of student work); it just meant I could count on a solid hour a day when I was fresh and rested and ready to grapple with the difficult stuff, ready to learn.

But now I've got a daughter, a commanding little girl. Reading? I read when Elysia tells me I can read. That first hour of the day? That's Fashion Polly hour now, or dress-up time, or American Girl hour. I mean, I'm playing *dolls*. But as I live the soap opera of the lives of those little plastic beings, I take comfort in the fact that once, a long time ago, for a certain golden period of my life, I read. And I take comfort in the fact that in years to come (missing that seven-year-old painfully, no doubt), I will have a morning reading hour again.

Oh, that's right. Sorry. You wanted an assignment.

Here it is: read every day. Make reading part of your job as a writer. And since that's easier said than done, let's make it more formal: for the next week (and every week hereafter), schedule into your days and evenings a little time for difficult reading, as much as you can manage, perhaps as much as is necessary to finish about a book of serious reading a week. Make real reading a priority, even if you have to forgo *Seinfeld* reruns or something else you value (obsessive gardening for me, at least back before Barbies and Littlest Pet Shop).

Kristen Keckler and I have included a much-expanded reading list in creative nonfiction at the end of this edition of *Writing Life Stories*, but make your own list, tailored especially for your serious reading hour. Make it eclectic. Include books and authors you don't normally go for. Haunt the used-book stores, browsing the sections you normally avoid. Probably there's just the right book in art history or psychology or engineering. Don't always head to the literature section (but head there often enough). And search your own bookshelves for those good volumes you bought or borrowed with best intentions to read and haven't quite yet cracked. And of course, go to the library—chase down new authors, appealing subjects, new lines of thought. Sunday night, pick a difficult or important or intriguing book from whatever source and assign it to yourself (sternly, if necessary) for the seven days ahead. And see to it the job gets done.

EXERCISE THREE: *A Writing Circle*

Many readers of this book will have come to it because they're taking a class. Good. Many readers more will be working on their own. For the latter group, I'm going to suggest creating some kind of writing circle. Writing is lonely enough! You may already have plenty of writing friends and acquaintances—make a project of bringing them together a couple of evenings a month to share work, even to follow the exercises here.

Then again, it's just as likely you know no other writers, aspiring or otherwise. Try making posters or putting a small ad in the paper:

Writing Circle Forming

And give a sense of the level you think your group will be on. No matter where you live, you'll get responses, gain readers, and make new friends—friends who will support your writing endeavors.

If you live in Timbuktu (is that still remote? Does it even exist? I better do some research), you might create a *virtual* writers' circle online, or even the old-fashioned way, by mail.

Very likely, you won't have to do the work of instigation: many such groups exist all around the country, all shapes and sizes, some formal (and costing money), some very informal. Check with your local librarians and your friendly neighborhood booksellers; they usually know who's meeting and when. Groups shrink and swell, come and go—take your time, find the right circle for you.

EXERCISE FOUR: *A Writing Schedule*

Writers write. But one of the big challenges is finding and defending time to do the writing. Any craftsperson knows that a regular work schedule makes for consistent production. Writers credit consistency with greater access to the unconscious (if you're working consciously every day, you'll be working unconsciously every day, too, and all night). The most popular excuse for not writing is this: I just can't find the time.

I have all kinds of sympathy for busy people (new parents, graduate students, and college athletes tops on the list), but if you look into successful writers' lives, you'll find unbelievable burdens: full-time jobs, children, multiple deadlines, car trouble, weddings and funerals, family expectations, illness, exhaustion, depression, imprisonment, and on and on. Yet the work gets done.

Here's how it gets done: every day. A little or a lot, but every day. Okay, maybe a day off every seven or so and two weeks vacation a year and a little sick leave and time for goofing off. Otherwise, every day, if you're going to call yourself a writer. (Some people I know are binge writers—nothing much for months at a time, then sixteen hours a day for three weeks; if that works for you, good, especially if the hours average out to a solid number daily, or if you can keep at least some kind of daily practice going alongside the bingeing.)

Your assignment here is to make up a reasonable writing schedule for yourself. I'd suggest making a fresh schedule every week, say on Sunday evening. Even if you can only manage fifteen minutes on Monday (what with the kids' activities and all, and your job, and the phone calls from your ailing mother), schedule it in. Twenty minutes Tuesday, fine. Wednesday, two hours. Thursday, fifteen minutes. Friday, two hours. Saturday, four hours. Sunday, off. For example.

Then, *use the time*. For creative writing. No letters to agents. No reading (your hallowed reading time is scheduled separately). No submitting or printing stories. No reorganizing your computer files. No wedding announcements. No column for the church bulletin. No surfing the Web for Paris Hilton's new white sunglasses or Grady Sizemore's astrological sign. Just creative writing. Be at your writing place. Even if you daydream or fret the hour away, be there.

Don't be surprised if at first you just sit there staring. But do sit there. And as the weeks go by, don't be surprised if that little fifteen-minute block before dinner Mondays and Thursdays turns into a half hour, then an hour. The regular schedule will help words start to flow, make "writer's block" disappear.

Perhaps most importantly, your schedule becomes your shield. With schedule in hand, you feel (and are) fully justified in saying to family members or old friends or insistent temptations, "I can't. I have to work that night." There it is, right on your schedule. *Work*. Writing is your job. The one you do alone at your desk. Make a sign like the one my sister had over her potting wheel in a busy academic studio: "Don't Bug Me."

If you've got childcare duties, try making a schedule with the kid or kids. Recently, Elysia and I sat down with a pad of paper at the start of a wonderful free day together. I had a blog deadline, as it happened, and told her I'd have to work at least a couple of hours.

She's just starting to write herself, took charge of the pencil, blocked out our day: 8 A.M. breakfast; 9 A.M. Pollys; 10 A.M. work time; 11 A.M. swim; noon lunch. And so forth, three work blocks in all, three precious hours among precious hours. While I typed, she drew, she built blocks, she read books, she sang songs. She left me to my work. Why? Because it was right there on the schedule, along with lots of things she dearly wanted to do in their allotted time slots.

The time to begin most things is ten years ago.
—Mignon McLaughlin

EXERCISE FIVE: *First Lines*

One of my favorite experiments in getting started is first lines. How do other people do it? I ignore the fact that most first lines weren't first till after much revision and just walk around the bookstore or library pulling down volumes and examining how books and book chapters and essays and stories and memoirs commence. What makes each opening compelling (or not)? How is my readerly interest caught (or lost)?

One of my favorite first lines is from a novel, Joseph Heller's *Something Happened*: "I get the willies when I see closed doors." Another is from a personal essay by Scott Russell Sanders called "Under the Influence": "My father drank." Another is from a memoir I mentioned earlier in this chapter, *The Glass Castle* by Jeannette Walls: "I was sitting in a taxi, wondering if I had overdressed for the evening, when I looked out the window and saw Mom rooting through a dumpster."

I didn't have to look up any of these lines—they are caught forever in my head, along with a long list of others.

Your assignment is to look at first lines, as many as possible in an afternoon's browsing. Head to the library or bookstore or even your own shelves, and read—first lines only. Type up a list of your ten or twenty favorites. What makes them work?

Having looked at the work of others, take some time to type up your own first lines, from across your body of work, however large or small that body of work might be. (If you're new to the writing game, try opening your notebook or random computer files—even e-mails, and pull out first lines.) Which ones work best and why? When you look at them side-by-side with the first lines from exercise five, what do you see? Here's a good place to start with a new writing circle, too: try giving this assignment to the group, then swap first lines around, start a discussion. Which of your lines get the best or most heated reactions? Which of your colleague's lines most caught your interest?

 Life is not an orderly progression, self-contained like a musical scale or a quadratic equation. ... If one is to record one's life truthfully, one must aim at getting into the record of it something of the disorderly disconti- nuity which makes it so absurd, unpredictable, bearable.
—Leonard Woolf

Go Easy

Now that you have your schedules set for reading and writing, don't be too harsh a boss! What's it going to hurt if sometimes you daydream on the job a little or goof around in the kitchen? As long as your working hours are clear, you at least know you *ought* to be working. You have to have a schedule to know when you're messing up.

Then Again ...

It won't do to coddle yourself. Not at your desk when you're supposed to be? Call yourself on the phone. Throw a tantrum. Ask yourself where the hell you are. Demand that you get yourself to your desk and get to work. Give yourself the business. Fire yourself, if necessary. There are plenty of writers to go around.

A little guilt is a good thing sometimes.

Onward.

CHAPTER TWO

MEMORY

Initially, I was unaware that time, so boundless at first blush, was a prison. In probing my childhood (which is the next best to probing one's eternity) I see the awakening of consciousness as a series of spaced flashes, with the intervals between them gradually diminishing until bright blocks of perception are formed, affording memory a slippery hold.

—*Vladimir Nabokov*

Gow Farris said, "I don't do that kind of thing." He looked at me and the whole class looked at me and it was as if he were talking about mugging elderly women or smoking crack, as if I'd suggested something he found immoral. Worse yet, several heads nodded.

What we were talking about was an exercise I'll outline a little later on in this chapter, an exercise in mapmaking. What Gow was saying was roughly this: I've written daily newspaper stories for forty-five years and have never once done an exercise of any kind.

All I could really say was, "Gow, you'll have to trust me." But as a newspaperman Gow had learned not to trust anyone, of course, especially those with benevolent smiles. He just looked at me. I wanted to say more but didn't. Wanted to give a little speech about how it was time to disconnect that scolding part of the brain that demands to know where you're going before you start in all endeavors. Wanted to say how writing isn't a trip up the Amazon. Not exactly. How you won't die if you get on the wrong tributary. You'll maybe revise, at worst. Or maybe have to admit to being stuck. But any poison-tipped blow darts that pierce your hide in this particular rain forest are going to be fired by yourself, and some might have "I don't do that kind of thing" printed right on the shaft.

Just, "Trust me," is what I said, kind of lightly, as if it were a joke, and people took it that way, including Gow, and we all mildly laughed, breaking the tension.

CHALLENGING THE LIMITS OF MEMORY

One of the many curious things about the act of writing is the way it can give access to the unconscious mind. And in the hidden parts of consciousness lie not only hobgoblins and neurotic glimmers, but lots of regular stuff, the everyday stuff of memory. The invisible face of your grade-school bully is in there, somewhere, and the exact smell of the flowers on vines in your grandma's backyard, along with most everything else, perhaps including borrowed memories, even false ones. Some memories are going to be painful, but some pleasurable, too. An awful lot is just informational, the stuff of lost days.

And—I'm just realizing this—memory is what people are made of. After skin and bone, I mean. And if memory is what people are made of, then people are made of *loss*. No wonder we value our possessions so much. And no wonder we crave firm answers, formulae, facts and figures. All are attempts (however feeble in the end) to preserve what's gone. The present is all that's genuinely available to anyone, and the present is fleeting, always turning instantly to the past. Even facts distort: What's remembered, recorded, is never the event itself, no matter how precise the measurement—a baseball score is not the game. Memoir is never a re-creation—that's impossible. At best, what we can do is listen to memory and watch memory (the other senses are involved, as well—who hasn't been transported back by a taste, a fragrance, a touch?) and translate memory for those we want to reach, our readers.

All my stories have been written with material that was gathered—no, God save us! not gathered but absorbed—before I was fifteen years old.
—Willa Cather

MEMORY HAS ITS OWN STORY TO TELL

If you've written fiction at all, you know that detail is required to make a vivid scene. What's in the room? What sort of day is it? Who exactly is in the scene, and what exactly do they look like? All well and good writing fiction: you make it up. But writing nonfiction, the challenge is different: how to remember. For, of course, if we're going to call it a true story, the details better be true, right? Then again, we all know memory is faulty. Don't forget Tobias Wolff: "[M]emory has its own story to tell."

My sister, Carol, likes to tell the story of the time our younger brother, Doug, sucked on a hollow toy bolt till it suctioned onto his lips. He was maybe four. She and Mom and Doug were at Roton Point, our run-down beach club in Connecticut, end of the day, marching to the car carrying blankets and towels and pails and toys. Doug was a stocky little kid (we sibs meanly called him Bullet Boy till he shot up into a slim young man), and he looked cute as hell stumbling along carrying the Scotch Cooler with this big blue bolt suctioned onto his lips. In the car he still wore it, all the way to the guard booth, where he liked to say good-bye to the genial old guard who watched the beach gate. Carol tells the story at Thanksgiving and Christmas about every year. And I believe she told it at Doug's wedding rehearsal dinner. Anyway, at the gate, The Bullet tried to pull the bolt off to say hi to the guard, but he'd sucked on it so long and so hard it wouldn't come unstuck. Carol grabbed hold of the threaded end of the thing, wrestled with it a little, till (*pop*) it came loose.

Carol looked at Doug and Doug looked at Carol and then Carol said, "Oh, my God!" and so Mom turned and said it, too: "Oh, my God!" Doug's lips—poor Doug!—were ballooned up like some character's in a cartoon, so big even he could see them. Doug freaked! Carol freaked! Mom freaked! Doug cried and cried, even though it didn't hurt, but before they could even get near the doctor's, the swelling had disappeared.

That's it. Cute little family story. But the trouble is, Carol wasn't there. *I* was there. And the bolt wasn't blue; it was yellow. And that guard was a nasty old guy. I can still see him, all crabbed in his cheap uniform. And Mom didn't freak; she laughed. She laughed despite herself, because poor little Doug looked so comical, and because—this is important—she knew he'd be all right. And I laughed and laughed, "Bwaa-ha-ha!" because I was a big brother, and big brothers laughed at the misfortunes of younger brothers, at least they did in 1963.

I let Carol tell the story at meals, only occasionally challenging her, and now that's part of the family story, how we both claim the memory. I know she's wrong. She knows I'm wrong. Whom do you believe? Does it matter? Maybe we're both wrong. Doug can't remember. Mom has died. Is something more important than swollen lips at stake here?

Memory is faulty. That's one of the tenets of memoir. And the reader comes to memoir understanding that memory is faulty, that the writer is going to challenge the limits of memory, which is quite different from lying. One needn't apologize. The reader also comes expecting that the writer is operating in good faith, that is, doing her best to get the facts right.

Listen to Darrel Mansell, a teacher of writing, in his article on nonfiction in the Association of Writers & Writing Programs' journal *The Writer's Chronicle*:

> You just can't tell the truth, the whole truth, and nothing but the truth about that amorphous blob primary substance—language, with its severely limited and totally unrealistic rules and regulations, won't permit it. Furthermore the aesthetic and rhetorical demands of writing won't quite permit it either. The best you can do is to be scrupulous about facts and conscientious about what you and only you know to be the essential truth of your subject. That way you have a shot at telling one modest aspect of what really happened—something true, up to a point.

EXERCISE ONE: *Mapmaking*

Please make a map of the earliest neighborhood you can remember living in. Include as much detail as you can. Who lived where? What were the secret places? Where were your friends? Where did the weird people live? Where were the friends of your brothers and sisters? Where were the off-limits places? Where did good things happen? Where did you get in trouble?

MAKE THAT MAP

Go on, you, go make your map. Notice the ways (if any) you resist—get away from that refrigerator!—but make your map, no matter how simple. (One young guy made an X with a pencil and wouldn't go further, at least not until he saw the maps of others.) Or no matter how complex. (Another student, over fifty, reverted completely to childhood, went to work on a huge sheet of poster board with colored markers and tempera paint, magazine cutouts, bits of cloth to represent lawns, complete lists of house occupants, dioramas of two school yards, three churches, and her grandparents' house. She spent so much time that she came to our workshop all exhausted and without any writing to show.)

However you approach your map, enjoy yourself. Then come back and read on. See you in fifteen minutes, an hour, a week. But do make that map, or drawing, or $35,000 fiberglass scale-model relief, complete with working grain elevator and talking puppets.

DISCOVERING LOST WORLDS

We're back. Remember Gow Farris, our retired journalist? Well, Gow surprised me with a wonderfully detailed map, stiffly drawn, showing his childhood neighborhood in St. Louis. His family had left there when he was ten. A squiggly line behind his house denoted a ravine, he told us, and the ravine, judging by his small smile as he pointed it out, seemed to hold fond memories. Mindy Mallow-Dalmation, my Colby undergrad, just didn't feel like drawing a boring old street map (and besides, her parents still lived in the same "whack" neighborhood she'd grown up in), so she drew the three-dimensional plan of the funky old apartment building in which her late grandparents had lived in Indianapolis, where Mindy had spent two summers during an all-but-forgotten family crisis.

You may have used maps before in your writing. They work well for fiction, especially as a way of delineating territory, aiding imagination, creating a world. But maps can aid memory, too, unlock memory, release a lost world, bring it forward.

And that's the thing, isn't it: the world of your map is gone. In the introduction to his collection of short memoirs, *Excursions in the Real World*, William Trevor writes:

> Places do not die as people do, but they often change so fundamentally that little is left of what once they were. The landscape of the Nire Valley that spreads over a northern part of County Waterford is timeless, but the Dublin remembered here is the Dublin of several pasts.

My own map would be that of a neighborhood in Needham, Massachusetts, where I lived till I was five. Only five. Young, young, the earliest rosy light at the dawn of my memory. But I remember Fuller Brook Road (or is it Fuller Brook Avenue—it won't be hard to find out, when the time comes). Fuller Brook curved into the woods from a busy main road, made a crescent sweep, then turned back out to the highway.

After sketching a rough crescent, I'll draw a little box for Ellen's house across the street. I remember the big picture window of that house, and the name Ellen, though not Ellen herself particularly. I'll draw the sidewalks, and in doing so images will come to me unbidden, images of chalk and crayons and cracks one best not step on. Few cars passed by there. I'll draw our short driveway and our enormous brown station wagon, which suddenly I can picture so clearly I know it's a Ford, though I wouldn't have known that then. Oh, let's see, the year is 1959. We moved to Connecticut that year in August, which I know because Douglas was born just before the move, his birthday two days after mine. So now I'm five. That car smelled a certain spicy way, and the headliner—the material on the ceiling—was soft and crushy as felt. Of course, drawing the confines of our yard, I think of my older brother, Randy. And I think of the older of my two younger sisters, Carol—you've just met her, the one deluded about her whereabouts on bolt-lip day. I see my toy bass drum and Mom's garden taut with strings to make the rows straight, and certain adult neighbors and a rusty wagon. The more I draw, the more comes to mind, lost stuff: the second corner of the crescent had a dirt road off it. The houses ended and there was this dirt road and big fields and then a lot of woods. I draw, I draw. Heroic Randy (who stabbed the head of my bass drum repeatedly with a fork) was stung by yellow jackets in the edge of one of the fields. I was tagging along and didn't get stung. I can clearly see the place he stepped and the cloud of vespids coursing out of their ground nest. And thinking of this fear makes me remember another fear: the Nike missile base.

Yes, of all things there was a Cold-War Nike missile base. I draw it on the map at the other end of the crescent of Fuller Brook Road (or Avenue) and remember the high fence and barbed wire. Am I really remembering this? Later (in chapter seven, to be exact), I can be a reporter and check. One call: *Hey, Mom.* And while I'm at it, I'll ask about Dougie's lips. But for now memory's the thing.

Nike missiles? Yes, and Sputnik went over—you could see it—a moving star in the night sky. Checking (I can't wait for chapter seven, I guess), I find out I'm not quite right about Sputnik: the first sputnik was shot to the heavens in 1957—the one I saw that summer was part of a series of uncapitalized sputniks (the word being a generic, like satellite). But hey, without bothering Mom I remember our windows rattling with sonic booms. (Research note: How come there aren't any sonic booms anymore, yet far more supersonic activity up there?)

And school, the Dwight School, was over that ridge. I draw the ridge and recall Randy and some other bigger boys climbing the missile-base fence: a shortcut to school. I recall some man in a uniform yelling at us. I recall (and draw) the approved route to the Dwight School, out Fuller Brook (among my first jokes was to call it Fuller Brush road—I remember my dad laughing and seeming impressed with my humor) on the sidewalk along the busy main street (Great Plains Avenue? All I need is a street map to find out), a long walk. Then take a left. The classroom is clear to me. And Mrs. ... Mrs. ... Can't get her name, though I bet my mother knows. Mom would have been thirty-two, thirty-three. Last, I'll draw some rudimentary bulldozers in the fields. Just before we moved they started development on those pastures. I loved the bulldozers. They were dinosaurs.

Time Passes

The previous several paragraphs were written ten years ago, for the original edition of this book. I've resisted revising them in the efficient way I've been revising the rest of the book because in them my mother is still alive, still available as a resource to memory. (She did know my kindergarten teacher's name when I asked, but now I've forgotten it again, having failed to write it down.) On April 16, 2006, about a year and a half ago as I write, Mom died. So very much has changed in ten fleeting years. (Street map? What about Mapquest?) And I realize as I sit here at my desk and revise that I must have made a good many of my readers feel sad, cavalier as I was about having my Mom around to query, when so many people do not.

Hey, Mom. What's it like in the next world?

Forget thirty-two. Reba Pearl Elaine Burkhardt Roorbach would have been eighty-two this coming July as I write, or rewrite. In chapter seven, "Finding the Facts," I'd better add some recommendations for interviewing relatives—especially older relatives—before time overtakes them.

I'm thinking of the last line of *The Great Gatsby*, F. Scott Fitzgerald's now classic novel (if you haven't read it since high school—it's far better than you remember): "So we beat on, boats against the current, borne back ceaselessly into the past."

> *Often there is a human tendency to obliterate happiness—to live in one's painful memories. But for me, going through my life gave me back the good things I had forgotten, and I've captured them for good. It gave me back my happy mother.*
> *—Jill Ker Conway*

EXERCISE TWO: *Map Story*

Once you've made your map, it's time to write. Here's the assignment: tell us a story from your map. "One day back in Anchorage ..."—and off you go, elaborating on your recollection that you and Ellie Tottenhammer used to throw frozen fish through garage windows. Don't edit yourself much; don't try for anything finished. The story needn't be long. A couple of pages is fine (but keep going if you get inspired).

Perhaps it will help to broaden the definition of the word *story* for yourself. Consider this quote from Flannery O'Connor: "If nothing happens, it's not a story." That makes a pretty simple definition, and very broad: in a story, something happens.

Now, go write. Stop reading this book right now, and get to work. Yes, even if you're in bed or on the subway or at the coffee shop or seated on a jet. Pull out that notebook you've got with you always and get started.

A Sample Map Story, Complete With Disclaimer

Here is Gow Farris's response to the map-story assignment, written quickly and in longhand, no cross-outs.

It's July in St. Louis, 1936. My younger brother Frank and I want ice cream, but we're not allowed.

I am ten and Frank eight.

If we go off down the street there's hell to pay.

We have a plan. Climb down through the ravine. Down there we will be hidden. Then sneak out to Four Corners along the tracks.

I don't remember what we thought we'd do at Krock's store for money. I don't remember being in the store. The store I remember all right. Large jars of candy. Licorice, is the one I remember. And Mr. Krock. I remember him, he was very far off and quiet, but friendly enough. He was sad, I now see. Or maybe depressed. That may have been the time we stole. Anyway, we would walk down there along the tracks and take our time, even though we knew we had to be home by supper. Oh, we would walk to the road and then down to Krock's and get candy. We would do this daily right up until the time we stole. Then, of course, Mother got into it.

Those were days when kids thought about candy instead of Nintendo and TV.

That's it. Nothing finished about it, obviously, or meant to be, just a penciled draft written on the busy front stoop of a vacated sorority house in the twenty minutes between lunch and a lecture at that summer writing conference in Vermont (Gow had no trouble shutting out distractions), but full of life and possibility nevertheless, and the force of memory.

He read it to us the next morning, but not before apologizing profusely for how rough and unfinished it was going to be: he'd had little time; he hated writing with a pencil (arthritis, horrible); he wasn't trained in this sort of writing. Lots of self-doubt.

Gow didn't know it, but he was speaking for all of us. Most people have something similar to say just before presenting new work, whether to an editor, a friend, a writing circle, or a class. In fact, what's said is so similar that I have come to call it the generic disclaimer, or even Generic Disclaimer, or better yet GENERIC DISCLAIMER. You can save a lot of time just by raising a hand and saying, "GENERIC DISCLAIMER," when the impulse to apologize for your work strikes.

Exercise Three: *Generic Disclaimer*

Make up a little card, or maybe a big one. Write GENERIC DISCLAIMER across the top in big letters, then write a paragraph or so apologizing profusely for how rough and unfinished your exercises and first and second drafts are going to be. Talk about how little time you had, how tired you were, how ornery your computer is, how dull your pencils, how you're not used to doing exercises, how you just couldn't think, how you write and work and think differently than other people do. Get it all down, all your best excuses and reasons, all your self-doubt and blaming and delusions of grandeur. Make it a nice card, and pull it out and have a look at it whenever you feel discouraged about your writing, whenever you feel everyone in the world is farther along than you are.

Having given the GENERIC DISCLAIMER, Gow turned red and stammered a little. Then he read his piece. We all sat quietly when he was done, drawn, despite the roughness of the writing, into the past. Then we talked. A young woman said she liked the part about the candy; she could really see those jars. A fellow, not young but not yet Gow's age, said, "I can relate to the wanting to get away."

Other people in our group noted the shift from direct narrative to the "I don't remember" stuff.

Gow (a touch defensive) said, "I won't and can't write something I don't remember."

"But, Gow," we said, "you remember so much!"

We all agreed: the ravine, the store, on and on, even in such a short piece.

Next, the woman across from Gow noted the terse short sentences, one or two per paragraph.

Another workshopper said, "Newspaper style, ma'am," in a kind of Joe Friday voice. And he knew a little more: those narrow newspaper columns make single sentences look like paragraphs, and the eye needs those breaks. But Gow was entering a new world, one in which long paragraphs are welcome alongside short ones.

He seems to know it, too, judging by that last block of his effort, the "don't remember" block. Here, Gow lets the paragraph get longer, makes at least some of his sentences longer and more complex.

Despite his writerly protestations, we all agreed that Gow had managed to evoke Krock's store and Depression-era St. Louis pretty admirably for twenty minutes of scratching on a pad of paper.

<hr>

EXERCISE FOUR: *Sentence and Paragraph Length*

You'll want to learn to look at your own writing the way our class looked at Gow's. We'll talk about language more as we go along, and especially in chapter nine, but since language is so important, let's start now. Note without judgment the length of your standard sentence, the length of your standard paragraph. Where do odd lengths turn up, and why? Is there a dearth of short sentences? Do you never make long paragraphs? The next step as you do your daily writing is to consciously experiment with sentence and paragraph lengths, using more of whatever you avoid now, and getting a lively mix.

<hr>

TAKING DOWN THE SCAFFOLDING

Perhaps you noted the important who, where, what, why, when, and how information Gow spins out in his first lines, not a bad habit by any means, though first sentences probably need to do more than offer basic information. Gow's working to a formula that's so familiar to him (and to many of us) it's become unconscious.

The truth is we're all working with formulas that have become so familiar they seem handed down to us by God himself, or by Mother Nature. Even if we're not writing for newspapers, we've been taught, for example, that essays start with introductions.

If you look at the end of Gow's effort (and probably at your own), you'll find the traditional conclusion, too. The question is, does it add much here?

We've all been told from first grade that a good essay has an introduction, a body, and then a conclusion, and we've been praised for delivering, even when our introductions were too neat, our conclusions pat (or clever mirrors of introductions that repeat language to form a frame: a tired structural cliché). That structure—or formula—made it easy for our teachers to teach large groups of students, but there's nothing inherently wonderful about it.

Man, oh man, when I think of my college essays: "In this essay it will be shown that William Faulkner's use of the first person ..." Then to the body of the essay, where I'd talk to the assigned page length about Faulkner's brilliant use of first person. Then, hallelujah, the ringing conclusion: "In this essay it has been shown that William Faulkner's use of the first person ..." Arghh! Forget all that. No matter how painful it is to do so, chop those intros and conclusions away. Just for now. Just for an experiment. Please?

This will help you become aware that the introductory impulse (let's call it) runs deep, that the conclusion compulsion (ditto) has been carefully beaten into all of us.

But introductions and conclusions aren't necessary. Good stories, good essays, leap right to their subjects, perhaps not in draft one or draft six, but at some point. When the introductory apparatus is cut, it's seen for what it is: scaffolding. You put up the elaborate and complicated and even beautiful scaffolding and build the cathedral. When the cathedral is complete, well, you take the scaffolding down.

Why not take the advice of Aristotle (via Horace, hence the Latin) and start *in medias res*, in the middle of things. And keep in mind it's possible and permissible (what a word!) to end in the middle of things, too. Often conclusions are neat but redundant. Sometimes they just lead us off in a new direction that as readers we didn't want to go.

Have a look at Gow's piece. What would you identify as introduction? What as conclusion? Where's the story here, the something happening?

EXERCISE FIVE: *Point of Entry, Point of Exit*

Have a look at your own map story with the same critical eye you turned on Gow's. Have you built an elaborate introduction? How about a subtle one? I know you meant it to be there, but—just as an exercise—delete your introduction. Where does the story really begin? Where do you stop explaining? Now delete any conclusion you find. Is there a story left there?

Sometimes I've deleted my introduction and conclusion and had nothing left: I was so busy making scaffolding, I never got to the cathedral.

Generic Mode

We spent probably twenty minutes talking about Gow's piece. Near the end of the discussion I pointed out the switch to what I like to call "generic mode" in the last paragraph. Instead of something like "We walked down there," Gow gives us "We would walk down there," that *would* meaning that over time and probably in several summers, Gow and his brother walked down those tracks many times. Generic mode is a useful way to condense time to move a story along, to tell a long story in summary, but in this case it puts distance between the reader and the action. It also creates a safety net for Gow: he doesn't have to remember any particular day, just a set of similar days. Fine, fine. But notice how one particular day is emerging despite him: the day he and Frank stole.

A Neighborhood in Brooklyn

Let's look at some more responses to the mapmaking exercise, points of comparison for you to use with your own work. Here's one from Wendy Guida (she's a cheery, very hip high-school English teacher from Brooklyn who was in another of my summer workshops in Vermont), which I'll type up from her rough handwriting on pink notebook paper, skipping the cross-outs and the false starts (though the cross-outs and false starts are interesting, too, of course).

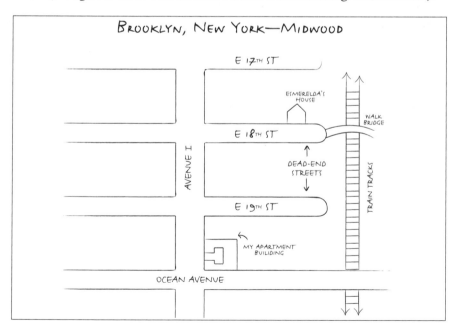

> Esmerelda's house was way better than mine. It was better in all ways, which is hard if you consider all the possible ways there are, but it was. Most of my childhood was spent coveting. Esmerelda had a house (not just an apartment like ours), with a sprawling, cluttered porch. She had cats, where I only had a dog. She had Ralston cereal and my family only had farina. Her things were, by definition, better than mine. I figured any time my family was different we were low class.
>
> Somehow I believed that song lyrics were maps to my future, not lessons to be learned from to avoid pain. I mirrored Esmerelda's taste in music, adoringly purchasing Carly Simon's Greatest Hits, James Taylor's White Album, every Barry Manilow album. I could probably still sing my way thorough every Barry Manilow song. But Carly, Carly was our love.

Obviously, this is a response to an exercise, quickly rendered. Wendy, I'm sure, would like to invoke the GENERIC DISCLAIMER at this time. Of course it's not a finished or polished or structured piece. There's quite a jump here from feelings of lower-caste unworthiness to the record collecting. Some of the sentences are a little ungainly. But there is no abstract opening, no scaffolding. We get right to the point and quickly arrive at a promising discussion of a kind of musical nostalgia. Material is arriving.

EXAMINING YOUR PRECONCEPTIONS

Here's another response to the map assignment, by Nancy Kuhl. You'll remember her note about resistance, from the introduction. This is the first assignment she wrote for me, and you'll see signs of her resistance, which I hope will help you detect any resistance of your own. Nancy's work was produced in the course of an academic quarter, when she was a graduate student at Ohio State. She had five days and a weekend to work, so another thing you'll see is the result of more time spent than Gow or Wendy had, perhaps more the kind of time you yourself have been able to spend. Before reading what follows to the class, Nancy invoked the GENERIC DISCLAIMER with vehemence.

THE BIKE

> The house I lived in until I was five sat on the corner of a street that dead-ended into an elementary school parking lot.

The lots nearest my backyard were still meadow from which you could see the square, skeletal frames of new houses.

I have no story from that neighborhood or that house; I have only disconnected bits of memory. For instance, I remember a green bedspread, and a baby, named Evelyn, born to the couple who lived across the street.

Though my memories of my life in the house are few and flawed, I think of one fragment often. My brother is pulling me in a wagon. The wagon tips over and I crack my front teeth on the pavement, knocking one of them out.

That's it. The whole thing. Yet, like a piece of cloth between my fingers, I worry that memory, until it is only bare threads. I was four, Schuyler was eight. He was wearing blue tennis shoes. It was a Saturday in late spring. The wagon was bright yellow.

My mother would have stepped outside in response to my brother's calling for her, which I also remember.

This memory stays with me, perhaps, because of the question it poses. If this memory is impossible, as it surely is, how then can I trust any memory? That I remember this, of all the falls and bumps and scrapes I must have suffered as a kid, makes it remarkable. My memory of the moment stands as the middle ground, somewhere between what could never have been and what is.

Wow. Nancy declares there is no story, then produces a story, then proceeds to analyze her memory and challenge the assignment. Wonderful! Yet evasive, too. Note the concluding paragraph; observe her instincts toward making a rounded essay with beginning, middle, and end. All good. But the assignment was to tell a story from the map, not to write a traditional essay. Part of the explanation for such a remarkably intellectualizing response is just more resistance, no doubt. But part of it—the greater part—is Nancy's half-unconscious insistence on a preconceived notion of what nonfiction is or can be. I asked for a scene; she gave me the first draft of a taut little essay. What gives?

Well, she's a writer.

I'm not trying to box her in, or you. Any response to the assignment is of intense interest to me, and your own should be of intense interest to you, not only as a piece of writing but as evidence of your notions about nonfiction, as example of your eye and ear for sentence and paragraph, as evidence of your modes of resistance, as a small laboratory in which to begin the work of growth. Try hard to give the same tough scrutiny to your own writing exercises. That's why they're there: to help you develop your critical eye.

Then again, you may be having a ball with these storytelling exercises. But don't get smug, or the other kids in class are going to beat you up on the playground. The harder work for you may come in chapter four, "Big Ideas," which will be a breeze for a writer like Nancy.

Easy or difficult, right now we're just trying to tap into memory. Right now we're just learning to trust our sub- or preconscious minds. Think of all the material in those vaults, all the subjects. Anytime in the next months or years, you might make more maps of other neighborhoods you've lived in, tell stories from all the eras of your life. Always, rich material will emerge, especially if you do the exercise without thought of making publishable work. Not yet, okay? That's for chapter eleven, all the way at the other end. For now we're just bringing ore out of the mine and into the light.

Remember Janet Bellweather? Janet didn't do exercise one at all. Nancy Kuhl only became aware of her resistance gradually. Mindy Mallow-Dalmation got so involved in her apartment-building drawings that they became a project in themselves. That was fine for her art class. But I was teaching *writing*.

How about you, gentle reader? Have you read this far without writing anything? What? You haven't even drawn a map? Are you thinking, Well, I'll just read through the whole book here and then come back and do some of these exercises?

Come on, pal. What makes you so special? Anyone can lie around and read. Let's get to work!

COLLECTING MATERIAL

Here are some exercises to try after the map: I wouldn't spend huge amounts of time, though perhaps one will catch your imagination and keep the keys clicking. Just write and collect a nice pile of pages—rough, polished, good, bad—it doesn't matter at this point. The important thing is that you're writing every day, or nearly every day, creating a file or files of material. Forget the introductions, the conclusions, the impulse to round stories off, the powerful need to make completed pieces: just get things that happened when you were however-many-years younger onto the page for possible future use. And don't forget that practice is always one of the main objectives of all these exercises. Allow yourself to be a learner. Practice, practice, like a kid at the piano. We'll get to the finished product in good time.

Think of what you are making as solid, clean rocks for an eventual stone wall. When the time comes to make the wall, you'll want a variety of rocks to choose from: all sizes (within a range), many shapes, many colors or subtle shades, many textures. Most of the rocks you collect in preparation for the wall won't be used in the final product. Some may be discarded, some broken, some used in a different project. And then again, some rocks are beautiful all on their own.

EXERCISE SIX: *Time Lines*

Life goes by in such a tumble of events that it can be hard to reconstruct even the big picture, much less remember particular days. "Time Lines" is akin to the map exercise, in that it not only provides a frame for remembering but provokes memory. And it's simple. You just make a chart for any year of your life. Not quite a calendar: a box for each month of the period will do. (Detail beyond that—weeks, days, hours—is up to you, and certainly beneficial.) Then fill in the boxes with what you were doing. Last year will be pretty easy. But what if I pick, say, my sophomore year of college? 1972. What was I doing then? Ithaca, New York: Ithaca College. But when exactly was it that I went to Maine to work on Mike's cabin? When was it that I worked for Dave Conway, the electrician? When was it that I met Bob Meyer, who would later become such a good friend? When did my not-quite girlfriend Gail Campbell and I break up? Harder than it looks, but one clue leads to the next, and after a couple of days of puzzling over it, I figure out that Dave Conway was a year later, Bob Meyer and I met November of freshman year, Gail and I broke up in January, and Maine was that summer, in August.

Once you've got one year figured out, you might want to go on to the next year, or the year previous. My book *Into Woods* covers about ten years of my life; eventually, my time line—much revised and recopied—covered all ten years, full of notes and arrows and surprises. It helped immensely in keeping time straight, for sure, but also helped me remember lost days and events and people as well.

And one of my students in Vermont—a minister, seventy-six years old—spent a whole year and made a chart of her entire life, color coded. What a catalog it was, the uneventful alongside weddings and funerals and relocations and religious awakenings. And what a valuable tool the chart became as she worked on her memoir. (In chapter seven we'll dig deeper with a little personal research, but for now the idea is simply to see what memory will yield.)

For years I have worried that if I turn all my life into literature, I won't have any real life left—just stories about it. And it is a realistic concern: it does happen like that. I am no longer sure I remember how it felt to be twenty and living in Spain after my parents died; my book about it stands now between me and my memories. When I try to think about that time, what comes to mind most readily is what I wrote.
—Judith Barrington

EXERCISE SEVEN: *Time Lines, Part Two*

Back to the writing: look for the stories in your time line and tell some of them in quick versions. The idea isn't to produce finished stories—not yet—but to create a collection of rendered memories. Chances are there'll be a lot of stories—truckloads—far too many to write. So make lists, more or less detailed. This is enjoyable work, great on a day when you are otherwise stuck or not sure what's next for your writing.

EXERCISE EIGHT: *Idea Notebook*

This is something you might already have going, in one form or another, a common writerly habit, used in varying ways by different writers. I've got a loose-leaf notebook that's almost a scrapbook, full of ideas I've had—bad and good—for essays and stories, full of odd sentences that have passed through my head, full of cryptic phrases and snatches of conversation. I settled on the loose-leaf book years ago, because I can punch holes in any odd piece of paper I've written on and file it away. I tape napkins in it and staple in notes hastily made on the backs of credit-card receipts. It's a wild mishmash but gives me a resource when I can't get started. F. Scott Fitzgerald went so far as to keep his ideas in file folders, alphabetized by subject.

I also have an absurdly large collection of miniature notebooks for various pockets and glove compartments and desk drawers. I'm crazy for these things, buy them in threes and fours whenever I see a cool version for sale. I also keep a pen in my pocket always, always, always, just like my keys.

Got an idea? Write it down.

Lost an idea somewhere in the fairy-tale forest of your thoughts? Don't worry, many more where that one came from. And especially good ideas have a way of returning, sometimes in a new suit of clothes.

The past is really almost as much a work of the imagination as the future.
—Jessamyn West

EXERCISE NINE: *New Leaf*

You must have heard about Ernest Hemingway's young first wife, Hadley, packing a suitcase full of the only copies of his early stories in order to surprise him on a visit in Europe. She lost the suitcase on a train. At first, of course, old Ernie was displeased, to say the least, but in the end he said it was the best thing that ever happened to him.

So here's a painful exercise: collect all you've written (well, at least up to the day you started reading this book; keep your exercises for now, okay?), Published or not (whether on paper, on old floppy disks, or downloaded from that hard drive), and put it in a box or boxes. Next, tape the boxes shut dramatically. And finally, take a thick marking pen and write phase one on the side of the box, or apprentice work, or perhaps old leaf. Do all this theatrically, with lots of moaning and shouting. Ululate, if you know how. Tear your hair. Then put the box of retired work in the attic. Or leave it on a train. Then take yourself out to dinner and celebrate.

Next morning, dawn of a new era, get to work.

CHAPTER THREE

SCENEMAKING

*The scene is the single most important element in
your screenplay. It is where something happens—
where something specific happens.*

—Syd Field

When I think about my existence, any stretch of it—any month, any year, any
minute, really—I'm thinking in fragments. Perhaps a meadow comes to mind,
and a stone wall, and my high-school girlfriend Linda, sitting on the stone wall
kicking her feet waiting for me. The snatch of conversation I can hear is Linda,
too, but it seems to take place in a room imbued with a certain light ... morning
sun ... her parents aren't home. But the meadow was later, wasn't it? Yes, college
years. I can immediately start spinning vignettes, and those quick stories of my
life come so fast I can't believe it. The more I think, the more I remember. The
more I write what I remember, the clearer it all comes to me.

True stories depend on memory, of course, but what do you do once the
great gates are open? It's a painful truth of memoir making: you can't tell it all.

The secret is in scenes; scenes are one kind of rock for that stone w̶a̶
spoke of last chapter. Scene is vital; it sits at the heart of all dramatic wı̶ı̶ı̶ı̶ı̶g̶.
And scene is nearly always what's missing when a piece of creative nonfiction
fails to come to life.

SCENEMAKING IS SHOWING

A good scene replaces pages and pages of explaining, of analysis, of telling,
what Mindy Mallow-Dalmation called "blah-blah," with her usual ironic flair.
Instead of a passage about your family's socioeconomic status, you show your
dad pulling up in the brown Ford wagon, muffler dragging. Or does he pull up
in a shiny Mercedes? Or does he walk up the hill with his jacket over his shoulder, car traded for shares in a new invention? Let the reader infer your message
about class issues. In one house, the furniture is polished wood. In another, it's
painted metal, showing rust. Trailer park? Butler? Ranch house? Elvis Presley
clock? Trust the reader to gather all that's implied, and get on with your story.

Also trust the reader to discover emotion in your real-life character's actions. Instead of a lot of explaining about how much you loved a boy or a girl
and how good-looking he or she was to you and how awful it was that he or she
never paid much attention to you, show the beloved. Give a whiff of the orangey
scent you associate with him or with her. Show him smile at the prom queen
just the way you'd hoped he'd smile for you. Show her hug the football captain
when she thinks you can't see. The difference between telling and showing is
life. And, of course, *life* is the root meaning of the word *vivid*—high praise for
the scenemaker.

Narrative, which is simply the act and art of storytelling, makes use of several modes of discourse: scene, summary, and exposition among them. Every
narrative makes use of all of these, with different writers giving different emphasis to each. A *scene* takes place in a specific time and place, records events,
actions, talk, stuff happening ("Rick threw the javelin with a stumble and a
roar"). A *narrative summary* collapses events, gives the gist of your story in
condensed form, paraphrases talk, mentions people and places with briefest of
descriptors, speeds the story along, and generalizes time ("those were unhappy
weeks"). *Exposition* is the most abstract and seeks to explain things, to convey
information, to offer analysis, to put forth ideas ("Athletes express their anger
through acts of strength and poise"). It's good at giving the facts ("I had a serious girlfriend named Linda for a year in high school back in Connecticut") and

has a prominent place in the making of successful narrative (more about this in the next chapter).

But there are jobs for which exposition hasn't got the credentials, respected as it is. Emotion, when presented as a fact ("I was in love with her"), starts to fade, dies on the page. Instead, consider the following:

> Linda stood up when she spied me coming through the tall grasses. She fixed her blouse, inspected herself—that freckled cleavage—looked up and grinned, then frowned, the scent of faint vanilla in her hair as I pulled her in, kissed her ear, kissed her salty mouth. "Potato chips," she said, her hand on my chest.

When presented as scene emotion fills the reader's head and heart, as well.

So, exposition is telling. Scene is showing. Summary is somewhere in between. Aristophanes gave the command first, and every drama and creative writing teacher since has repeated it: "Show, don't tell."

A good scene can succinctly exemplify and illuminate whole sections of a life, give the reader all she needs to go on, make a writer's point clear, make further discussion unnecessary.

Listen to this from *Going to the Territory*, a memoir by Ralph Ellison. Ellison, author of *Invisible Man*—the great and funny and harrowing novel about being black in 1950s America—is recalling a time he heard some men arguing heatedly (behind a closed door) over which of two Metropolitan Opera divas was the best soprano. Curious, he knocks.

> For a moment there was an abrupt and portentous silence; then came the sound of chair legs thumping dully upon the floor, followed by further silence. I knocked again, loudly, with an authority fired by an impatient and anxious urgency.
>
> Again silence—until a gravel voice boomed an annoyed, "Come in!"
>
> Opening the door with an unsteady hand, I looked inside, and was even less prepared for the scene that met my eyes than for the content of their loud-mouthed contention.
>
> In a small, rank-smelling, lamp-lit room, four huge black men sat sprawled around a circular dining-room table, looking toward me with undisguised hostility. The sooty-chimneyed

lamp glowed in the center of the bare oak table, casting its yellow light upon four water tumblers and a half-empty pint of whiskey. As the men straightened in their chairs I became aware of a fireplace with a coal fire glowing in its grate, and leaning against the ornate marble facing of its mantelpiece, I saw four enormous coal scoops.

"All right," one of the men said, rising to his feet. "What the hell can we do for *you*?"

Ellison tells the men what he's doing—collecting signatures for a petition (significantly, at least for our purposes in thinking about the nature of memoir, the writer tells us he can't remember what the social cause was: some things don't matter to the drama). They rib him and make jokes and decide to trust him, then deign to sign his petition. But something else is at stake here.

Then I blurted it out. "I'd like to ask you just one question," I said.

"Like what?" the standing one said.

"Like where on earth did you gentlemen learn so much about grand opera?"

For a moment he stared at me with parted lips; then, pounding the mantelpiece with his palm, he collapsed with a roar of laughter. As the laughter of the others erupted like a string of giant firecrackers I looked on with growing feelings of embarrassment and insult, trying to grasp the handle to what appeared to be an unfriendly joke. Finally, wiping coal-dust-stained tears from his cheeks, he interrupted his laughter long enough to initiate me into the mystery.

"Hell, son," he laughed, "we learned it down at the Met, that's where ..."

"You learned it *where*?"

"At the Metropolitan Opera, just like I told you. Hell, we been down there wearing leopard skins and carrying spears or waving things like palm leafs and ostrich-tail fans for *years!*"

Now, I have no way of knowing how the writing of that scene went for Ellison, no way of knowing except my own experience: it was hard. The natural flow, the vivid description, the humor all came piece by piece till the scene was whole. He remembered imperfectly a scene from his youth, did his best to recreate it, complete with feelings. I've left out most of the fine dialogue he creates (knowing you'll be heading to the library later), but the dialogue, too, came with many revisions, much testing of memory, much willingness to re-create.

Let's look at Ellison's passage more closely.

First, note that it's all scene. Every word. Even the expository stuff, the explaining. Ellison opens with a knock: We feel that knock on our knuckles, we hear it, we see the hand hitting the door, the youth waiting. The grown man—the writer at his desk—doesn't intrude here. Now's not the time. The reader is as involved in the silence as the teenager was, so long ago. We hear chairs move. More silence. Ellison is carefully remembering the particulars of the event, the full sequence, confidently getting it all in. Some details will have been pure in his memory, some will have been filled in—stuff he knows would have happened after such a knock.

The last line of the first paragraph I've reproduced ("I knocked again, loudly, with an authority fired by an impatient and anxious urgency") looks a lot like exposition. That, of course, is because it *is* exposition. But it's exposition that doesn't interrupt the reader's picturing the scene, but instead heightens it, giving a picture of the youth's nature: impatient, urgent. And those aren't exterior words: "Impatient" is a feeling in the breast and not just the mind. "Anxious," "urgency": These are gut feelings, even if offered in exposition.

Then a voice. Dialogue is always immediate, always takes place (and place is the exact word) in *time*, as stories must. The door opens (how clearly we see this!), and the room and men inside are revealed. Here, Ellison spends a whole paragraph setting the scene and giving us the characters. The room details he chooses are significant, not arbitrary: sooty lamp, pint of whiskey, water tumblers (note the specificity of word choice, tumblers over, say, glasses or cups), four coal scoops leaning on an ornate fireplace (analogous, of course, to the four laborers when they turn opera extras). He uses the senses: yellow light, rank smell, warm fire, a heard voice. Sight, smell, touch, sound. More than a few readers will taste the whiskey, too. Some writers would have put in creaking chairs or any of a number of other sensory details, but Ellison knows when enough is enough, when to let us imagine the style of the chairs, the size of the table, and so forth.

There's character development going on here, too: the men straightening in their chairs, their scoops at rest, the use of the mild curse "hell" in dialogue. The class issues being investigated live in the coal dust; nothing else need be said. These are working men. The author—destined for a life in letters—is distinctly other, despite shared race.

All this in what amounts to a single typed page.

CUTTING TO THE CHASE

One danger of my accenting scene is that some students get the idea that I'm saying scene is the only way to go, the only tool we've got, that scene is tops on my list, king of the realm. Listen: Expository passages play as big a role in memoir as they do in fiction. And an even bigger role in the making of essays.

It's perfectly understandable that people come to creative nonfiction and think in terms of exposition instead of scenemaking, "blah-blah" instead of motion pictures. Still, I used to be surprised when able fiction writers in my classes approached nonfiction as pure telling (sometimes as pure pronouncement, though years ago they'd learned the mantra I don't mind repeating: show, don't tell). These were makers of vivid and intense scenes who seemed to forget all they knew when it came to memoir. If it's going to be true, they seemed to reason, it has to sound like, well, like a newspaper article. Or an encyclopedia entry. Or maybe a sociology paper. Or like Emerson, Thoreau—lots of big ideas thrown around and fast.

In the next chapter, "Big Ideas," I will give the expository end of our enterprise its full due. But here, let's think about exposition's counterpart (not to say opposite): scenemaking. And don't forget we're still experimenting: actively trying to change our writing. You may want to say, "I like my style, exposition and all!" Good, good! Say it! But give pure scenemaking a go. And don't worry. Your style's not going to go anywhere while you try something new and different.

SWEET DREAMS

No one's found better words for the effect of scenemaking than John Gardner did in his landmark book *The Art of Fiction*:

> [...] whatever the genre may be, fiction does its work by creating a dream in the reader's mind. We may observe, first, that if the effect of the dream is to be powerful, the dream must probably be vivid and continuous—*vivid* because if we are not quite clear about what it is that we're dreaming,

> who and where the characters are, what it is that they're doing or trying to do and why, our emotions and judgments must be confused, dissipated, or blocked; and *continuous* because a repeatedly interrupted flow of action must necessarily have less force than an action directly carried through from its beginning to its conclusion. [...] [O]ne of the chief mistakes a writer can make is to allow or force the reader's mind to be distracted, even momentarily, from the fictional dream.

The reader is made to dream by the writer: She sees active characters in her head, she pictures settings, almost as if watching a film.

Let's run with the movie comparison for a moment. Think of all the work that's done by the camera before the actors ever say a word. There's the church; there's the main street of the town. And there are the actors, mouths agape in surprise, or whatever. *Scene* is what the movie's characters are up to in a specific time and place, the action we're seeing and interpreting as viewers.

Then what in a movie would correspond to exposition in writing? Stage directions, for one thing. Casting notes. Advice on the settings. Camera angles. Necessary stuff, but note that in the finished product all of that is carefully hidden from most viewers. What's left is people (or animals or monsters) doing things. In a movie drama, there's seldom any kind of analysis, any big pronouncements, any setting forth of ideas in words. But when there is, where does it come from? It comes from a character's mouth and has thereby been rendered as action.

And then there's voice-over. You know, the credits are rolling, the camera is dollying in on the village in the Appalachians, our protagonist's voice comes in out of the blue, kind of quavery, saying: "Life was sure different in those days. Why, America was in a depression, the papers said, but in West Virginia, we didn't feel a change at all. In fact, people felt a little better knowing it wasn't only us poor as mice." Life in general, life in a flow of time, life in a series of places: summary.

Then the little boy pops out of the general store, his arms full of clearly stolen baseball mitts: scene. Soon enough we'll figure out that the mitts are for his town league team and that he's destined to be a star pitcher. No one need tell us now—we're too busy watching the store clerk lose a comic chase (mitts flying) past the town's three churches.

STAY IN THE MOMENT

When you are engaged in scenemaking, know it, and make a project of removing anything that interrupts Gardner's dream. Stay in the time and place of your scene. If you're edging into summary, events in general, you're usually filling in background that should have been set up earlier in the narrative (or will turn out to be unnecessary—try cutting), or you're giving away the future when you should just let the future unfold with events.

If you offer a block of explanation, of judgment, of information, of opinion, you wake us from our dream. Exposition is interruptive. It doesn't make us see or smell or hear, but rather makes us think. Not a bad thing for words to do, don't get me wrong, but when we're in the middle of a scene, exposition can be like ice water in the face. Or, okay, it's like you're lying in your hammock dreaming peacefully of tropical island breezes and found money and perfect schnoogie love and someone leans over you to say, "Did you know that napping reduces stress and can help lower high blood-pressure?"

Here's a rule of thumb to help you weed out what's not needed: scene occurs in a specific place and at a particular time. When the time changes or the place changes (even just a move to another room), the scene changes.

Exposition doesn't need place or a time frame. Learn to separate it from your scenes, at least for now. Yes, put it at the opening or close of a scene or chapter or essay to provide context, overview, philosophy, opinion, appropriate facts and figures, transition. But don't put it in *the middle of the action*:

> My sister Sandra rolled onto the subway platform, grabbed the terrorist's ankle, pulled hard. He fell on top of her, his assault rifle popping off shots that rang against the cement. The second amendment to the constitution protects the right to bear arms. But an assault rifle can shoot up to two hundred rounds a minute. Hundreds are sold at trade shows nearly every week in cities such as Chicago and New York. Sandra felt the hot barrel of the gun against her neck. The barrels of assault rifles can reach temperatures of 450 degrees. In shooting tests performed by the Denver Police ...

No, no! Do the expository work before the scene, do it after, or don't do it at all. (Remember that cutting is a virtue.) If you're writing about assault rifles, give assault rifles a whole section of their own, all the information you can find, wonderful. But when you're in scene, when your sister Sandra is saving the day, *let her save the buzzin' day.*

Summary, too, can take the reader out of the moment. Summary, remember, covers the sweep of time, limns out the course of events in general. Best to use summary as connective tissue between scenes, not as sudden background information for the scene at hand:

> Jack, the neighbor's son, rushed into the kitchen, wielding a huge butcher knife. His uncle cowered, cried out. Jack had gotten the butcher knife on sale at a very nice kitchen-supply store in Jackson Hole, Wyoming, back when he was in college, just before he met Leslie, who became his wife in 1997. They were both skiers, Leslie, in fact, a champion. Jack had always liked knives.

Hey! What about that cowering uncle! Stay in the moment!

Anecdotes don't make good stories. Generally I dig down underneath them so far that the story that finally comes out is not what people thought their anecdotes were about.
—*Alice Munro*

EXERCISE ONE: *Dead Frog*

Go to a favorite work of memoir or other creative nonfiction, and sacrifice its careful construction to science. Take a pencil and mark all the scenes, even number them, as screenwriters do. Then, maybe with a different color, mark all the summary you find. Choose another color, and mark other kinds of exposition. You might even get out a whole box of colored pencils and mark different kinds of exposition, noting how the author is operating. Does she keep her scenes in the moment? If she interrupts them, what does she interrupt with? How does she move from one scene to the next? Where does she locate her blocks of expository writing, of summary? How does she fit in passages and phrases of description?

Next, do the same for some other favorite work: What differences do you find, writer to writer?

Now turn the scalpel on your own work. Are you finding all the same organs you found in the other writers' passages? Are they in similar places?

Can you move things around to more closely emulate your models? Can you add things that are missing? Subtract what's extra?

The title of this exercise comes from Mark Twain: "Explaining a joke is like dissecting a frog: you understand it better, but the frog dies in the process."

Sorry to kill your frog.

EXERCISE TWO: *Cracking Open*

Please go back to any of the exercises you've written from this book so far—perhaps your map exercise—and look for a sentence or even a phrase of summary (or other exposition) that condenses or skims over or rushes past a possible scene.

Now, get to work writing. Expand the sentence or phrase you've identified into at least two pages of scene: no voice-over, no explanation, no facts and figures, no analysis, no summary. The idea is to start to develop an eye for scenes that can move a memoir forward. Also, cracking open will help you begin to clearly see the difference between scenemaking (action, talk, gesture) and expository writing (explanation, summary, opinion, information).

A Scene Grows in Brooklyn

Remember Wendy Guida's map story about her friend Esmerelda? Let's look at the scene Wendy cracked open. The expository sentence she found rich with meaning was this one: "Somehow I believed that song lyrics were maps to my future, not lessons to be learned from to avoid pain."

I don't think it's coincidence at all that the sentence she picked is rather awkward. She's trying to do so much, say so much that needs to be shown. For Wendy, this exercise really took off. I'll just reproduce the opening page or so here, but Wendy's cracking open took five pages and then grew further into a tight little essay that proceeds from the childhood confusion and dreams about sex and romance and power displayed below to a clear-eyed (and yet entertaining) analysis of her failed marriage.

The Vocabulary of Love

Esmerelda and I learn the vocabulary of love as we sing "Haven't Got Time for the Pain" on the way home from P.S. 152. At least, I am learning. Esmerelda already has a stockpile of useful terms from her 16-year-old sister, Malerie, such as "hand job," as in, "if you don't want to sleep with a guy, you just give him a hand job." I figure this is something like lanyard, something to keep the guy's hands busy while you make your escape.

I reassure Esmerelda about the safety of my own virginity: "If Starsky ever comes to my house, I'll just give him a hand job," I tell her.

"Hutch is cuter."

"No he's not."

"Is, to infinity," she says, raising the stakes so high I fold.

Esmerelda is shorter than I am, but she's taller as we walk because she wore Malerie's clogs this morning without asking. We wear our hair in long braids, hers dark blond, mine brown. I do our hair alike each morning before school so people will think we're sisters. Our bodies are soft and rounded yet strong from gymnastics; we have been in the eight-week beginner class for six months. I do sloppy cartwheels so we can stay in the same level. When the instructor tells Esmerelda to do a series of rolls, she retorts, "My mother is paying you. I don't have to do anything."

One thing Wendy's cracking open shows is how much material hides beneath the most unassuming sentences. Note, though, that Wendy hasn't absolutely stayed in scene. Have another look. Where has Wendy gone back into voice-over, jumped out of the place and time of her scene? Where is she most purely in her scene, in the realm of the senses, *in the moment*?

The scene is two girls walking home from school. Wendy the writer interrupts the scene—nothing wrong with this, as I keep saying, nothing wrong when the time comes to make an essay, but in this exercise I just want you to be aware of such interruption—to fill in some history for us: sometime in the recent past, Esmerelda has given Wendy some curious advice. She tells us how the girls look: "soft and rounded yet strong." Description like this can't really be considered an interruption because that's how the girls look during the time frame of the scene.

(But if Wendy were to cut it, how might she get the important information she provides—how the girls look—more into the moment of her scene?) The interruption comes when Wendy goes on to tell us how the girls got strong: gymnastics class. The interruption escalates as Wendy tells us more about the class.

To stay in scene is to stay in the moment. Very difficult, of course, not always necessary, but a sense of the moment—knowing the temporal boundaries of your scene—is critical.

After you've given Wendy's cracking open a good inspection, after you've thought about her use of exposition and interruption, inspect your own work. Where have you gone into voice-over? Abstractions? Explanations? Fulsome description divorced from action? Where are you speaking as a writer sitting at a desk, removed from the events of your scene? And by contrast, where are you most firmly operating in the realm of the senses, staying in the moment, trusting the scene, hiding the writer?

WALKING THAT MILE

Janet Bellweather is a little behind the rest of us by now, but eager to catch up. She came to our second class meeting with a simply drawn map and, having heard the other writers read their stuff, was visibly less threatened, less convinced that everything she wrote had to be perfect. She showed her map around, shrugging, invoked the GENERIC DISCLAIMER to especial hilarity, and read:

> Mother carried Great Aunt Ellen's famous quilt hugged up in her arms like it was Great Aunt Ellen herself. She asked us to lay down on the blanket she's brought and she wanted us to wait until after we ate to swim. Which we did, then we walked a mile along the beach and I always think of that mile. That's when I learned what a mile was walking it. To Grandfather's house where we visit, then walk back. This is on the Cape. And the blanket had blown away. Its into the water, we guessed. And Mother yelled at us in an explosion and called my sister several very serious names and blamed us for losing the blanket and that was like the mile, I always think of it that's when I learned that mother was not well.

So much in this passage, so roughly written. In class I decided not to mention the differences between the verbs *to lie* and *to lay*, and the difference between *its* and *it's*. Not yet. Also, there's plenty to say here about run-ons and fused sentences and fragments and verb tenses. Later, later. Janet had already shown she was pretty defensive, after all. And the truth is, we're all defensive when well-meaning readers start in on our grammar and seem to ignore the important content of our pages. Heck, this is a rough draft, not even a first draft! Better to just note her (extremely common) grammar and usage difficulties in pencil in her margins, then talk to the class about such things later, when no one is in a defensive position.

(But you, gentle reader, you are not in a defensive position at the moment. So go look up a few things, right now. You might even mark Janet's paragraph, naming precisely each problem you find. Use a handbook if you're not clear on a given problem. To name it is to know it, and all that. Are you sure you have the difference between *it's* and *its* straight, for example? A lot of writers, even accomplished writers, don't. The point, of course, is to make you an expert on your own sentences. But more on that in chapter nine.)

In class, we didn't say much about Janet's small errors at all. What we did first was praise what's good here. Someone pointed out what a great line that was about the mile. Janet had "learned what a mile was walking it." And the picture of her mother, hugging that blanket, then yelling. The admission at the end that Mom was mentally ill. As for setting, we only have "the Cape." I think of Cape Cod. Someone else might think of Cape Canaveral or Cape Ann or the Cape of Good Hope, or Superman's cape, on and on. Turned out it was a cape in Oregon. So "the Cape" is probably not precise enough, at least for first mention.

We talked about what Janet might crack open. And folks, by the time we were done, we'd highlighted every line as rich with promise. The writer—Janet—was going to have to pick out her own line to work with.

GOW CRACKS A SCENE, IF NOT A SMILE

Gow Farris was infuriated by his faulty memory as he worked on cracking open a line from his map exercise, refusing to add one word that he couldn't safely testify (before the hanging judge in the court of his mind) was true and correct. First, he told us, he tried cracking open this line: "Those were days when kids thought about candy instead of Nintendo and TV." Even on his own, Gow came to see the evasion in picking the line the group had singled out as conclusion-compulsion stuff and, as such, expendable. His cracking open of this line rendered a bunch of sentences, all right, a kind of rant about kids and TV, an editorial, at best, but not a story, which is what he was after.

So, taking advantage of the fact that writing is endlessly erasable, he tried again, cracking open the line "Then, of course, Mother got into it." Let's see how he did:

> Mother was on the back stoop when Frank and I got home. We saw her as we came up out of the trees from the ravine, and she saw us. My pocket was purely bulging with candy, two kinds I'd stolen. Jawbreakers and root-beer barrels.
>
> We were caught, no way around it. My knees about gave out.
>
> Frank marched right up to the porch and without a second thought he plain lied. He said, "We have bought some candy at Krock's." I remember that line clearly. Mother said, "I see." I remember that line, too. Unforgettable.
>
> She saw, all right, because around Frank's neck were licorice whips, maybe a dozen he'd liberated, a penny each. You see, mother knew how much money we had to spend. A nickel apiece on the very richest day.
>
> Next thing we knew we were on our way back down to Krock's. This time, however, we arrived in a pony cart, one ear each pinched in Mother's sharp fingers.

After Gow read, we in the workshop told him what we admired about his cracked-open piece: mother's sharp fingers, the image of Frank with the incriminating licorice whips around his neck, the strong sense of the place, the strong feeling we all had that a story greater than the vignette is just beginning to unfold. And all without lying.

Someone around our workshop table pointed out the expression "purely bulging," saying she loved it, that it was an example of the success of Gow's voice.

Gow said, "Oh, heavens," at this compliment. He hadn't even noticed that "purely." He said he never talked like that anymore, had spent years purging his vocabulary of such old-time expression. I just grinned: Gow had unintentionally remembered something very important as he re-created this scene—his childhood voice. How wonderful that this bit of truth had slipped by all of Gow's prodigious fortifications.

Then we talked about the idea of voice-over, the author interrupting the reader's dream. Do you find any voice-over or other exposition in Gow's piece?

Where exactly? Where does the author, sitting at his writing desk, intrude himself into the reader's "dream"?

What we picked out as voice-over in Gow's piece is the stuff our favorite retired reporter has included about how clearly he remembers, and the forgettable "Unforgettable" that he throws in, trying to convince the judge in his mind of his veracity. But readers aren't like judges, not really. They just want to believe. No need to wake them up to tell them to do so: their dream is proof of their belief.

And then, some joker (I'm afraid it was I) had the temerity to say that there was still much to crack open here. How about "she saw us"? How does a boy know when his mother sees him? How did Gow? Did she stiffen? Wave? What exactly?

Or how about "Next thing we knew"? Hidden in that conventional phrase is Mother's entire response to the boys' crime. But how did she act? Is she a mother who shouts? Who smolders? Or is she forgiving, understanding? We know she pinches ears. What else? (We'll do a lot more with this kind of consideration in chapter five, which is about characters, but for now, let's simply note how closely character and character development are related to scenemaking.)

We talked, too, about language in Gow's exercise. I took the liberty of pointing out one small construction I would have liked to change: "Mother was on the back stoop." A simple verb switch can do a lot of work here. How about, say, "Mother loomed on the back stoop"? Or use any verb (as long as it's just right: Gow's job) except that pesky verb *to be*.

Now it's time to closely inspect your own work. Can you give yourself the same clear-eyed look we've given Wendy, Janet, and Gow?

EXERCISE THREE: *Exposition Patrol*

Get out your box of colored pencils and examine your own cracking-open exercise. Where are you interrupting the reader's dream with pronouncements and explanations and analysis? Where are you summarizing the past, predicting the future, leaving the moment? Look for the places you're speaking as a writer at his desk and not acting as a movie camera. Try cutting all the voice-over you find, all the expository writing.

What's left?

Scene, that's what, things happening.

And remember, I'm not trying to turn you into an exposition cop. Exposition is scene's sober sister. We need exposition to drive scene home after the party. You won't be leaving it out when it comes time to write your short memoir, your essay, your book, because exposition has its place, and it's an important place. It's just that that place isn't here and now.

So just for now, for the sake of the exercise, be merciless: identify exposition and summary, and cut it all. When you lose important information doing so, figure out ways to get that information in the moment, into your scene, all in a specific time and place.

EXERCISE FOUR: *Cracking Open II, The Sequel*

Please go back to your cracking-open exercise and see what's still there to crack. There's always something. For the sake of this exercise, try cracking a phrase that doesn't look very promising, something transitional, like Gow's "Next thing we knew." Or try cracking open pronouns. Who do you mean by "we," exactly, or "it" or "they"? Almost any sentence or phrase (or even word) will yield not just verbiage but important surprises.

EXERCISE FIVE: *Day of the Week*

Saturdays aren't like Mondays aren't like Wednesdays. Find a passage in your cracking-open exercise (or your Cracking Open II, The Sequel) that's set in generic mode, which is one of the forms of summary. You know: "When I was a kid we would go to Jones Beach." Or "In the months before our trip we would sing with father." Try starting with a particular day of the week: "One Saturday ..." The idea is to go from generic summary and life in general—the kinds of things you would do in childhood summers, say—to a specific day and time, and therefore firmly into scene.

And the day of the week is vital.

Did our writer sing with father every day? Or was it in reality only on Saturday nights? Perhaps from there our writer will recall that Dad wore jeans on Saturday night only: "One Saturday, Dad couldn't find his dungarees." And now we're in the midst of a scene. If it's Monday, a certain mood prevails, right? Fish on Fridays? Choir rehearsal always on Wednesday? Board meetings on Monday? And so forth. Note how the expression *one day* puts your work, and therefore your reader, in a particular time and not only a particular place: both are necessary for scene.

EXERCISE SIX: *To the Movies*

Rent two or three movies you've liked a lot and are familiar with and watch them in a new way, thinking about scene. How does the director manage scene? What exactly is the starting point of a given scene? Scan back and watch the scene several times. Where does it end? Are there interruptions of any kind? If you were to convert the scene to writing, what would be necessary to provide a similar mood? What information comes from the actors? What from the cinematographer? What from the director? What from voice-over? Try blocking out a favorite scene from a film on paper (Jane walks to dresser, picks up purse. Richard takes it away from her, rifles through it ...), then try writing a section of it in your fullest sentences.

Now turn back to your own writing. How would a director (and her huge staff) film your scene? What directions would you have to give to have it come out just the way you see it? Try turning your scene into a film script, including not just dialogue but camera directions, advice to the actors, casting and location notes. What's needed? What's extra?

Last—back to memoir mode—revise your original scene to reflect what you've discovered.

EXERCISE SEVEN: *Apology*

Think about Gow Farris. How might someone who will under no circumstances lie manage to make a vivid scene—including dialogue—that is true despite relying on re-creation?

Try this: Start a vignette by confessing to your reader that you simply cannot remember all the details of, say, the day you fell in the well, then apologize profusely for your memory. I'm sorry, I'm sorry, I'm sorry, but I can't remember what people said. Then apologize further: I'm going to have to make a few things up. Now make the scene. You aren't deceiving anybody, right? The idea is to free you of ethical baggage—just for the moment—so you can attend to drama.

When the scene's written, can you go back and cut most or all of the apologizing?

WRITING LIFE STORIES

EXERCISE EIGHT: *Telling the Goddamn Truth for Once*

If, unlike Gow Farris, you have tended toward easy fiction in these exercises—lying, Gow would call it—you might want to try this exercise. Gow Farris is a journalist. You, perhaps, have been (until now) a fiction writer. No one has to tell you how to make things up, or when. If it's more convenient for your story that Grandma live in Seattle, by God, she lives in Seattle. (Journalists, please go back to exercise seven. Go on, shoo.)

Okay, if you're still reading this exercise, you must belong here. Embellisher! You know who you are.

Here's your special assignment: Look back to your map or your cracking-open or other exercises and pick a scene to dramatize. Only this time the first line is "For once, I'm going to tell the truth."

And go on to write (or rewrite) the scene in a way Gow Farris would approve. It might help to imagine that a team of fact-checkers from *The New York Times* is going to investigate every single word. I've worked with these people. They're very, very good and very, very stern; not even mild exaggerations are going to get by. If that isn't enough, just picture yourself on Oprah's couch when the fact-checkers give their report.

EXERCISE NINE: *Seeing*

My daughter, Elysia, is seven as I write, a very funny person, smart and organized, uncannily observant. After a week at bug camp—an actual day camp dedicated to insects—she was an entomologist. I delighted in pointing out insects, and one fall day, I showed her one of those brown bugs with great, not-very-painful pincers off the front end.

"Earwig," I said.

"Boy or girl," she answered, unimpressed.

Boy or girl?

Impatiently she took the bug from me, examined its pincers. "Girl," she said. "See, the pincers are curved. Boy pincers are straight." For good measure she said, "And boy monarchs have spots on their wings."

In the autumn woods she picks up a brightly changed poplar leaf, says, "This one's different from the others."

"Well, we've got maple leaves here and oak leaves and basswood leaves and all kinds of others," I say.

"No, I mean different from the other yellow ones, the heart ones."

And I look closer. The leaf in hand is a heart, but unlike other poplar leaves it has a bold, sawtooth edge. It has blown in from somewhere across the neighbor's fields—we can't find the tree it's come from. Later I look it up: big-tooth aspen (called big-tooth poplar around here). And later again, we find the tree—it holds its leaves a week later than the regular heart trees.

Elysia's teaching me how to see.

Here's the exercise: Go sit someplace—an office, a park, anyplace— and just really look. How are trees put together? How are chairs made? How is this rock different from that rock? How do shadows and distance affect color? Why is this footprint wet and that one dry? And so forth.

I always think of an Edward Hopper retrospective I saw some years ago at the Whitney Museum of American Art in New York. His early work was good—showed his great talent—but was different from his later. The early paintings tended to use hundreds of small and rather fussy strokes, many shades of color carefully smoothed and blended. In one painting, a seascape, I took notice of a seagull for some reason and examined it. Loosely represented by about twenty small brushstrokes, the bird had a stiff quality; but no mistake, it was a seagull.

Gallery to gallery in the Whitney I followed Hopper's growth. Across one large room I spied another seagull in a painting that came thirty years after the first (the painting newer, the artist older), very plainly a herring gull, standing proudly, gazing the way herring gulls do, this one on the peak of a barn. Up close I could see the artist's hand motion— flick, flick—and see that the seagull was a matter of two quick and well-controlled dabs of paint, one white, one gray. Two strokes. Hopper was learning to see precisely and to simplify his work into mastery.

So just look. How would you put what you see into words? Take some notes next time you go out; try some sentences. How few words can you use to get an exact impression of, say, a stone wall? What's the simplest way to describe the sky? Get a good drawing pencil and make sketches with your words and phrases, thinking of them as strokes, as colors.

A variation is to look at people, preferably from a distance. Just see. What exactly are the visual clues that tell you someone is angry or intelligent or old or unhappy or high or a potential friend?

I'm trying to write a particular kind of scene, and I see corn on the cob. To "see" corn on the cob doesn't mean that it suddenly hovers; it only means that it keeps coming back. And I try to figure out "What is all this corn doing?" I discover what it is doing.

—Toni Morrison

Exercise Ten: *Hearing, Smelling, Touching, Tasting*

This is just exercise nine adapted to all the senses: Go back to your favorite places and, this time, hear, smell, touch, taste. What's to be sensed in a room? What's to be sensed in a field? How exactly are these sense impressions apprehended, and what effect do they have? How is a walk in the woods on a black, cloudy night different from a walk in moonlight, in sunlight? To disconnect overpowering sight, you might try a blindfold.

One caveat: When it comes to smelling, touching, and tasting people, discretion is advised, and, at the very least, permission.

Exercise Eleven: *The Photo Album*

You know, the one in your closet, buried beneath the piles of hand-knitted cardigans, gifts from Aunt Sue, or the box in the cabinet by the fireplace in your parents' house with loose photos from every conceivable era of their lives, and intersecting yours. The older, the better.

Flip through the pages, dig through the box, give yourself a slide show. (Remember those old carousel projectors?) You are looking for a scene. Avoid face shots, class photos, school portraits, and the like. Scenes need action, as well as a time and a place. You don't have to be in the photo yourself—perhaps you are the one taking it. Let the photo carry you back, not to a general past, but to a single time, a single place. Keep digging, make a pile.

Later, at your desk, pick a photo. What do you see? Perhaps Grandpa is cutting the cake, blue frosting-fish around the edges: *Congratulations Kenny Catfish!* There's a dog lurking (Alphie, the mutt!), eyeing the frosting on Grandpa's sleeve. Grandpa appears to be mid-sway—he's been sipping from his flask, secretly (he thinks). Who's that in the background?

Ugh—Uncle Pete's "date," Arlene (how could a skirt be that short)? Most importantly, what's just outside the frame? Your mother and your aunt whispering about Arlene, paper cups of sweet tea splashed with Seagram's, secretly (they think).

Then write. Jump into the scene, into the singular moment the photo holds. No exposition here, no summary, no voice-over, no setup, no background, no leap to the future. We don't need to know how we got here, nor where we're headed, just that we are here.

What's happening in the moment and location captured?

Use your words.

Taking Time to Grow

Before you move on in this book, I'd suggest a period of studious reading and writing. Analyze the scenes of favorite writers, perhaps with the help of your writing circle. Think again about how good writers separate scene and exposition (sometimes line by line). Do the seeing exercises; take some time to look. Dig through your photographs, stare at your timelines, and draw some new maps.

Then just make scenes.

This can be a lot of fun when the pressure of writing a finished piece is off your back—just make scenes for the sake of making scenes. Notice the connections between scenes, the emergence (perhaps) of themes and subjects and ideas, but don't work these up just yet. For now, just crack those scenes open sentence by sentence, then crack open the crackings open, make rocks for the beautiful stone wall that's coming.

Take all the time you wish.

CHAPTER FOUR

Big Ideas

Believe those who are seeking the truth; doubt those who find it.

—Andre Gide

In the last minutes of the last session of a two-week summer course I taught at the University of Vermont a decade or so ago, I turned with mock gravity to one of my favorite students ever—Jane Renshaw—and asked her a tough question, not expecting an answer: "Jane, tell us, what's the secret of life?"

Jane was eighty-five. Within a few months she would pass away, succumbing to a condition she had told us much about in a very short and blunt essay called "On Illness," which she'd written in fulfillment of an exercise I'll give later in this chapter.

The secret of life. Some question! I was making a joke about the process of our course, I guess, acknowledging a bit too sardonically that there weren't going to be any final answers, that the questions we'd raised about writing were going to have to be the answers.

Jane had arrived each morning in the van from her modest retirement home, had presided patiently at her end of our conference table, listening to my foolishness, asking for clarification when the younger troops (their ages ranging from twenty to sixty-six) were nodding their heads as if what I said made perfect sense. She was quick to smile and had a sweetly wandering laugh. Always her criticism of the other students' work was gentle; always it was tough and wise: "I wonder why a man would act like that," she'd muse, getting to the exact heart of a classmate's memoir about his rotten father when our writer hadn't really thought through that all-important *why*. And once, after I'd given one of my impassioned speeches about the need to care strongly about our material, Jane nodded to indicate a young man at my right hand and softly said, "That young fellow doesn't understand." She was right, of course—Chuck looked 100 percent dazed and confused—but she'd also picked up the quiet fact that it was that young fellow's callow and careless work that had got me speechifying.

So, last session: "Jane, tell us, what's the secret of life?"

Jane smiled benignly, forgiving me my sardonic nature, tilted her head, and said without the slightest pause: "Searching."

An indignant Chuck said, "Not finding?"

"No, no, no," Jane said emphatically, letting her beatific smile spread. "Searching."

FROM IDEAS TO ESSAYS

Ideas are abstract by nature. Unbidden, ideas (like memories) arrive in our brains in pieces: a bit of evidence, a blast of emotion, a sentence of logic, a shot of paranoia, a visceral reaction to film on the news, a vision clear as wind and descended as if from heaven. The pieces float around, coalescing in various and partial shapes, wrapped and then rewrapped in layers of preconceptions, blankets of family custom (or pathology), clear sheets of wisdom, sturdy pockets of knowledge. The problem is getting what seems whole and vital in our brains onto the page whole and vital. Seldom as we sit with pencil in hand will the idea come at once (though many experienced writers are skilled at doing earliest drafts in their heads). Most often, an idea will reveal itself fully—move from amorphous blob to elegant artifact— only in the writing. Honest first drafts often look like the mind as described above: aswirl with conflicting notions, half-baked insight, generous impulse, hackneyed platitude, opinionated surety, brilliant strings of words, silence.

How often have you had a heated argument with someone about a subject the two of you gradually came to realize you substantially agreed upon? Or left a pleasant conversation and understood only slowly that you have nodded your head to erroneous thinking and said things you didn't believe? In conversation, as in drafting, ideas take shape sentence by sentence, retraction by retraction, statement by revised statement.

Ideas. What I'm talking about in this chapter is sometimes called *theme*, sometimes called *thesis*. But theme seems too one-dimensional to cover what I want to cover here, too purposefully invoked by the writer, too easily grasped by the reader.

Thesis, as you know, is the point of a traditional essay (which point is traditionally made in a succinct thesis sentence, then supported). The term *idea*, as I use it, is a little broader: idea is the deep and cool well from which the waters of theme and thesis are drawn. When I talk about idea in an essay or memoir, I'm talking about the underlying conception or conceptions that give a piece of successful nonfiction its unity—the kind of unity that plot sometimes brings to fiction.

To convey an idea, you must have an idea. Where do ideas come from? How to get from the whorled mists of the mind to the straight lines of the page? How to develop belief into the background for a rich and convincing essay? How to build the vignettes of memoir into evidence that supports an idea?

Read on.

EXERCISE ONE: *Automatic Writing*

Automatic writing was a tool of Gertrude Stein's and other modernist writers and has been used by everyone from clairvoyants to psychoanalysts, philosophers to statesmen, from Jack Kerouac to Kristen Keckler. It's a simple way to disconnect the overweening editor in our heads, to let what's in our heads hit the paper or computer keyboard raw so that we can *see* what's in our heads. All you do is pick a prescribed time limit (start with one minute, work up to ten or more), get your notebook in hand, and say, "Go." And then, well, go. Write. Don't stop, don't think, don't worry, don't edit; just go-go-go, till the time limit is up.

Ding!

If you get stalled, just write anything, any nonsense ("I hate you Bill Roorbach for making me do this, I hate you Bill Roorbach for making me do this, I hate you Bill Roorbach for making me do this," to quote Mindy Mallow-Dalmation), but do not stop writing.

The goal is simply to see what comes out. Often, the issue at hand will be defined: you're about to start a new job, you're in the throes of grief, you're pregnant, you're in love, you're in New Orleans with your soul mate after Katrina. So that's what appears. But how you feel about the issue at hand turns up, too, often in surprising ways. And, so frequently as not to be coincidental, a new way of saying and seeing arrives. Sometimes a key turns up for that locked door you've been yearning to open.

This one is best done daily over time, perhaps when you first wake in the morning, and has the distinct excellence of not requiring excellence.

THE *I* IN IDEA, THE *I* IN THE ESSAY

I was taught as a kid and in high school that an essay was an argument of a particular kind. It had to have the thesis sentence we've mentioned earlier, clearly stated, and all the stuff you wrote had to support that thesis. And, of course, I learned that an essay had parts—a beginning, a middle, and an end—and that these parts had names. This format is the soul of what's commonly called academic writing, the kind of writing that makes a category and a term like creative nonfiction necessary. For me, as a kid and well into college, one of the defining characteristics of academic writing was that it was no fun. You couldn't be yourself but had to be someone else, someone deathly serious, someone formal, someone who shared the moribund and officious voice of an encyclopedia. A conformist, in other words, someone who wouldn't challenge the overburdened teacher. Things are changing drastically, and academic writing is often beautifully made these days, with voice and without obfuscation (in the form of prolixity and specialized jargon), with soul and not simply intelligence.

This "new" approach to academic writing suggests something your professors knew all along, even while they were drilling that five-paragraph monotony into your head: There's another kind of essay out there, the kind you find most often in *The Best American Essays*, or in the work of writers from E.B. White to Adrienne Rich to Janet Malcolm, George Orwell to James Baldwin to Nicholson Baker, and contemporaneously in all the best literary magazines, even some of the bigs, like *The New Yorker*, *The Atlantic*, or *Harper's*. It's a more wandering sort of essay, an essay in which one gets the sense of a person, a person who is, well, *searching*. An authorial opinion isn't enough for an essay like this: an opinion gets examined, turned inside out, flipped, flopped, mugged, comes out the other side bruised but burnished, or disproved and left for dead. Facts get stacked in various combinations, are interrogated for meaning. Objectivity isn't ever a value—objectivity is a myth. People aren't objects. People are subjects. Subjectivity is the whole point. And truth emerges. But truth can't gloat—as soon as she shows her head, she gets examined, too. Nothing is taken for granted in the personal essay. Everything is fodder for further thought, investigation.

The writer is learning, discovering something that the reader will discover, too. As I noted earlier, the term Phillip Lopate uses for such work is the *personal essay*. (And I repeat: Please see his anthology *The Art of the Personal Essay* for not only examples of the genre, but for the genre's history and for Lopate's illuminating and defining introduction. Read his personal essays, too, for strong examples of the form.)

When I say personal essay, I don't mean that the work contained therein is private or somehow small; I don't mean that it's work only one's family should read or that there's nothing universal there; I don't mean that there is no argument, no thesis; I just mean that the author speaks as a person rather than as a disembodied voice of knowledge, that the writer speaks from the heart, with no great worries about so-called fairness. That is, the writer speaks honestly, admits that he is there behind the words—complete with prejudices, interests, passions, hatreds, tastes, pet peeves. The writer writes something that only he could possibly write, sometimes grumpily. And the writer writes for a general audience, for all intelligent readers, for anyone who cares.

TAKE BACK THE ESSAY!

A little history:

The origin of the term *essay* to refer to a particular kind of writing is usually placed in Renaissance France and attributed to Michel de Montaigne (pronounced in English to rhyme with Fontaine, and not to be confused in either person or pronunciation with the Italian artist Andrea Mantegna, who died in 1506).

In *The Art of the Personal Essay*, Phillip Lopate lovingly calls Montaigne the "fountainhead," and goes on to say that Montaigne "may well have been the greatest essayist who ever lived." You might want to pick up Donald Frame's readable and thoroughgoing biography of our man, but here's the way-too-quick version: Michel de Montaigne was born in 1533, son of a patient and doting father (Montaigne himself tells us quite a bit about his father in his *Essais*), who gave him the best education money could buy and set his son up as a lord. Montaigne loved the Latin poets and philosophers and statesmen, Seneca and Plutarch, Virgil and Tertius, Martial, Catullus, Horace. He was a practicing lawyer, a member of the *Parlement* of Gascony, and later, mayor of Bordeaux. But it was at *Parlement* that he met Étienne de La Boétie, a poet and thinker and statesmen with whom Montaigne talked endlessly. According to Frame, "La Boétie satisfied [Montaigne's] deepest need, for complete communication."

But after five years of a deep friendship, ideal conversation, and constant companionship, La Boétie died, aged "32 years, 9 months, and 17 days" (in Montaigne's tellingly obsessive reckoning), of a sudden intestinal ailment. Frame fills in many details of La Boétie's life, but readers of Montaigne already know much of the story from Montaigne's essay "On Friendship."

Donald Frame: "There is much to show that the *Essays* themselves are—among other things—a compensation for the loss of La Boétie."

Phillip Lopate: "Indeed it has been suggested that Montaigne began writing his book so that he could talk to someone; the reader took the place of La Boétie."

So the *Essais* of Montaigne are an ongoing conversation with Étienne de La Boétie. And centuries after Montaigne's death, a reader feels the writer's presence: Montaigne's essays separately and in total remain a conversation with readers—readers who become stand-ins for La Boétie, one at a time.

EXERCISE TWO: *The Conversation*

What if you were to begin to think of your writing as a conversation with a reader, just one? Two people intimate over a meal, say, or over a cocktail, or coffee, head-to-head. What if your audience was not a huge roomful of frighteningly various souls but one single person, the king or queen of good listeners, always nodding in interest, always with you, and a genuine friend, always ready to question your logic? What if you started to think of your writing as a conversation?

Here's the exercise:

Pick a dear friend with whom you enjoy conversation and argument. Now picture that friend reading over your shoulder as you sit down to

revise any of your exercises to date. What must change? Will your ⫶
admonish you for a certain pomposity? Will your friend yawn as y
peat old information? Will your friend take issue with some of your f̲ ̲ ̲ ̲ ̲.
Argue your opinions? Where will she laugh? Where will she grow sad?
Where will she nod her head in understanding and agreement? Tailor
your sentences to the needs of one reader, and you'll tend to make your
work more accessible to all.

If you find it hard to imagine your friend listening, why not bring the
work to the actual person and read it aloud to her? What reactions do
you get? Why? What do you hear as you read? Where do your own words
trip you up? Again, what needs to change?

And if as yet you are (understandably) too shy to read your stuff
aloud to anyone, take heart: even contemplating such a reading will result in necessary revisions.

YOU ARE AN EXPERT, TOO

Montaigne is said (by himself) to have worn a medallion around his neck inscribed with his motto, which I will render in modern French: *Que sais-je?*
"What do I know?"

And indeed, when it came time to write, he would look into himself and
report what was there—good or bad, ugly or beautiful. He was an expert on
himself (as we all are, or should be) and so reported confidently, as an authority
(note the word author lurking in that common word).

It's difficult, these days, to ascribe much value to our own thoughts on, say,
friendship. The editors of *Newsweek* don't call one of their friends if they wish to
have a report on friendship. They call a psychologist or a sociologist. Yet we all
are experts on the subject, just as Montaigne was. Even if you have no friends,
you know something about friendship, perhaps more exotic stuff than the rest
of us. So, look inside yourself. What do you know? The answer is that you know
a lot, about myriad subjects.

If I asked you to write on, say, ants, you'd have plenty to type: you've dealt
with ants all your life. And your take on ants would be different from anyone
else's. Sure, someone like Edward O. Wilson, the renowned myrmecologist (and
fine memoirist, by the way, read *Naturalist*), knows more about ants than you

do, but you know more about the day the ants carried away your great-aunt Minnie. And you could always study up to add to your knowledge, bolster your authority (but more about that in chapter seven).

Here are a few titles from Montaigne's essays. Note that anyone—even you, especially you—could write about any of these subjects: "On Sadness," "On Idleness," "On Liars," "On Prognostications," "On Fear," "On the Power of Imagination," "On Drunkenness," "On Books," "On Cruelty," "On Valour," "On Anger," "On Smells," "On Experience."

Other writers have taken over and made use of this form of title, too, for books as well as for essays: *On Love*, by Stendhal; "On Shaving a Beard," by Phillip Lopate; "On the Morning After the Sixties," by Joan Didion; "On Embalming," by F. Gonzalez-Crussi; "On Living Alone," by Vivian Gornick; *On Becoming a Novelist*, by John Gardner; "On Coffee-House Politicians," by William Hazlitt (the elder); "On Failure and Anonymity," by Mira Schor; "On Ambition," by Donald Hall; "On Apprenticeship," by yours truly (see appendix C).

Let me forthwith reproduce in its entirety Montaigne at his most basic, as translated (with probable debt to John Florio) by Charles Cotton in 1685–86 and revised by William Hazlitt (the younger) in 1842.

Of Thumbs

Tacitus reports that amongst certain Barbarian kings their manner was, when they would make a firm obligation, to join the right hands close to one another, and twist their thumbs; and when, by force of straining, the blood mounted to the ends, they lightly pricked them with some sharp instrument, and mutually sucked them.

Physicians say that the thumbs are the masters of the hand, and that their Latin etymology is derived from *pollere*. The Greeks called them *antichier*, as who should say "another hand." And it seems the Latins also sometimes take them in this sense for the whole hand: —

sed nec vocibus excitata blandis
Molli pollice nec rogata, surgit.

It was at Rome a signification of favour to depress and turn in the thumbs, —

Fautor utroque tuum laudabit pollice ludum

"Thy patron, when thou mak'st thy sport
Will with both thumbs applaud thee for't,"
and of disfavor to elevate and thrust them outward: *converso pollice vulgi Quemlibet occidunt populariter.*
"The vulgar with reverted thumbs
Kill each one that before them comes."
The Romans exempted from war all such as were maimed in the thumbs, as having no longer sufficient strength to hold their weapons. Augustus confiscated the estate of a Roman knight, who had willfully cut off the thumbs of two young children he had, to excuse them from going into the armies. And before him, the senate, in the time of the Italian war, had condemned Caius Vatienus to perpetual imprisonment, and confiscated all his goods, for having purposely cut off the thumb of his left hand, to exempt himself from the expedition.

Someone, I forget who, having won a naval battle, cut off the thumbs of all his vanquished enemies, to render them incapable of fighting and of handling the oar. The Athenians also caused the thumbs of those of Aegina to be cut off, to deprive them of their precedence in the art of navigation.

In Lacedemonia, pedagogues chastised their scholars by biting their thumbs.

[Note that translators Cotton and reviser Hazlitt have decided not to translate the first Latin passage. John Florio, 1603, was not so shy: "It will not rise, though with sweet words excited/Nor with the touch of softest thumb invited." And if that's still too cryptic, how about this 1987 translation from M.A. Screech (he titles the essay "On Thumbs"): "Neither sweet words of persuasion nor the help of her thumb can get it erect."]

Did you notice the lack in "Of Thumbs" of introduction or conclusion? The quotes, the bits of history? What does Montaigne know about thumbs? Our man reaches into his well-stocked mind and lets us know. When he can't remember the thumb-chopping general's name, he says so and goes on contentedly. Of course, he could have looked up this information, but he sees (even through multiple revisions) that the name is not the important thing. But translators like Hazlitt Jr. simply cannot let Montaigne's insouciance about sources go: there's often a footnote and the general named.

Reading Montaigne, I feel time telescope and collapse, five hundred years like nothing; I feel very much in the presence of an interesting person, someone talking just to me.

Pass the wine.

The True Nature of the Essay

Montaigne called his chapters *essais*. This term, as you may already know, comes from the French verb *essayer*, which means "to try." So an essay is a try. That's all. An attempt. An effort to get some little bit or large chunk of thought into writing. (Sir Francis Bacon brought the word to England and to the English during Shakespeare's lifetime, publishing some of his own writings as "Essays.")

So an essay, dear writer, is just a try. Doesn't that take some of the pressure off?

EXERCISE THREE: *Trying*

One more conceptual exercise: think of each day's work as a try. Nothing more, nothing less. This may be a radical bit of thought restructuring. And instead of applying the labels *memoir* or *essay* or *piece* or *article*, say, "Try." Just to yourself. Just for now.

Remember Jane Renshaw: "Searching."

And Chuck: "Not finding?"

"No, no, no. Searching."

A GENTLE GOAL

One more note: My talk in Jane's class about essays as *tries* reminded another student, Joe Deffner, of his days in the Peace Corps, teaching English in Kenya. One of the many cultural differences between Kenya and the United States became apparent as Joe taught: the greatest compliment, the thing his students told each other and most wanted to hear from him, was, "You have tried."

This one's easy to start. You just write the word *On* at the top of a piece of paper (or type it at the top of your screen), then add an abstract noun. One I like to do in class is "On Separation." Everyone seems to have something rich to say about that subject. Montaigne's list of titles, or Bacon's, may give ideas, too. But go with the word that popped into your head first. (It's probably hanging there right now, worrying you with the honesty it's going to take to discuss.)

This exercise should be as close to automatic writing as you can make it: Pick your title, think for a minute, then write. No pausing, no editing. Just tell us what you know about, say, humiliation, or ecstasy, or what have you, that word that's in your head right now. And don't pre-edit by searching for an easier word to use. The word now peeping its name from the depths of your cerebral cortex has great value in itself. Why that word at this moment?

But please be sure it's an abstract noun. Not a concrete noun (like ant), not a proper noun (capitalized, like Joe or New Jersey). Abstract. Note that many students try jokes: "On My Husband." Tee-hee. "On My Way to Work." Ha-ha. But the joking interferes with the purpose of the exercise, which is to get you saying true things about abstract notions. That is, to get you working with ideas.

Oh, by the way: no storytelling, no scenes. Here's a chance to speak from your desk, from the present.

One page is fine. More if you like.

Go!

PURE EXPOSITION

How'd it go? Not so easy? Piece of cake? Either way, this is an exercise you can try again and again. It will help you find ideas—even if you struggle mightily with it—and *Idea*, as we've said, is one of the main engines that powers an essay or a memoir. This exercise will also show how you can use yourself, your indivisible *I*, to illuminate a particular subject, however simple or however abstruse. It may lead you, as well, to begin to find your voice, find the power of your unique way with words (but more about that in chapter six, "Stage Presence").

What you write in this exercise might not make its way verbatim into your finished work but may explain to you what's at stake, or what you're getting at. Always and at the least, it will leave a flavor. Often it will provide your essay or memoir with a strong sentence or two, sometimes the very pivot of your piece.

In the previous chapter, I asked you to make scenes, show events, keep the voice-over and the analysis out. Now I'm asking you to do the opposite—speak from your desk directly to your reader, offer information, opinion, ideas, categories, hierarchies, facts, figures, all in the most elegant sentences you can manage. When I say, "No narrative," people sometimes go into shock. Certain writers (I'm like this) are *made* out of narrative—characters doing things, dialogue, action—that's all they really know or care to do. But, let me repeat something I said earlier (and let it become a refrain): learning is changing, doing the hard work.

Then again, some readers of this book (maybe you?) will have struggled more with the scenemaking exercises, the cracking open. More comfortable writing exposition? Okay, here's your chance.

Some definition, or redefinition, is probably in order:

NARRATIVE	EXPOSITORY WRITING
· needs a time and place	· ideas exist outside of time
· tells a story	· examines, explains
· portrays events	· analyzes events
· exemplifies ideas	· expresses ideas directly
· puts a dream of events in a reader's head	· uses those events as evidence for an argument

High exposition is exposition that's aphoristic (an aphorism is a saying, an adage). Some examples? Here's a classic, from Jane Austen, her opening sentence for the novel *Pride and Prejudice*: "It is a truth universally acknowledged, that a single man in possession of a good fortune, must be in want of a wife." Or how about this sentence from the opening of the chapter called "Reading" in *Walden*, by our friend H.D. Thoreau: "In accumulating property for ourselves or our posterity, in founding a family or a state, or acquiring fame even, we are mortal; but in dealing with truth we are immortal, and need fear no change nor accident." Or this, from Katharine S. White's *Onward and Upward in the Garden*: "For gardeners, [spring] is the season of lists and callow hopefulness." Or Kathleen Norris, from *Dakota: A Spiritual Geography*: "Dakota is a painful reminder of human limits, just as cities and shopping malls are attempts to deny them." High exposition has a quality of grand truth, of universal applicability. God probably thinks in high exposition when He or She is not making up the stories of our lives.

Note that in using the term *high exposition* so blithely, I don't mean to imply any value judgment. I'm only calling it *high* because I'm picturing a ladder, a ladder that's not going anywhere better than where it started, a ladder whose bottom rung is just as sturdy as the top. I could have easily as flipped the ladder, called personal exposition *high*. But that would subvert the old terms, and I don't want to cause confusion among people my age and older, who heard all these terms in school. Notice there's no exposition I'm calling *low*.

Other forms of exposition include *informational exposition* (the facts—newspaper journalism is mostly this); *exposition of opinion* (op-ed pages, columns, polemics); observational exposition (description); *personal exposition* (the grand *we*, speaking for us all, is replaced with a humble *I*, speaking for itself); and *narrative summary* (what happened over periods of time beyond the immediate).

Have a look at this passage from Diane Ackerman's book *A Natural History of Love* (which, by the way, might as easily have been titled *On Love*).

> Many lessons about whom and how to love, and what's sexually chic, bombard us from the media. Whenever I open a magazine these days, I half expect steam to rise from the pages. Perfumes war in the visual Amazon of the ads. To make their zest more potent, one rips a slit open, smears the all-but-invisible, exploded beads of scent along one's wrist or inner elbow, and inhales the aroma. We crave sensory experiences. In that, we're no different from most people.

It's all exposition, of course, but note that the first line and the last two are high exposition and use the grand *we*. The rest is good writing, of course, but note the differences in sweep and grandeur, the different styles of exposition, sentence to sentence.

Please look back at your "On ..." exercise. Have you written any sentences of high exposition? No? Try to add a couple. Not easy, I know. A lot of first stabs at saying something grand about love, for example, will get you slogans from drugstore greeting cards. But keep going. Use the grand *we*. Say a great truth. Don't get embarrassed; no one's looking. It might take many tries, but keep going till you get a sentence you can use, even if it means making stabs at your "On ..." exercise ten minutes (or more) a day for two weeks.

The acid test for high exposition? It should be unarguably true, unequivocal.

Jeez, is that all?

I thought everything you wrote had to be about England; nobody ever told me you could write about growing up in Ireland.
—*Frank McCourt*

MORE EXAMPLES FOR COMPARISON

Gow Farris, you'll be glad to know, used the opportunity of the "On ..." exercise to blast me as a knee-jerk liberal and a general clown with an essay called "On Ponytailed Professors." I would gladly reproduce it here, but for some reason Gow hasn't offered it for my use. Suffice it to say, it was very funny; the class roared with laughter. You have never seen so many red faces and teeth and tonsils. I took the piece as proof that Gow was falling in love with me. My response after laughing a long time was to point out that *Ponytailed Professors* is not an abstract noun. The old company man hadn't followed instructions. I asked him to do the assignment over.

He did:

On Grief

Time heals nothing. Those that are gone, stay gone. Your heart like a balloon with it, a gloomy balloon. The kind that rolls on the floor after bad parties. Swollen and dejected. Might explode at any minute. Lord help us. We are made of dust and ashes and to dust and ashes shall we return. That's not original with me, by the way. I am TRYing to get the exact feeling. O, liberal professor, I am essaying (do you know that word?). In grief the air around us is filled with the heaviness of loss and our chest is filled like a rising balloon. A sinking balloon. Our chest is filled too full with some gas heavier than air.

Gow is getting there, folks, battling his defenses, battling me, battling memory, working toward the idea that has made it so important that he write. And sometimes the search is a battle. In fact—let's face it—sometimes searching is the whole damn war.

Jacki Bell on Memory

Let's examine another student's response to the "On ..." exercise. Note that a lot of fine things can happen even while no high exposition (or very little) turns up.

Here's a try by Jacki Bell, a talented writer of fiction, working in creative nonfiction for the first time. Look for traces of narrative, for examples of high exposition, for examples of other expositional styles, especially personal exposition, where the humble *I* replaces the grand *we*.

On Memory

There should be more choice in memory. It should be a kind of video store where we can go and choose what we want to remember clearly—and obscure, no delete, that which we no longer need or that which serves no good purpose.

Memory should be reliable. Like the lungs or the heart.

A child's happiest moments should be preserved absolutely in memory, emotional responses intact—both for the parent and the child—and readily available any time they are needed.

The opposite should be true for the worst moments.

People who love you should have only fond memories of you. People who don't should have no memory of you.

Memory is too inaccurate to have so much power over our lives.

Jacki is playing with the concept of memory in grand terms, but, clearly, personal terms are emerging here. Which of her lines would you consider to be high exposition? Which might more appropriately be called personal exposition? Is anything here unequivocal or unarguable? How might Jacki rephrase certain sentences to get the more universal sound of high exposition?

Perhaps it will help to think in terms of bumper stickers: MORE CHOICE IN MEMORY! perhaps, or MAKE MEMORY RELIABLE! I love this line (let's revise it into one sentence): "Memory should be as reliable as the lungs or the heart." It's so plaintive. And complex, too. Jacki doesn't say "reliable as the sunset"; she invokes our mortal and thereby unreliable human organs, seat of much suffering and many deaths. Lovely depth there. And clearly Jacki's take on memory indicates struggles in her own childhood.

EXERCISE SIX: *Bumper Stickers*

Simple: Think up ten or more slogans for bumper stickers you wouldn't mind putting on your car. Or maybe on a T-shirt. They're all exposition, aren't they? What sort of exposition in each case? Any great lines you might feed into a memoir or essay?

Here are a few I've seen lately, from commands to pronouncements, from the sublime to the ridiculous:

"Hug a Logger. You'll Never Go Back to Trees."

"In God We Trust. All Others Pay Cash."

"These Colors Don't Run."

"War is Wrong."

"Nietzsche is Dead. —God"

"Moose Don't Back Up."

"Dog is my Co-Pilot."

"Nothing Happens."

"Mean People Suck."

"Don't procrastinate—masturbate!"

Janet All Alone

Now an excerpt—the last paragraphs of a long piece—from Janet Bellweather's try, "On Solitude":

Solitude is the only natural state for a human to live in. In Solitude comes peace. The patter of little feet to me is like hailstones knocking my head. Alone, we face the edges of the Universe more squarely, and know the eternal more fully.

So where's the peace?

The early portion of her try was six pages of aphorisms about solitude. Some sounded awfully familiar. Many had the sharp tone and edgy meanness that Janet brought to class; many had the humor that went with all that. But look at that last line. Something's happening. In the effort to make high exposition, some marvelously revealing personal exposition is emerging. The first cracks are appearing in Janet's armor, in her castle wall.

Gow Leaves the Joking Behind

As for our friend Gow Farris, I've refrained from analyzing his "On Grief" till now to reproduce the silence that filled the room after he read his paragraph. Note that the angry stabs at "professor" aren't the least unusual in students at this phase. Note, too, how well he's done at leaving the joking and teasing behind, getting at something important to him.

He finds his own way through his thoughts, doesn't rely on preconceptions about structure, on his old way of doing things.

THE EXAMINED LIFE

Difficult as it is to begin to see Janet's and Jacki's and Gow's defensive armor, and then to see the cracks therein, it's more difficult still—exponentially more difficult—to see our own armor. Sometimes the cracks are what we see first, those places where the stuff of our lives oozes out, perhaps embarrassingly, perhaps painfully, perhaps joyfully. But turn from Jacki and Janet to your own work now; see if something formerly invisible is taking on ghostly outlines. No right answers here—it's enough for now to begin to take serious looks at the ideas that power our lives, that lurk behind jokes and defensiveness and vagueness and facility and laziness.

Remember Mindy Mallow-Dalmation? In the end, following her pierced nose after writing dozens of edgy responses to the "On ..." exercise, she put together a connected series of short essays about food, inspired by a cooking course in France and the chef's assistant she fell in love with there. He was the very first man who'd expressed not just googly-eyes but great enthusiasm for her particular zaftig shape and for her angry mind, her black and gloomy humor, his warm attention that first made her realize how cold and narcissistic her family and all previous boyfriends had been, he that also turned her on to heroin, injected intravenously.

EXERCISE SEVEN: *Left-Brain Workout*

Please pull out one of your own scenes, perhaps one of the rocks you cracked open in the last chapter. Read it once or twice, then ask: What's this try about? Make a list of ten possible answers.

One student of mine in Maine, Shermaze Lawrence, had written about a camping trip. Her list was roughly as follows: (1) camping, (2) scenery, (3) my ex, (4) my father, (5) my brother, (6) my son, (7) my husband, (8) different tempers, (9) marshmallows, (10) anger.

Shermaze was surprised. She didn't clearly see that her piece was about relationships with men till she made her list. And—wow!—the word *anger* seemed to come out of nowhere, since the piece was just about a pleasant excursion to the hills of Michigan.

Once you have your list, write a paragraph or so analyzing your scene. What's it about? What's going on in it exactly? Think of the scene you made as evidence; then, in your paragraph, tell us just what is evident. Keep going till you've got it right: true and elegant and hard as a diamond.

Difficult work.

EXERCISE EIGHT: *"On ..." Again*

Pick the most compelling or most mysterious abstract noun from your list above, whatever word intrigues you. Write a page, "On ...," using that word. Then go back to your narrative and revise according to what you have learned.

Shermaze wrote "On Anger." It isn't a fabulous piece of writing—not at all and nothing she'd want anyone but her teacher to read, but when she went back to revise her narrative, she knew the subtext of the charming marshmallows-over-the-campfire scene, and suddenly a piece of narrative that had been slight—light, humorous, and adequate—was poignant, deep, layered, meaningful.

Yet somehow still funny.

EXERCISE NINE: *Write Something Awful*

My friend Van Santvoordt is a fine set designer and a smart, subtle actor. Also a generous friend. Years ago, a couple of us lived with him (and, okay, various girlfriends) in his loft in SoHo, New York City. We did lots of projects in the place, built walls, painted, added plumbing. Sometimes it took Van a long time to get a project done. Sometimes a very long time. Why? He wasn't lazy, that's for sure. He worked twice as hard as I did, yet (for better or worse) I finished my projects twice as fast. The problem was he wanted things right. He'd reject warped 2x4s, he'd sand knots endlessly; he'd strip paint off old French doors till there wasn't a speck left. This kind of obsessive exactingness, he realized, was alive in his acting practice, too, and was holding him back. So he wrote a message on the loft wall in dark black charcoal (later adding a red border).

A JOB WORTH DOING IS WORTH DOING BADLY.

Your exercise, if you find that some form of perfectionism is holding you back, is to write something bad. I give you permission. Write something horrible, some awful exposition, and put it on the wall for a day or two. Resist all temptation to fix it up. At the end of a suitable display period, revise it. Or throw it away. So what?

You might even make yourself a facsimile of the permission slip below, which I hope you'll pull out when necessary, especially during the making of rough drafts.

> I, Bill Roorbach, being of sound mind, and I, Kristen Keckler, holder of many advanced degrees, do hereby grant and concede permission for _____, who resides at _____, to write something horrible and to display this miserable verbiage upon the living room wall for a period of _____ days.

EXERCISE TEN: *What Do I Know?*

Simple: Make an exquisite medallion of solid Mayan gold to wear around your neck, inscribed *Que sais-je?* If you don't have sufficient solid Mayan gold, an index card will do: *What do I know?* And then make a list of subjects upon which you are an expert. Start with your big subjects—the stuff stemming from your work or from your hobbies. But then keep going; faint expertise is fine for our purposes here. Your list in the end should be very long, and will certainly contain many abstract nouns: love, friendship, forgiveness, discretion. Along with the concrete: beer, chicken thighs, oxy-acetylene torches, ballet slippers, xanthan gum.

The idea is simply to uncover your subjects, large and small, subjects meant for you, good stuff to get your motorcycle started on a cold day, or to feather into the essay at hand, whatever its primary subject.

If you can't explain your theory to a bartender, it's probably no good.
—Ernest Rutherford

Exercise Eleven: *Loafe and Invite Your Soul*

This exercise will be very difficult for most readers (except perhaps certain college students I know, who had better skip it), but I recommend it highly. Spend your writing time this morning or afternoon or evening just doing nothing. You'll want to pick a place where no one will bother you at your task, because people hate to see someone doing nothing, and they will do their best to see you doing something. To them, quote Walt Whitman:

> I loafe and invite my soul
> I lean and loafe at my ease observing a spear of summer grass.

And let me quote Brenda Ueland, from *If You Want to Write*:

> So you see the imagination needs moodling,—long, inefficient, happy idling, dawdling and puttering. These people who are always briskly doing something and as busy as waltzing mice, they have little, sharp, staccato ideas, such as: "I see where I can make an annual cut of $3.47 in my meat budget." But they have no slow, big ideas. And the fewer consoling, noble, shining, free, jovial, magnanimous ideas that come, the more nervously and desperately they rush and run from office to office and up and downstairs, thinking by action at least to make life have some warmth and meaning.

EXERCISE TWELVE: *What Have You Been Thinking About?*

I had the good fortune to meet the filmmaker and visual artist Rudy Burkhardt at a gathering of filmmakers and artists and writers and students. He was in his eighties, had given a stirring talk, showed one of his quirky, beautiful films (rapid-fire takes of New York City—almost stills—interspersed with long, long takes: two full minutes just gazing at the East River in one of them, a crow flying from extreme right to extreme left of the frame in just that time, jangly original music). I gathered my gumption and walked up to him in one of those awkward social moments that find the guest of honor alone at his own party. I gave him the usual compliments, told him my mother was a Burkhardt.

"There are a lot of Burkhardts in the United States," Mr. Burkhardt told me warmly, quavering voice. He wanted to hear *my* name. I had time only to say it before the party's hosts rushed up with cocktails and quick banter. My moment with Rudy was over.

The next year, same setting, Rudy Burkhardt and I attending some other dignitary's party. This time the old artist shambled up to me. "Hi Bill," he said. I was impressed he'd remembered me at all, much less my name. There was a certain urgency about him, something I couldn't quite put my finger on.

"Hi Rudy," I said.

And then we departed from the cocktail party script. He didn't say the usual *how have you been*, nor any of the usual social pleasantries. He hadn't time for that, was the sense I got, hadn't time for small talk. Instead—that quavery voice, that amused blue eye—he said, "What have you been *thinking* about?"

There was no stock answer. The question required a serious reply. No matter that it took me a minute to know what to say (*take all the time you wish*), the actual, honest thing: "I've been thinking about, um, loneliness."

"Ah, loneliness," said Rudy, and we went on to have a satisfying talk about our struggles with the solitude inherent in creative work.

When that wore down, I gave him back his question: "What have *you* been thinking about?"

"Pain," he said.

A month later, as it happens, he walked into the pond at his summer house, in his clothes, and drowned, a probable suicide. He'd been thinking a great deal, apparently.

The assignment is to tell an ideal reader what you've been thinking about. And not the surface stuff, either. Again (for the purpose of experimentation with the possibilities inherent in expository writing): no scenes.

You'll notice I've attached this assignment to the end of a couple of scenes linked by summary. Do as I say, not as I do.

The Secret of Life (and Ideas)

Learning to write about ideas is largely a matter of learning to have ideas, learning to see the ways experience contains ideas. I'll give Jane Renshaw the last word: "Searching."

And good old Chuck the second-to-last: "Not finding?"

"No, dear, no, no. *Searching.*"

CHAPTER FIVE

CHARACTERS AND CHARACTER

[Characters] need to exhibit enough conflict and contradiction that we can recognize them as belonging to the contradictory human race.

—Janet Burroway

My first spring in Maine, I got to work making a vegetable garden. My mother had kept gardens all my life, and to me a garden was a form of love. I started at the corner of a hayfield where no garden had been before, so the first task was breaking sod.

Right away, I got blisters on my thumbs. I worked the dirt up with a borrowed roto-tiller, raked, added manure, and dug out stones. I planted cucumber and squash and radish seeds along with a couple of flats of tomatoes and peppers and basil from the makeshift nursery down the hill. My nails broke and got so much black under them I couldn't get them clean. My hands had gotten awfully soft in the new life: full-time professor, full-time writer at his desk. Pol Pot's brigade of children would have shot me for certain.

In the garden, my hands were starting to look and feel as they had just a few years earlier (but in a different life), when I had worked in New York City renovating bathrooms and kitchens: demolishing walls, tearing out toilets, running pipe, laying tile, building, building, building.

With my vegetables nearly planted, I was struck by a bolt of inspiration, a vision of an essay, the whole thing clear as my new garden's view of the foothills of the White Mountains. I picked up an empty seed packet and scratched *Hands* on it with a broken pencil.

And then I carried on with my life, finishing up my first year of tenure-track teaching at the University of Maine at Farmington. I'd just published my first book and was struggling to get started on the next project, a novel (*The Smallest Color*, which would only be published eight years later). The seed packet made its way from the table in the laundry room of my rented farmhouse to the trash, where I retrieved it—pure luck—on recycling day, thence to my desk, and after a month or so more into my idea notebook. Since the novel was such hard going every day, I decided to give myself a break Saturday mornings. Those sessions, I'd work on a short piece instead: a story maybe, or a memoir, possibly an essay, something I could get done in a month or two. The first Saturday I spent half a morning flipping through the odd bits of paper in my idea notebook, came upon the seed packet:

Hands

That caught my interest, and I spent another hour trying to remember what I'd been thinking when I wrote it. I remembered the clarity clearly, but not really the idea.

I started writing. "Our hands make our worlds." No way. "My hands used to be tough." Nah. I didn't want to start with exposition. I wanted to start in the middle of things—a scene—but I didn't know what things I wanted to be in the middle of. What scene? What people? My hands, my hands. I certainly wasn't going to start with me standing in the garden, scratching the word *hands* on a seed packet: too self-conscious.

My clarity that gardening day had been a delusion, one all creative writers share, the one that keeps us going: vision. Drafting, revising, structuring, re-revising—all these are steps back to some version of an original clarity, that original inspiration, a lurching dance from delusion to execution, from *could be* through *would be* to *is*. Or *nearly is*, since perfection is impossible.

Okay, enough exposition.

Somewhere in the last hour of my writing time, I managed to write a bar scene that described the time I barely dissuaded a rough drunk in a Berkshire dive from his decision to kill me for being a yuppie by showing him my cracked and grimy and calloused hands. Just that much: I walk into a bar in the Berkshires, get into a small argument with a large man, show him my hands and am saved. Plenty for one morning.

During the week I worked on my novel, all fiction all the time, and I taught, and I did my committee work, cooked meals, cleaned up, all while that one scene from my actual life tumbled around in my head. Come the next Saturday, I seemed to know a little more: the issue around my hands was socioeconomic. I was a suburban kid, raised in a well-to-do town by well-to-do parents. I was different from the bar fighter, beat-up hands, work boots, and construction job notwithstanding. But in the rough draft of my scene, I'd made myself out to be as tough a tough guy as my tormentor, and thus played down our social differences.

So. My reluctance to be myself—college educated, privileged in definite ways, headed away from construction, strong but not particularly tough—became one of the things I thought I must be writing about. But there was something bigger looming, too: class distinctions in America. How'd I get such split sensibilities? How, for example, did I end up in so many shop classes in high school? Why had I taken wood shop over and over again? That Saturday morning I sat at my desk and fumed and ruminated, finally started a bit of a scene about shop class. Couldn't sustain it past about lunchtime, such a beautiful autumn day.

Saturday by Saturday, the essay grew. At some point, it (yes *it*, the emerging essay, up on its feet and thinking for itself) realized that my father was a big factor in my youthful need to seem and even *be* working class. Ineluctably, incrementally, despite my intentions, really, my relationship with my father became the subject of the essay. And my father, poor guy, got translated from walking, talking human being to a character on typed pages, a dual existence. Suddenly, the man had a doppelgänger (which just now went triple).

On one Saturday, perhaps the seventh, the essay reared back, snorted, and took off across the fruited plains at a gallop. Holding on for dear life, I kept working past lunch, and then kept working on it daily through the next weeks, pushing the novel (not for the last time) out of the way.

I certainly never worried what my dad would think of his portrayal, his transformation into literary character. This, he'd never see. If I were spectacularly lucky, my new work would be published in, say, *The Iowa Review*. My dad does not read *The Iowa Review*. Much less the *Wrinkly Elbow Quarterly*, where the piece was much more likely to appear, if at all.

Totally safe.

I got the essay written, or the essay wrote me, I'm not entirely sure which.

And to make a long story a little shorter, I'll just tell you that *Harper's Magazine* took the piece, which the editors confidently labeled a memoir and titled "Into Woods," throwing out my working title, which was "Woods II." (I've included it in this volume, as appendix A, starting on page 239.)

Harper's. One of my favorite magazines. Now, of course, the first thing you do when you get good news like that is tell a few people. Your colleagues. Your old friends. Your grad-school profs. Your *dad*.

Gulp.

I called home, told my dad that *Harper's* had taken a piece I'd written. He'd always called it a pinko publication anyway (partly kidding, partly serious)— not a chance he'd happen across my work.

"Oh, chief, wonderful," he said. "Can't wait. When's it coming out?"

THE SOUL OF A GENRE

Characters are the soul of what's come to be called creative nonfiction, an umbrella term that covers memoir, the personal essay, and literary journalism, among others. But characters in nonfiction present special problems: while characters in fiction are often *based* on real people, there's still that screen, that safety net, that legal loophole (not that it always lets a writer off the hook). Characters in short stories and novels are *made up*, do not represent people living or dead (to use the language of the disclaimer often found at the front of books of fiction). In nonfiction, by contrast, the writer is telling the reader: *These people I'm bringing to you are real.*

A lot has been written about characters and character in many good books about making fiction. Many of the same techniques apply to nonfiction: through detail, through gesture, through talk, through close understanding of whole lives before and after the scope of your story, you make your people vivid in your reader's head. If you're new at writing, you owe it to yourself to study the techniques of fiction, especially as regards characters (I'll list some good books in the bibliography at the end of these pages—enjoy them, apply the lessons to the nonfiction at hand). If you're coming to nonfiction from a background in fiction, you've got a head start.

When you are writing nonfiction, much of the work of characterization is done for you. The character has been made, characterization is complete, the family history is in place, the physical description is a given. But that doesn't make anything easier. The chore is merely different: doing justice to a person that you and many others have known, while also doing justice to the fact that you know that person in your own way, filtered through your own emotions, biases, and experiences, including your experience of the person.

In *The Glass Castle*, a memoir by Jeannette Walls (you'll remember the first line of that book from earlier in these pages, the one about Ms. Walls spotting her mother Dumpster-diving in New York City), we don't meet her father right away. The first scene in the book gives us little Jeannette, age three, cooking hot dogs for herself, life as normal in her nuts household, at least until she sets herself on fire. We meet her father, the redoubtable Rex Walls, when he comes to the hospital to visit her—she's been badly burned. He thinks the little girl should have been taken to the witch doctor that cured her older sister's scorpion sting. He threatens a doctor with a beating for saying that bandages are necessary, finally gets thrown out of the hospital bodily by a guard.

Then we see him again (and hear him, smell him, touch him, very nearly *taste* him):

> A few days later, when I had been at the hospital for about six weeks, Dad appeared alone in the doorway of my room. He told me we were going to check out, Rex Walls–style.
>
> "Are you sure this is okay?" I asked.
>
> "You just trust your old man," Dad said.
>
> He unhooked my right arm from the sling over my head. As he held me close, I breathed in his familiar smell of Vitalis, whiskey, and cigarette smoke. It reminded me of home.
>
> Dad hurried down the hall with me in his arms. A nurse yelled for us to stop, but Dad broke into a run. He pushed open an emergency-exit door and sprinted down the stairs and out to the street. Our car, a beat-up Plymouth we called the Blue Goose, was parked around the corner, the engine idling. Mom was up front, Lori and Brian in the back with Juju. Dad slid me across the seat next to Mom and took the wheel.
>
> "You don't have to worry anymore, baby," Dad said. "You're safe now."

We see the man in action, but we see him from the little girl's point of view. She doesn't judge her old man—he's a hero, her knight in shining armor. Later, Ms. Walls will report from her writer's desk: "In my mind, Dad was perfect, although he did have what Mom called a little bit of a drinking situation." But here, early in the narrative, it's all in the moment, all from a particular point of view. We see the hospital, but only as required to give the action a context, and only as the three-year-old sees it. A nurse yells—that's our reality check—this guy *is* over the top. We burst out an emergency door, feel the air, hear the alarms going off without Walls having to say anything about these things. We get the name of the family car, the sense that it's not exactly a Mercedes, that they're not exactly Mercedes people. And off they go. Rex is established, in fact all but literally burned into the reader's mind. We suspend our readerly judgment, adopt the child's point of view: she does seem safer. We're in a particular time and don't leave it. We're in a particular place. We're seeing things from a particular point of view. The mode is action, action, action, and it's effective.

The burned girl and her family are only home a short time before Dad gets it in his fiery head that the FBI is after them. And off they go in the middle of the night, traveling light, leaving all their bills and memories and belongings behind.

Now that we've seen her dangerous father in several scenes, Walls takes a long paragraph to describe him in exposition:

> Everybody said Dad was a genius. He could build or fix anything. One time when a neighbor's TV set broke, Dad opened the back and used a macaroni noodle to insulate some crossed wires. The neighbor couldn't get over it. He went around telling everyone in town that Dad sure knew how to use his noodle. Dad was an expert in math and physics and electricity. He read books on calculus and logarithmic algebra and loved what he called the poetry and symmetry of math. He told us about the magic qualities every number has and how numbers unlock the secrets of the universe. But Dad's main interest was energy: thermal energy, nuclear energy, solar energy, electrical energy, and energy from the wind. He said there were so many untapped sources of energy in the world that it was ridiculous to be burning all that fossil fuel.

Walls is still working from the kid's point of view, trading in family stories. Of course, not everybody thought Rex Walls a genius. The adult writer is standing back, withholding judgment, letting us readers come to our own conclusions, make our own judgments. Later in the memoir, the writer-at-her-desk will have more to say. She'll condemn her father in some ways, while loving him, missing him. But for now, early pages of the book-length memoir, Walls is content to stay in the moment, put her wild father in front of us as he was.

EXERCISE ONE: *Put Your Dad on Stage*

Here are some pages to write just for yourself, always a good exercise in itself. Not everything need be for readers, for the distant idea of publication.

The drill here is to think of a particular way your childhood perception of your father is different from your adult perception. Then come up with a scene that shows that childhood dad in action. If your dad wasn't around, write about whoever ended up playing the role. Write the scene twice, once from your childhood point of view (language and all), once from your adult point of view, the view from your desk as you write.

I'm thinking of my own father jumping athletically from a maple tree in our front yard, only to land on a garden rake, one of those hoe rakes with four curved tines, sharp tips. These were facing up. All four went all the way through Dad's foot. Not wanting to scare us, he didn't cry out, didn't curse. He just leaned down and pulled the rake off his foot very calmly, calmly put a hand on my big brother's shoulder, said, "Randy, you're in charge here. I'm going to just drive myself to the hospital."

Got it? Two scenes? How are they different? Can you work to make them even more different? Now try another angle: write the scene from your dad's point of view. Let's call this fiction-in-the-service-of-nonfiction, since you can't truly know what it was like to be him.

EXERCISE TWO: *Bring Your Mom on Next*

Of course you can switch Mom and Dad in these two exercises, even plug in anyone else—but moms and dads are hard to write about, call up our worst guilt, our worst fears of exposure, failure. Again, this is writing just for you.

Write a long passage of exposition describing your mother. Get the physical characteristics, yes, and put a picture of her in our heads, but also try for gesture, her favorite phrases ("I'll snatch you bald," my mother would say when angry), characteristic dishes, dress, hobbies, work, fingernails, figure, the works—including her subtlest subconscious methods of inducing your guilt. Keep it expositional.

EXERCISE THREE: *A Wedding*

Now write a scene featuring your mother and father together, a time when things were strained, perhaps. If from happy times, do be sure you're working toward dramatic tension. Again, two tries, first from the child's point of view, second from the adult you, the one sitting at your desk typing.

WHAT DO WE OWE OUR CHARACTERS?

When we go to write about the people in our lives, in fact before we even start, we run into an ethical problem, even when—maybe especially when—they are aware that we are writing about them. Janet Malcolm says it sharply and well in her good book *The Journalist and the Murderer*:

> Every journalist who is not too stupid or too full of himself to notice what is going on knows that what he does is morally indefensible. He is a kind of confidence man, preying on people's vanity, ignorance, or loneliness, gaining their trust and betraying them without remorse. Like the credulous widow who wakes up one day to find the charming young man and all her savings gone, so the consenting subject of a piece of nonfiction writing learns—when the article or book appears— his hard lesson. Journalists justify their treachery in various ways according to their temperaments. The more pompous talk about freedom of speech and "the public's right to know"; the least talented talk about Art; the seemliest murmur about earning a living.

Memoirists don't have the same immediate and practical need to exploit the stories of others, yet others come into our own stories in unavoidable ways. What do we owe our families? Our friends? Our lovers (past and current)? Our enemies?

I once sat on a panel to benefit the Graduate School of the Arts at Columbia. On the panel with me were other, more accomplished alumnae of the writing program there—Mary Gordon, Kim Wozencraft, Rick Moody—all of us writers who have written memoir or autobiographical fiction. The title of our talk was, I think, meant to be a little tongue-in-cheek: "Autobiography and Guilt: Managing Your Loved Ones."

The novelist Rick Moody spoke first. He had used parts of real people in fiction, he said, was delightfully unremorseful, looked archly over his glasses at the crowd as he read. Kim Wozencraft, author of *Rush*, was next. She was very serious. She had written her fine novel based on events that had landed her in prison. The stakes were getting higher.

When my turn came I was nervous but managed as planned to quote Scott Russell Sanders (from his essay "The Singular First Person"): "The *I* is a narrow gate." And to explain what I thought Sanders meant by that: You can't—impossible—put your whole self on the page. Always, you pick and choose, construct an *I* that has a select and manageable few of your traits and quirks and inconsistencies. Generally, you make the best self you can out of the raw material of reality; generally, you are careful to put in a humble flaw or two. We are all made of ten thousand traits at least, from our principles to the ridges on our toenails. In an essay, in a memoir, you might display a hundred or so of these traits. One hundred carefully selected traits. And never the ten thousand.

My point, when I finally made it, was that all the people in our true stories are narrow gates. It's possible to make the person you wish—every journalist knows this, and every packager of political candidates—picking and choosing among perfectly real facts, real qualities, real events. You can make someone bad look worse; you can make someone good look better; you can make someone bad look good, and you can certainly make someone good look bad. Every writer's ethical stance is going to be different: How far do you go in the service of drama, for instance, or in the service of your prejudices? Do you leave out traits that don't support your story or scenario? How can you tell when you're going too far? When does memoir turn into prosecution? Invasion of privacy? These are not only rhetorical questions but questions you might want to ask yourself once your work is done.

After my first book, a memoir called *Summers With Juliet*, was published, I felt nervous about the way I'd described certain friends, major characters in my life, minor characters in the book. I was going for comedy in many cases, choosing their most amusing traits, showing the funny gesture, the pratfall. In the chapter called "Bachelor Party," very near the end of the book, I showed my friend Kurt being stern with me in various ways, and then fishing with me in 1980s Central Park, New York, something we did for laughs, missing the country, missing our hobby. In the book, I called him "jaunty." He'd fish with his tie thrown over his shoulder, his briefcase hugged between his knees. People would watch us, bother us. After he read the book, we went out for a drink, ostensibly to talk about it. But he didn't say anything. Finally, I swallowed my pride, asked what he thought.

Silence. Then a cloud crossed his face: "You called me 'jaunty,'" he said, genuinely hurt, "*Jaunty!*"

You just don't know what people will find insulting. I guess Kurt thought of jaunty as a kind of Dandy's mode, silly and shallow. To me, it just meant cheerful. All I could do was say I was sorry. And then, of course, call him jaunty every chance I got, just for fun.

At readings, I'd look up from my pages to see the very people I'd written about while alone at my desk. I'd made copies of them out of words. But those friends and acquaintances in the book *perforce* are not the people who sat in the audiences, were not and could not be. Kurt, slightly miffed about being called jaunty. My friend Jon, irritated to be depicted as clumsy. It's seldom you like your own photo. (Then again, the reviewer for *The Boston Globe* said my sketches of people I knew were "merciless.")

At the panel, when finally I finished my monologue, Mary Gordon spoke. She was articulate and impassioned, said how awful she thought the phrase "managing your loved ones" was, how we ought more think about respecting their privacy than managing them. Further, said she, we as memoirists ought to remember that our characters are people and that we owe them not only the truth but every courtesy. We ought to manage *ourselves*, if anybody. Finally, she said she's never shied away from writing about people very close to her. She writes without a qualm. She writes it all. Then—simple solution—she doesn't publish.

It's My Story, Too

I agree with Mary Gordon, and of course I agree with myself. But there's another twist that only Kim Wozencraft really touched on: what about bad people?

Some of the most dramatic stories, some of the stories that most need to get told, are about bad people. In criminal activity, in conspiracy, the rule is *don't rat*. In abusive families, one of the primary refrains is *don't tell anybody*. Don't tell anybody: that's what pederasts tell their victims (adding, "You'll get in just as much trouble as me"). That's what violent husbands tell their wives; that's what we all say at different times and in different ways about any weirdness at home (insanity, violence, deformity, perversity, venality): Don't tell anybody. And it's not just negative stuff that gets hidden under blankets of enforced shame; sexuality, illness, bodily functions, sadness, and lots more are hidden, too. Why? There are cultural answers to that fine question, of course (good subject for an essay), but every case of secrecy has its own whys and wherefores. And not all (not even many) secrets are big, obvious ones (murder, addiction, unfaithfulness); some secrets are so subtle, we are able to keep them even from ourselves.

What's a writer of memoir (or a writer using memoir as evidence for personal essays) to do? Just go for it and risk hurting people? Isn't it better to lie?

My vote is to tell whatever story you have to tell exactly and truly, leaving nothing out, at least in a first draft. And those places where you catch yourself changing the facts should be alarms, grand signals, signposts saying: *Here's the place to examine most closely for meaning*. Dig in. Tell the story right. Later you can adjust so as to protect privacy, if necessary. (Though if you really want privacy, why are you telling your story?) Later you can change names (of towns, of states, of characters). Later you can disguise characters in ways that hide them without damaging your drama, your story, your point. Later you can choose to leave out part of the story that doesn't bear on the eventual focus your essay takes.

Later.

In the rough draft, let it all arrive.

And don't gut the first draft as you revise. Later will always be there, right up till the time you publish (if you publish). And when that time comes (if it does), you'll have the advice of an editor to help you make adjustments, if any still seem necessary. Disguises, name changes, composite characters, all of these are time-honored and ethical ways to protect the privacy of your people, to protect the safety of your people, to protect yourself, both from physical harm and from lawsuits. And all of them can be effected at the very last minute. Note, though, that it's not easy to disguise, say, your father. You can give him a new first name, new last name, a big mustache, a lisp, a limp, a prosthetic nose. That will protect him as he goes about his life among strangers.

But the guy's going to be your father no matter what, and people close to him are going to know.

If you have half a conscience, of course, there will be the urge to protect people in your life. They never asked to be put on the page. You're not a journalist, exploiting others for their stories. But listen: it's your story, too. If, like Scott Russell Sanders, you had a parent who drank, that drinking happened to *you*. If, like Mikal Gilmore, your brother was a murderer, those murders happened to *you*. Do you have a famous grandfather? That fame happened to *you*. Was your father crazy? Your mother a master of guilt? Your brother a big success? Your old lover manipulative? Your wife preoccupied with career? It's your story, too. Negative emotions and traits, such as jealousy, greed, misery, and meanness, are all part of the story—*your* story—and shouldn't be left out any more than the good stuff should be left out: generosity, love, happiness, health. The truth is the whole story, never half.

When the voice in your head (or the voice of an actual person) says, "Don't tell anyone," that voice (or person) is taking away your story, and your story is *you*, baby. It's your life. In the end, what we owe our people is exactly what we owe ourselves (and this is exactly what we owe our readers, what readers will demand): the truth.

But what is the truth?

The truth is what happened, but it's also the effects of what happened, ramifications that transcend the realm of facts. The truth will arrive and will announce itself character by character, some of them kind and sweet and good, some of them mean and bitter and bad, most of the rest in between. And you will have to shape those characters so as to serve the truth, not some sense of propriety on the one hand, revenge on the other.

EXERCISE FOUR: *Roast, No Leftovers*

Then again, revenge might be kind of fun. Is there someone in your life, past or present, whom you just can't stomach? Well, then. Using both exposition and scene, write a few pages *eviscerating* that person. Tell all. Be mean. Let 'em have it. Pick your way through traits to make the person ugly, inside and out. Find dumb or sinister things to quote. Tell tales. Expose lies. Describe warts, pimples, farts. Abuse the abuser.

Later, throw it away.

That's right, you heard me. Throw it away. Burn it. This hatred is just between you and yourself. We're in this game for expression, not revenge.

But if you can write this exercise truly (or maybe you'll roast a dozen bad eggs), you can begin to approach the truth in other ways. These raw pages, not for the world, will be a good start at questioning the sanitized versions of lives and events with which we and our families and our friends and our cultures face the world. Are you going to flinch when the subtle stuff arrives in the course of writing this exercise? Or are you going to stare it down?

Probably, if you're like me, you're going to flinch. At least in the first drafts. And those places where you do so will mark the places where your writing is dying to teach you something.

Take the lesson, toss the pages.

Without the least idea of what is innately transgressive about the literary imagination, cultural journalism is ever mindful of phony ethical issues: "Does the writer have the right to blah-blah-blah?"
—Philip Roth (via E.I. Lonoff, via Amy Bellette)

RULE NUMBER 872

As you go about bringing your people to the page, remember this: Human beings are complicated; characters are simple. Human beings have the ten thousand traits I mentioned earlier in this chapter, probably more like a million. Characters have maybe thirty, with one or two predominant. You get to pick.

EXERCISE FIVE: *Hagiography*

One by one, take the same people you roasted above and treat them as saints. Write some paragraphs about them in which you laud all their best qualities, their best acts, their nicest clothes. If you really can't do it, can't get more than a line or two, try writing it from the other person's point of view (once again, let's call this fiction-in-the-service-of-nonfiction). After all, no one's all bad, no one's all good. The truth resides somewhere in between. But it's smart to investigate the poles, create a dialectic, in which thesis (the bad) and antithesis (the good) lead to synthesis (the person).

Rule Number 1

Do unto others as you would have others do unto you.

Exercise Six: *Classified, Top Secret, For Your Eyes Only*

First, you are the most important character in your memoir or essay. Even when you are offstage, just observing the lives of others, you are still telling a story from your point of view, looking at it through your lens. So, let's put *you* on the hot seat.

The exercise: Make a list of the top ten things you would not, under any circumstances, want a stranger to know about you (and not just your address and cell phone number). In other words, what are your top ten secrets? Forget the stranger, this can be stuff that even your significant other doesn't know. Go on. Be honest. Could be fun. You can always shred the list later and use it as kitty litter, or perhaps confetti for your New Year's Eve party, all those resolutions. If you have been particularly naughty, you might also e-mail the list to the authors of this book, as we could use a thrill.

Things to think about: What, if anything, do the items on your list have in common? How many of your secrets involve another person? Which have you left out of your writing until now? Why? Why do these things embarrass you? Is there a subject in your shame?

Before you shred your list, write up the darkest secrets, a couple of paragraphs, a scene, just something true that beats your inhibitions. Destroy and repeat. In some form, perhaps, corners of your confessions will come into everything you write, adding to the risk—readers love risk—adding to the truth.

Caliban and Company

In the early drafts of my book *Temple Stream: A Rural Odyssey*, I portray lots of people I know: scientists, friends, neighbors, shopkeepers, the poet Ted Enslin, a certain house sitter, mountain men. They were all positive portraits, sunny even, except for the last. Three people, three very large and angry fellows, whom I'm calling for want of a better rubric *mountain men*, didn't come off too well. They'd treated me poorly over the years, each in his different way, they'd broken the law, each in his different way, they'd said the nastiest possible things about me and my neighbors and our town, each in his individual voice. And one of them, a particularly ugly type, had threatened me, and more than once. And he was a great reader of books. My books, as a matter of fact, found in the town library, had brought me to his attention. He was a fierce critic of my work, he let me know: He hated it. He hated me, too, and everything I represented to him, which all centered around the word *professor*. He wrote me letters, he stopped by in person at my office, he came to my house, always with a jab, a rant, a cruel gift: I know it was he who put the dead porcupine in my mailbox, he who drove his truck through the decorative row of cedar trees in my dooryard, sheering them all off at the ground. Worst of all, he told people we were *friends*. But that stuff I hadn't put in the book. It didn't fit. The stuff I put in the book was worse.

My editor asked if I didn't want to disguise these people. "They didn't ask to be in your book," she said. "And there are legal issues as concern their privacy. And Bill, sweetie, in some ways I'm worried about your safety." My editor called me sweetie as a matter of course. Good editors are manipulative. But that's not the point here.

In the next draft of *Temple Stream* I gave disguises a try, changing names where negative portraits were involved: four cases, four people—the only people in the book I wouldn't have formally interviewed, even though they were fully aware that a book was in the works. I changed a few physical characteristics, changed their names.

"Sweetie," my editor said holding the manuscript. "Everyone's going to know these people."

In the next draft (plenty of other issues to work on, as well—I cut nearly three hundred pages from the bloated early drafts), I tried further disguises, but they just weren't working. So I did something radical. I took all the negative people out of the book. Just excised them.

"Sweetie," my editor said. "The energy's gone."

Worse, without the bad people, my story was no longer true.

Next draft, after a lot of bad nights, after a lot of false starts, after a harebrained scheme to try interviewing my hostile characters (I gave up after the very first guy, the nicest one, whom I'd collared in the town diner, called me a fat little hippie shit before I even got started), after thinking about the strategies of other writers I admired, I hit upon a plan: make a composite character out of my three mountain men, make this composite into a kind of mythic figure, a north woods Caliban. His mythic qualities would tip the reader, as would a clear disclaimer in my acknowledgments page—I wouldn't be trying to fool anyone—but everything he said, everything he did, would be real, would have come directly from life, directly from one of the people he was made of.

This character, whom I named Earl Pomeroy, is more real than real in the book, larger than life (larger than three lives, that is), fills the hole my excisions made, keeps my story true without violating anyone's privacy, without endangering Yours Truly, a.k.a. Sweetie.

It wasn't an easy decision to make, but I think it saved the book.

EXERCISE SEVEN: *Composite Characters*

This is a method fiction writers use all the time, often or even subconsciously. In nonfiction projects, the composite character allows writers to approach people and situations they wouldn't otherwise be able to. Another example of fiction in the service of nonfiction.

We'll make the composites purposefully. Pick three people who matter to you—three people from the same category in your life, three people you won't easily be able to interview, three people you'd like to expose but know you can't, three people with bad habits, three people whose shabby behavior makes them great subjects for your true stories—and blend them. Three old boyfriends. Three former employers. Three aunts. Three siblings. Three professors. Three neighborhood tough guys.

Then again, it could be three lovely people, three gentle souls, three kindly angels who you know will be embarrassed to be called out in your work. Or three people with legitimate secrets: gay friends who aren't out to their parents, whistleblowers at your company, anonymous benefactors.

Can't come up with three people in a given category? Two will do.

Can't come up with two?

Maybe you don't need this exercise.

To work: Tell an important story, something that really happened to you or to others, but work with a composite character, a character whose disguise is so complete that no one will recognize him or her from real life.

Sometimes it works to make composite stories, as well, to make and strengthen your narrative point by way of concentration. Three old boyfriends wrecked four of your cars in four separate incidents; you write one incident with elements from all four crashes, using a single, meta-boyfriend.

This is only an exercise. Only you can make the ethical decision over whether to include such a character and his scenes in your nonfiction work. If you do, be sure to let the reader know, one way or another. The idea is art and truth, not deception.

Disclaimer

Gow Farris and Mindy Mallow-Dalmation are composite characters. Gow is made from three: a certain wonderful very old bird who had provided me work for this book and was excited to be included, but died. Another gentleman who was very hostile to the project and to me but let me use the writing you see here under Gow's name, as long as I changed identifying details and didn't say anything nice about him. Finally, a third, older student who provided the physical description.

Mindy Mallow-Dalmation is made from three as well, all undergraduate students of mine, but from different institutions. The writing I represent as hers comes from two people. Otherwise, you'll notice, I just *describe* her work. The personal history is a mix of all three. The physical description is a mix of a different two. I wanted to use one particular person, but she said no emphatically, being most afraid of her parents learning certain information. The others gave permission, but they just weren't as interesting, as useful pedagogically.

I can't say a ton more about how I made the composites without subverting the purpose of the composites, which is privacy for those who asked for it.

A pedagogical query: How do you feel about Gow and Mindy now? Are you mad at me? Does the disclaimer make things better or worse? Would this book be better or worse without Gow and Mindy? These are all questions I've asked myself. I find there are no easy answers. Rest assured, all the other people in this book are undisguised, come to you as themselves. Then again, I wrote them. And true as I was to the facts, how real can they be?

EXERCISE EIGHT: *Your Life—The Cast*

Find a nice, big piece of paper. In a small circle at the center, write your name, or *me* (or *moi*, if you're Miss Piggy). Now draw a circle for each friend and family member and co-worker and on and on, placing the circles as near or far from *me* as is appropriate to their importance in your life. Where might you draw a larger circle to enclose those names that could be called the inner circle? Who's in there? Who's just on the line? And who's not in there?

Try different versions of this constellation: One for family. One for friends. One for co-workers. One for your childhood. One for now. One for the people who give you the most trouble. One for angels. The idea is simply to get thinking about who's important in your life and why, always looking for ideas, of course, and stories.

 The first thing that makes a reader read a book is the characters. Say you're standing in a train station, or an airport, and you're leafing through books; what you're hoping for is a book where you'll like the characters, where the characters are interesting.
—John Gardner

EXERCISE NINE: *Characters as Traits*

From your constellation of characters, pick a friend. Type his or her name at the top of your screen, and make a list of traits. Include absolutely anything that comes to mind. What bugs you? What's endearing? What kind of humor? What kind of clothes? What's her favorite movie? What time does he hit the hay?

Next, do the same for a family member. Then an enemy. Then an employer. How well do you know each? What kinds of things do you know about one person in your life and not about the other? What traits would you leave out of a portrait? Which would you include? What traits would your subject like left out of a portrait? Which traits are needed for the story but uncomfortable for the person you portray? The idea is simply to start seeing the people in your life as characters, for as soon as you write about them in a narrative, that's what they will turn into.

For each person you reduce (I use this word pointedly) to traits in the previous exercise, try a paragraph or two explaining the central drama between the two of you. Drama can be defined as conflict, conflict defined as tension, but remember that not all drama is negative, nor is all tension. The pages you produce for this exercise should not be a story or a description of an event but a discussion of your relationship. As you do two and three and four of these discussions, the idea of a central drama will take on more meaning for you. Note how reducing a friendship or romance to one central thing simplifies, clarifies. And note how drama arises from character.

Would the person you're writing about agree with your assessment? Why not? Can you write from his or her point of view for a draft? What changes? What can you use? Does a voice separate from your own emerge? If so, that's a voice the reader would like to hear.

CHARACTERIZATION THROUGH DIALOGUE

As a memoirist, you don't have omniscience at your disposal, can't read your brother's mind, can't but guess or intuit motives (unless you ask). Still, your reader must be made to forget your presence as the creator of his readerly impression of a character, must be made to forget the filter of your bias. Your reader comes to trust you only slowly and is quick to take the side of your mother, say, if your portrait feels too bitter, or quick to disbelieve you if your portraits are too sweet.

So a good place to start thinking about characters in nonfiction is with dialogue. In dialogue, your characters, your people, are speaking for themselves, and if your characters are speaking, the reader can look over your writerly shoulder, have the feeling he's seeing past you to the person herself.

Dialogue in nonfiction poses the same problems as in fiction—drama, verisimilitude, intensity, surprise, storytelling—with the added burden that (to whatever extent your ethics demand) it must really have been said, or be representative of the kind of talk that did occur. When I'm engaged in journalism (and when the talk isn't merely straight quotation, an easier case), any dialogue I use is verbatim, though at times I have condensed a conversation or moved a sentence or edited for sense and grammar. That's as much as my journalistic ethics will allow.

John McPhee, a preeminent writer of literary journalism, says:

> The nonfiction writer is communicating with the reader about real people in real places. So if those people talk, you say what those people said. You don't say what the writer decides they said. I get prickly if someone suggests there's dialogue in my pieces that I didn't get from the source. You don't make up dialogue.

I get prickly, too, when we're talking about journalism. But in memoir I give myself more leeway, and I think my reader does, too. Writing about events twenty or thirty years gone, I use dialogue more freely than in my journalistic pieces, letting my people talk as characters in the rough drafts to aid my memory, then carefully editing their talk to make it as close to that of my real friends, family, and other characters as I can, to make the speeches I can't quite remember not only plausible but probable, even occasionally giving the reader markers like: "My father said something like ..." And then proceeding to the talk.

Amazingly, though, much of what I report as dialogue I do remember well, some of it very well indeed. I can hear my father as clearly as I did the day he caught me puffing at a cigarette (stolen from him) in my bedroom forty years ago: "You'll be a lucky bird if you don't start smoking."

I don't remember my reply, but you can be sure it was a squirming promise (unkept, by the way—I started smoking, all right, and had to go through hell to quit twenty years later, twenty years ago). If I were to write about my former smoking career and my quitting, I'd probably reproduce that promise, knowing the kind of words I used for such things, and not feel badly or unethical about it. And, to reiterate, if I'm really going out on a memory limb, I'll say so: admit to making plausible dialogue, then carry on.

New writers of memoir will sometimes let problems of memory—especially in matters of dialogue—freeze them up. And if nothing gets written, what difference does a high ethical stance make? If your first goal is verifiable accuracy, you're better off as a scientist or historian or traditional journalist than as a memoirist. Successful memoir requires drama. Readers demand it. The form itself demands it. Drama—characters in action—must be the first excellence. Accuracy comes in a very close (and very important) second, but *second*. Always keeping in mind that lying is lying.

Check out the boxed disclaimer at the very front of Augusten Burroughs's winning memoir, *Dry*:

Author's note:

This memoir is based on my experiences over a ten-year period. Names have been changed, characters combined, and events compressed. Certain episodes are imaginative re-creation, and those episodes are not intended to portray actual events.

Burroughs is at the far end of a certain continuum, willing to mix a little fiction in with his nonfiction (fiction in the service of nonfiction?), but he lets us know up front, and, in the end, I don't think he loses our trust. We know that memory is faulty (especially in a story of alcohol addiction); we know that a writer's people need to be protected in various ways.

Like other defenses, the refusal to write anything but verifiably accurate dialogue (even in a memoir's rough drafts) gets in the way of discovery. Memory holds a lot more, even in matters of dialogue, than we may credit at first examination. You probably do remember what was said, so let yourself hear it. And if you don't quite remember, let yourself write anyway. Your rough draft and first drafts are yours alone. What matters is that your last drafts are as true as memory can make them and that your reader always knows where you stand. If you want to be trusted (not busted), let the reader in on your process and methods.

Or, having written pages and pages of plausible dialogue that helps you hear your people's voices, hear the conversations you've had in life, cut it all back to the two or three lines you're sure of, the ones all the extra writing made possible.

EXERCISE ELEVEN: *Your People, Talking*

Pick a character from your constellation, and write two pages or more of the two of you talking. You might use as a starting point a remembered conversation, but don't get too technical at this stage. Just let the two of you talk about one of your usual subjects.

Do four or five or more dialogues, different characters talking with you, a page or two each. See if that central drama I spoke of in the previous exercise starts to emerge in each one. If not, see if you can make it emerge. See if you can get your people talking about stuff that matters.

Make at least one of your characters a good friend you could easily ask to read the dialogue you come up with, and show it to him or her. Does your friend feel well represented? Make sure, too, that one of your characters is someone you could never ask to read it.

Then, check your work against the following advice.

DIALOGUE TO AVOID

Wooden

> "Doctor Smith has just called, Jonathan, and says the tumor is not malignant after all."
>
> "Well, that is good news, Marilyn. I did not want to die so young."
>
> "Yes, Jonathan, that is good news to me, as well."
>
> "Marilyn, our life insurance agent, John Strauss of Wilton, called last night to say you have quintupled the policy upon my life. Is this true, Marilyn?"

These people sound too formal, inhuman. They are a couple, yet they use each other's names excessively. They speak without contractions.

Small Talk (and Lost Sequence)

> "Doctor Smith called, and you're going to be okay!"
>
> "That's good news!"
>
> "Isn't it?"
>
> "Quite good."
>
> "I'm so pleased."
>
> "Me, too."
>
> "Darling."
>
> "Darling."
>
> "I'm going to live."
>
> "Yes, you are."
>
> "Ah."
>
> "Ah."

> "Oh, honey!"
>
> "Relief!"

Real talk consists of a lot of filler and repetition. Your dialogue doesn't need to. All the relief here takes too much time, grows boring. And did you find the lost sequence? The speakers change places somewhere in the middle, not an uncommon problem in long stretches of unattributed back-and-forth.

Information Dumping

> "Jonathan, Doctor Smith, who lives just down the street, phoned while you were at your office in the most expensive building in Dallas and said that the tumor in your gizzard has turned out to be benign."
>
> "Darling, that is good news. Come here with your ample figure and long blonde hair and give me a hug!"
>
> "Watch it, your black eyeglasses that you've worn since the skiing accident in Tahoe are gouging my prominent forehead."

Information dumping is a matter of the writer trying to give readers important information through dialogue. These characters are telling each other stuff they certainly ought to know (and therefore needn't *say*). Better to just communicate it in exposition or show it in scene. Let the characters speak for themselves.

Too Much Dialect

> "I kin a' ha' na see a kenning tha' bless kinna wooffle nok."
>
> "Aye, an' is trey, matey, an is trey!"

Okay, how people talk is important, but all that's needed to indicate accent is a suggestion here and there to give the flavor of it. Trust the reader to add the rest. In this case, our writer might have said, "He's Scottish and sounds it." An "aye" here and there and selected unusual vocabulary will do the rest.

Mimetic Comedy

> "I uh-uh-uh-uh d-d-d-don't k-k-k-know, Ch-Ch-Ch-Charlie."
>
> "Uh, you, uh, don't, uh, know?"
>
> "N-n-n-n-no."

Again, the suggestion of a stammer is all the reader needs. She'll add the rest as part of her readerly dreaming.

Dumb Tag Lines

> "I guess we can cancel that insurance policy now,"
> he enthused.
>
> "Perhaps it can wait till Monday," she encouraged.
>
> "But we'll save eleven dollars if we do it now," he misered.
>
> "Who's we?" she queried.
>
> "Why you, darling, and I!" he exclaimed.
>
> "I'm more inclined to cancel *you*," she chortled.

I know your high school teacher told you to vary your tag lines. But there is nothing wrong with repeating *he said* and *she said* over and over. Every great writer does so. *He said* and *she said* provide fine rhythms, and when repeated, they fall into the background of readerly consciousness. Fancy, verby tag lines shake a reader out of his dream. Note that a question mark *means* "she queried," and that an exclamation point *means* "he exclaimed." "Chortled"? That's a marvelous word, coined by Lewis Carroll for *Alice's Adventures in Wonderland*, but how do you laugh and talk at the same time (if it's possible, show me, don't tell me ...)? "Enthused"? What's said ought to *sound* enthusiastic. "Misered"? Please! I'm not saying never use anything but *he said*, *she said*, just use anything else sparingly and carefully.

Adverbial Insanity

> "I'm going to live," he said gratingly.
>
> "Where?" she said mysteriously.
>
> "Why, I mean, I'll be alive!" he said meaningfully.
>
> "What makes you think so?" she said menacingly.
>
> "What's that in your hand?" he said realizingly.
>
> "A hunting rifle," she said explainingly.
>
> BANG, went the weapon loudly.

Your story ought to have provided enough context that only very rarely should you need to add an adverb to your tag line. As a matter of policy, try cutting all of them in your work. Which, if any, turn out to be really necessary?

EXERCISE TWELVE: *Read It Out Loud*

Gather all your dialogues from exercise eleven in this chapter and any dialogue you've written as part of other exercises, and one by one, try reading them out loud. One of the characters is supposed to be you—do you sound right saying what you've written? If you've got a patient friend, try reading together a dialogue meant to be between you two.

I always read all of my writing out loud at some stage of the drafting, often at many stages. My daughter thinks I'm nuts, lurking in the kitchen, ranting to myself in two or three voices: "Daddy! Who are you talking to?"

But anything I can't say right, a reader is not going to hear right in her head.

EXERCISE THIRTEEN: *Monologue*

I use a lot of long speeches by single characters, particularly in my journalistic work. Try re-creating five or ten minutes of someone giving a talk or someone passionately explaining an opera or someone giving you complicated directions. The trick is taking fast notes while you listen, writing them up immediately afterward, not putting it off. And do this one over and over.

Of course, a voice recorder will help, but the point of this exercise is training your memory. For the sake of the exercise, use your recorder only as an aid to check yourself: write first, then listen, superposing memory over record. What kinds of things do you tend to misremember?

EXERCISE FOURTEEN: *Real Talk*

Take that voice recorder to a gathering at which you know lively conversation will result: your poker night, a dinner party, reading club, family outing. You probably don't need to hide the machine; people tend to forget it's there very quickly, and you'll feel better operating in the open.

Next day, pick a lively section of the conversation, find it on the recorder, and go ahead and type it up, word for word. That is, *transcribe* it. Get it all correct, and add tag lines.

Chances are, you'll have a lot of pages before you're through, and chances are even the most scintillating conversation you remember won't flow smoothly, won't hold tension, won't work as dialogue.

The assignment is to make your transcript work as dialogue. What must be cut? How do you set off one character from another? How different are the voices? Can you get the funny way Aunt Esther coughs before each pronouncement? Can you get Charlie's lisp? And so forth. The idea is to think about how different actual conversation is from written dialogue, how much artifice is required to capture the truth of the mood and the timbre of lively talk.

LOOKING AT EXAMPLES

As with every other writing skill, when it comes to characters talking, it's a good idea to look at the work of fine writers.

So, let's look at some dialogue from a master, Philip Roth, this from *Patrimony*, a memoir of his father (and particularly of his father's death).

> When finally my father seemed to remember Benjamin's presence, he looked up and said to him, "Well, Doctor, I've got a lot of people waiting for me on the other side," and with his head jutting out toward the bowl, he dropped his spoon into the Jell-O and resumed the attempt to eat something.
>
> I walked out into the corridor with the doctor and his aide. "I don't see how he could survive two operations like that," I said.
>
> "Your father is a strong man," the doctor replied.
>
> "A strong eighty-six-year-old man. Maybe enough is enough."
>
> "The tumor is at a critical point. You can expect him to have serious trouble within a year."
>
> "With what?
>
> "Probably with swallowing," he said, and that, of course, evoked a horrible picture, but not much worse than envisioning him recovering not from one eight-hour operation on his head but now from two. The doctor said, "Anything can happen, really."

"We'll have to think it all through," I said.

We shook hands, but as he and his aide started away, he turned back to offer a gentle reminder. "Mr. Roth, once something happens, it may be too late to help him."

"Maybe it's too late already," I replied.

The drama here is clear. Between the doctor and Roth is the imminent death of Roth's father. No problem finding the dramatic center. I've plucked this bit of talk out of the middle of a scene in the middle of a chapter in the middle of a book, but note how much sense it makes; note the tension, the urgency. And note the parts that aren't talk. Roth's father says his poignant piece about people on the other side, and then there is silence. No one's talking. Everyone is silenced by the first line of speech. Roth fills this silence with his father trying to eat Jell-O. The silence lasts long enough for Roth and the doctor to get out into the corridor. Their talk fills in the facts, which we get as Roth gets them. His concern, his surprise, his worry become ours. "Probably with swallowing," the doctor says. Then there's another silence. Roth fills it now with his thoughts at the time. His worry about his father's swallowing has been made visceral and visible to us by the earlier image of the old man eating Jell-O.

More talk. Then a handshake, and one more silence in which we get the image of the doctor walking away only to turn and say the last devastating thing.

Roth's dialogue is never talk; it's always managed as a scene. How? For one thing, he doesn't forget the people who aren't talking. For another, he remembers that talkers aren't just mouths. He uses what's called *stage business*: characters doing things while they talk.

EXERCISE FIFTEEN: *Stage Business*

Again, get out one of your dialogues. Does it contain stage business? That is, are people doing things with their hands? Their faces? Are there silences? Are there moments when one character forgets to listen to the other? Are there background activities (traffic, music, wind)? Try adding the things that are missing. How much adds to the drama? At what point does too much start to take away?

What people do is as important as (and often more important than) what they say. The marvelous thing about nonfiction is that as writers, we already know what our people have done (the story needs only be dramatized, not made up) and, even better, how they have done it. We know the way Mom holds her mouth when she doesn't believe a word we're saying; we know the way Mr. Collins lurches when he walks through the office; we know how the gas station kid smirks when we ask him to hurry. That is, we know these things if we've been observant.

<hr>

EXERCISE SIXTEEN: *Write First, Look Later*

Pick one of your scenes from earlier exercises, one that portrays someone still in your life, a person you can spend time with. And then, go observe him or her. Have lunch, play tennis—life as usual—but as soon as you part company, write your person up: note gestures, typical expressions, stance, quirks of manner, whatever is available. Then go back to your scene. What can you use and where?

<hr>

GOOD OLD DESCRIPTION

I've saved description for last because a great deal of the work of character description gets done in the course of the scenes your characters make possible, in their dialogue and in their actions. But always, it's vital that your reader be able to see your characters clearly and that the picture in her mind have something to do with the picture in your mind as you write. Adjectives alone won't do the job; in fact, too many adjectives will serve more to obscure a character than reveal him. It's probably most effective to reveal your character in the course of a scene, trait by trait. And it's important to keep quietly reminding the reader of your character's physicality: gesture, hair style, clothing, posture, body-English, *affect*.

Let me define that last word the way psychologists use the term. First of all, it's pronounced with the accent on the first syllable. It's not the same word as *affect* with the accent on the second syllable. And it's very important as we think about making characters. Affect, the way I understand it, is the visible and otherwise tangible expression of personality, mood, and attitude. When

WRITING LIFE STORIES

we talk to a stranger, affect is what we see. Sad eyes, a downcast demeanor, sighs, and halfhearted shrugs might be read as a depressive affect. A big smile, bared teeth, and bright eyes might be seen as aggressive by one observer, happy by another. Some people—notably murderers in court—seem to have no affect. One's affect will change from interaction to interaction and day to day.

Affect is what we want to capture when we try to portray one of our people. I might lay out the depressive affect in the course of a long dialogue: first the sad eyes, later a shrug, and so forth, as my person speaks (perhaps cheerful words, subverted) and is spoken to.

As always, lots of practice is the best way to get better, and, in this case, the best way to simple, evocative description of your people. And, as always, reading as a writer is crucial. Here's a passage from *Great Plains*, by Ian Frazier (not incidentally one of my favorite books of creative nonfiction for the way it mixes so many elements of good writing and thinking, and for its humor). This is the opening of chapter six, and by now we know that Frazier is very interested in and very knowledgeable about the history of Plains Indians:

> One day, on the street in front of my apartment in New York (this was before I moved to Montana), I met a Sioux Indian named Le War Lance. I had just been reading a study of recent economic conditions on Sioux reservations. The authors seemed puzzled that so few Sioux were interested in raising sugar beets or working in a house-trailer factory. As I waited for the light to change, I noticed that the man standing next to me resembled many pictures of Sioux that I had seen. I said, "Are you a Sioux?" He smiled and said, "I'm an Oglala Sioux Indian from Oglala, South Dakota." He said his name and asked for mine. He had to lean over to hear me. He was more than six feet tall. He was wearing the kind of down coat that is stuffed with something other than down—knee length, belted around the waist, in a light rescue orange polished with dirt on the creases—blue jeans lengthened with patches of denim of a different shade from knee to cuff, cowboy boots, a beaded leather ponytail holder. His hair was straight and black with streaks of gray, and it hung to his waist in back. After I saw him, I never cut my hair again. In one hand he was holding a sixteen-ounce can of beer.

"Your name is Lou?" I asked. "Lou War Lance?"

"Le!" he said. He pronounced it kind of like "leh" and kind of like "lay." He said it meant "this" in Sioux. I had never before met anyone whose first name was a pronoun. Next to him was a compact woman with straight auburn hair. I had not thought they were together. "Do you know each other?" Le asked. She recoiled just perceptibly.

What is the center of drama between Frazier and War Lance? The center is the fact that War Lance is a Sioux Indian (as the scene goes on we learn the amazing fact that he is a grandson of Crazy Horse, who we learn is a special obsession of Frazier's). Note the luxurious paragraph Frazier devotes to describing War Lance as he first saw him. He doesn't need to supply a guess as to the Oglala's age; the gray streaks in the Sioux's hair help the reader make her own guess. Frazier shows his own height and War Lance's by way of a quick comparison. The orange parka, the blue jeans, the hair band all give us the man. That Frazier never cut his hair again is about the power of the presence of War Lance, and this power is part of his affect. War Lance smiles at the initial question, "Are you a Sioux?" That friendliness is affect, too. That sixteen-ounce can of beer is a stage prop, of course, and has its meaning. It's not an elegant bottle.

Only when the description has been delivered does Frazier resume the dialogue. That long descriptive paragraph represents the moment of observation, that burst of time when we first see someone and gather in all the clues there are as to character. And Frazier gives us as many of those clues as he can.

The minor character—the woman with the auburn hair—gets minor treatment, but not *no* treatment. We see her size, her hair, and an important bit of affect: she recoils when she has to interact with our writer. This lets us see the writer as a character, too. He's been studying the conditions of Sioux reservations in his room so long that women actually recoil when they see him. So all three characters are dealt with, none forgotten, even while War Lance is at center stage.

EXERCISE SEVENTEEN: *Characters and Their Telling Details*

I don't want to ask you to describe a character, because that will result in a block of description that happens outside a scene, a character doing nothing, a character who's not in the moment (and listen to me, Grasshopper: a person who's not in a moment is dead).

Instead, I want you to work up a clear picture of your character in action, in a scene, talking. So, once again, get out one of your dialogues. (If you don't have more than one, perhaps it's time to go back and write a bunch. Take your time. And quit paving the road to you-know-where.) Pull out one of your dozens of dialogues—you as character speaking to another person as character—and add character traits, give clues as to affect. Help us see the person even as she's speaking, even as she's walking; give us the person alive, with all her contradictions. And while you're at it, find ways to sneak in some description of yourself.

Assign each person several concrete details as you go, and pair each concrete detail with an abstract detail. A concrete detail is a sensory detail—some physical trait, some favorite article of clothing or jewelry, something obvious, something everyday in your person's life. An abstract detail is an emotional or metaphorical detail, a personality quirk, an emotion, an air. To complicate your character description, try to pick pairs of abstract and concrete details that contradict each other. Try numerous pairs and groupings until you feel you've caught something fresh about your person.

Here's an example from Kristen Keckler:

> My cheerful brother-in-law, Joe, also the family chef and fix-it man, cooks chocolate-chip pancakes on Christmas morning. Whistling like a winter wren, he flips the sizzling pan. The grim reaper tattoo on his thick forearm wiggles, dances.

Here, the abstract details are "cheerful," and "fix-it man," even "brother-in-law." These, along with the concrete chocolate-chip pancakes—gooey and hot and sweet—make contrast with the image of his tattoo—death, dark humor, misspent youth. The details arranged in combination, carefully juxtaposed, paint a more complex view of Joe and pique the reader's interest.

Minor Characters

A note on minor characters: Use them. Every person you mention should get a quick, sharp, devastatingly exact sketch. Help your reader see each person, no matter how inconsequential. If a ticket taker gives you directions, be sure to show us his toupee. If a kid down the street shouts an epithet as you drive past, let's see the kid's freckles and not just the upraised middle finger.

The travel writer and novelist Paul Theroux does remarkable things with minor characters in his travel books. With deft strokes, he nails the man on the train, the customs official, the idiot tourist. Joan Didion is magnificent at capturing the small player quickly, skewering doctors with simple portraits, hanging dictators and bureaucrats with their own words and gestures. John McPhee populates his books with unmistakably individual people, no matter how small the role, from Alaskan bush pilots who land on sand bars in rivers to merchant seamen waiting in a vast hall for work on a ship. George Dennison— who lived in the next town from me in Maine—describes neighbor after neighbor with such precision in his journals (edited and published posthumously as Dennison's last book, *Temple*) that I know them and recognize them in town. The best lessons will always come from your reading.

As a matter of revision, come back to your people over and over again. Crack open each person as you have learned to crack open each scene. Talk to those people who are available to speak, telling them (or not) about your project. Don't let them go till you've got them right, on paper, so right and so true that any complaint will be unfounded. The truth is always your best protection.

A CHARACTER TALKS BACK

I put my feet up and just daydreamed, sitting by the fire, home in Maine, teaching done for the week, new snow on the ground, perfect afternoon. My *Harper's Magazine* piece had come out, my novel was going pretty well. The phone rang. My dad.

He said, "I've been checking *Harper's* every month, and here it is; here you are! Wonderful, chief! Let me just take it home and read it, and I'll give you a call, tell you what I think."

"Sure, Pop." Oh, man. I'd sort of put off telling him any more about when the piece would come out. I just thought it best if I let life go on as always: my dad never one to read *Harper's*; I never one to insist he did.

My calm afternoon was busted. A *character* had called me on the phone and was about to pass judgment on his portrait. My editor had called the rendition of my father "loving." But still. I'd said stuff about my dad's and my relationship that I had never said to him, that had gone unsaid. I'd told the world what aftershave he used. I'd confessed to goofing off in school, and much worse.

When the phone rang again, it was my dad. He was crying. Sobbing and trying to speak. I had never heard the man cry before, didn't know really that he was capable of crying. I was alarmed. I had done this thing. He cried and sobbed and managed to say he liked the piece; it was a hell of a piece. He said a lot of stuff that hadn't exactly gone unsaid before, but now it got said directly: he was proud of me; he loved me.

He said the piece was true, that he recognized himself, that he was maybe a little sorry to recognize himself. He said I surely overdramatized a little, that I didn't get everything exactly right. He said, for example, that he didn't ever use Aqua Velva. It was Old Spice. He asked how the car was running.

Here we were, nearly forty and nearly seventy, and we were talking as we never had, taking the first firm steps toward a relationship as adults.

I didn't write "Into Woods" to communicate with my father. I just wrote it to say something I had to say, something that turned out to be true. But my dad and I talked. We talked.

CHAPTER SIX

Stage Presence

I search for language in which faith intertwines with desire, faith that we can recapture, with erotic accuracy, that treasured memory or vision which is the object of our desire. ... I think back to a phrase of Julia Kristeva's, the most interesting feminist thinker of our time, who speaks of "the voluptuousness of family life." I would apply the same phrase to the prose I most admire, prose I can caress and nurture and linger on, diction which is nourished by the deep intimacy of familiar detail, and yet is constantly renewed by the force of the writer's love and fidelity to language.

—*Francine du Plessix Gray*

Dear writer, I'd like you to do an exercise before I say a word about stage presence or anything else in this chapter. Later, I'll come back with some explanation and rationale (and all that other left-brain stuff). For now, just take an hour and work on the following exercise. That's what we're here for, after all. Right?

EXERCISE ONE: *Epistolary Discovery*

Please write a letter to someone you haven't seen in a very long time, explaining yourself. This should not be a letter you intend to send. The person may be alive or dead. Go on, okay? Write.

HAVING A VOICE

Mick Jagger has a distinctive voice, for example. So much so that when you hear him singing backup in Carly Simon's old hit song "You're So Vain," you know it's Mick Jagger. Couldn't be anyone else. Similarly for every great or even really good singer: Ella Fitzgerald is Ella Fitzgerald. Maria Callas is Maria Callas. Van Morrison is Van Morrison. Liz Phair is Liz Phair. Louis Armstrong is Louis Armstrong, both voice and trumpet, and there's no mistaking either. 50 Cent is 50 Cent, that gritty whistle-lisp a result of being shot in the jaw. Imitations amuse, but seldom (if ever) fool us completely.

What accounts for our immediate recognition? In singing, it's a matter of a thousand factors coming together, some a matter of study and control, others part of an innate gift. There's phrasing, timbre, modulation, the simple pronunciation of words, breathing, authority, mood and attitude, regional inflection, on and on, some factors a matter of utmost mystery, some of science.

Same in writing. How do you account for voice on the page? How is voice on the page the same as literal voice, the voices of your friends speaking, their unmistakable tones and cadences and enthusiasms, which, even recorded on the cheapest answering machine through static, even with the bar brawl in the background, are plainly their own?

I confess I don't know the answer. But every reader knows a false voice when he hears it, knows an imitative voice, knows an unsure voice. Officiousness, tentativeness, coyness, every form of dishonesty, vanity: it all comes through. If an essay is a conversation with the reader, then you must not only have a voice but be able to control it such that most readers hear the exact *you* that you want to project.

A Few Strong Voices

As you read the examples to come, think about what makes the person behind the words apparent to you. Whom are you picturing? What age? What face?

The first short excerpt is from *Dry*, by Augusten Burroughs. Last chapter, you'll recall, we looked at his boxed disclaimer. *Dry* is a hilarious, sad memoir of alcohol addiction by an ex-advertising executive. (The first hardcover edition has a great cover, too, designed by the author, bold font for the title, and a martini glass stuffed with a besotted fish.) Burroughs goes to rehab because there's been an intervention at work and an ultimatum: dry out or be fired.

> I have replayed my internal Rehab Hospital Tourism tapes over and over. My favorite goes like this: A discrete, Frank Lloyd Wright-ish compound shrouded mysteriously from public view by a tasteful wall of trimmed boxwood trees. Ian Schrager, of course, created the interior. Spare rooms, sun-drenched, with firm mattresses and white, 300 count Egyptian thread cotton sheets. There is a nightstand (probably made of birch with a galvanized steel top) and on it: *Chicken Soup for the Alcoholic Soul* and a carafe of ice water with lemon wedges. I imagine polished linoleum floors. (By allowing this one clinical detail into my fantasy, I believe I will be allowed all the other details I envision.) Nurses will be far too holistic and nurturing to wear white polyester; they will wear, perhaps, tailored hemp smocks and when they are backlit by one of the many floor-to-ceiling windows overlooking the lily pond, I will see the outline of their lean, athletic legs.
>
> There will be a pool. I will forgive its heavy chlorination. I will understand. This is a hospital, after all.

The tone is comic, ironic, Burroughs playing the stereotypical decorating-savvy homosexual, the tragic-romantic figure. He's kidding, but he's not kidding at the same time, and the disjunction drives the voice. There's something plaintive, very vulnerable, beneath the joking, and while we readers are entertained, we're also moved.

After rehab, Burroughs heads home. He's thirty days sober. He's been stripped of his illusions. He knows who's to blame for his drinking, for his various derelictions. The voice of the narrative shifts with the writer's fortunes, highlights the new, depressing clarity with which Burroughs sees his old life. There's no more kidding around, and our man lets the details speak for themselves:

> I am not prepared for what I see when I unlock the door to my apartment. Although I have obviously seen it before, lived with it even, I have never encountered it through the lens of thirty days' sobriety. My apartment is filled with empty Dewar's bottles. They cover all surfaces; the counters in the kitchen, the top of the refrigerator. They are under the table I use as a desk, dozens of them there, with a small clearing for my feet. And they line one wall, eleven feet long, seven bottles deep. This appears to be far more bottles than I remembered, as though they multiplied while I was gone.

He cleans up the bottles, gets started in his new life. But of course, nothing's easy.

A CALM, RICH PACE

The next example is from *Minor Characters*, a memoir by Joyce Johnson, who is also a novelist (*In the Night Café*) and a journalist (*What Lisa Knew*). *Minor Characters* is a coming-of-age story set in the fifties. The title gives reference to the fact that Johnson was a minor character in the story of a major literary figure, Jack Kerouac—she was his girlfriend for a time. In her own story, of course, and in her own conception, and, very quickly, in the reader's mind, she's a major character. The tension of these two points of truth—minor, major—make the dramatic center of this book. Here's the opening paragraph of the second section of chapter three:

> It's the spring of 1949 and I'm thirteen and a half. With my best friend Maria, I am sitting in the very front seat of the top deck of a double-decker bus as it makes its way down lower Fifth Avenue toward Greenwich Village, which I've been assured is the very last stop—thus impossible to miss. Suddenly we see it, the famous arch that's supposed to be the entrance to Washington Square and to lots of other things—perhaps a life of romance and adventure—that I've heard about from four older, very knowledgeable Trotskyite girls whom I've met in the basement of Hunter College High School. Juniors who disdain the bourgeois cafeteria upstairs,

they lunch secretly on yogurt deep in the locker room. They carry bags of knitting under which there are copies of the *Militant*, which they hawk around Fourteenth Street nearly every day after school. They have Trotskyite boyfriends whom they make sweaters and argyle socks for and endlessly discuss. They never quite explain to me what Trotskyite is, but it seems that if you are one, you're headed for trouble not only with the fascists but with detestable teen-age Stalinists who've been known to harass sellers of the Militant and even beat them up. I admire the daring of these girls tremendously, their whole style, in fact—dark clothes and long earrings, the cigarettes they smoke illicitly, the many cups of coffee they say they require to keep them going. Friendly as they are, however, they never invite me on their rounds. With Olympian disinterest, they delineate a territory that it's up to me to explore for myself.

You'll note, I hope, all the background information seemingly effortlessly provided: who, where, what, when, why, and how. But let's think about what makes this brief passage so unmistakably Joyce Johnson. For one, there's the length. This paragraph is long, with a calm, rich pace. There's a sense of capaciousness and time, of confidence, of comfortable, adult intelligence. She's going to tell us what needs to get told, and we're going to listen. The tone is slightly ironic throughout—this is a thirteen-year-old self she's writing about, after all, and, of course, all these years later she knows infinitely more about life and knows how silly the longings of youth can be. And yet, there's an elegiac tone as well, a whiff of nostalgia, an acknowledgment that for all the silliness of Trotskyite girls there was real romance in the air in 1949, and real possibility. The tone is compassionate, as well: Johnson does not judge her younger self, and only mildly the Trotskyites.

I could go on (and I hope you will continue this analysis on your own terms), but the most important thing to note is how many layers really exist here, how it is possible to be both ironic and compassionate, how it is possible to mingle the present (the writer sitting at her desk, remembering) and the past (the writer as a present-tense teen), the elegance of these sentences juxtaposed to the awkwardness of young adulthood.

VOICE

Voice arrives in contrasts. And voice isn't a matter of conscious artifice so much as it is a matter of personality, of *affect*, when you think about it.

When a new writer defends his "style," the teacher smiles, because real style isn't an artifice; real style—voice—arrives on its own as an extension of a writer's character. When it's done self-consciously and purposefully, style becomes affectation and as transparent as any affectation (an English accent on an old college chum from New Jersey, for example).

More than anything, voice, the magic of a person appearing on the page, is the result of years of writing practice, of a writer getting so fluent in her medium that the medium itself—in this case words—doesn't get in the way of expression.

But voice is also a matter of urgency. Of passion. Of the clarity of a writer's caring about her subject deeply, and deeply caring about communicating it to her reader. Voice is personality on the page.

A STYLISH OBSESSION

Let's look at another example, this one from *U and I*, by Nicholson Baker, a funny, poignant, honest, and urgent account of Baker's fascination (that's not to say obsession, which Baker admits is a tad bizarre) with John Updike. What follows is the first paragraph of his chapter nine:

> I would never have done it either—drag in *The New Yorker* name so obviously to get his attention—except that life was too short not to. Those ticking seconds of signature might be the only chance I would ever get to embarrass myself in his presence. When the excessively shy force themselves to be forward, they are frequently surprisingly unsubtle and over-direct and even rude: they have entered an extreme region beyond their normal personality, an area of social crime where gradations don't count; unavailable to them are the instincts and taboos that booming extroverts, who know the territory of self-advancement far better, can rely on. The same goes for constitutionally ungross people who push themselves to chime in with something off-color—in choosing to go along they step into a world so saturated with revulsions that its

esthetic structure is impossible for them to discern, and as a result they shout out some horrible inopportune conversation-stopper, often relying on a word like "pustulating," when natural Rabelaisians—who afterward exchange knowing glances with each other that say "Sad—way out of his league"—know to keep their colostomy sacks under wraps for the moment. Which referenced sacks bring us to the second time I met Updike—for I did, as it happened, get a further opportunity to embarrass myself.

Nicholson Baker is a stylist, no doubt about that, but style—the choice of words, the speed of phrasing, the grandness or plainness of syntax—is only one of the many layers that create voice. Because, honestly, almost anybody can elevate his language. Almost anybody can reach to the heights of sesquipedalianism. Almost any good writer can throw together a wry passage, full of allusion. But almost nobody (one person, in fact) can make a Nicholson Baker paragraph. His sense of humor is alive in there. His irritable and almost microscopic vision of the world (compare this to Joyce Johnson's more sweeping and romantic view) makes us laugh or bridle. His willingness to invoke colostomy sacks alongside mortality, his ability to show himself while hiding—all of it is a matter of voice, all of it uniquely Nicholson Baker.

A COMFORTABLE INTIMACY

Now I'll reproduce a much different example, this from *A Childhood: The Biography of a Place*, by Harry Crews:

My fifth birthday had come and gone, and it was the middle of the summer, 1940, hot and dry and sticky, the air around the table thick with the droning of house flies. At supper that night neither my brother nor I had to ask where daddy was. There was always, when he had gone for whiskey, a tension in the house that you could breathe in with the air and feel on the surface of your skin, and more than that, there was that awful look on mama's face. I suppose knowing what the night would bring, not knowing if it would be this night or the next night, or the morning following the second night, when he would come home after a drunk, bloodied, his clothes stinking with whiskey sweat.

Compare Crews's sentences with those of Burroughs and Johnson and Baker. All of their sentences are beautifully grammatical, all of them musical, but Crews's music is a different kind altogether. That last long sentence staggers and jerks like a drunk coming home. There's the sound of the language of his childhood and very little of the sound of the writer at his desk, looking back. The imagery is sweaty and bloodied, not figurative (as are Baker's colostomy sacks), not grand and ironic (as is Johnson's invocation of the arch at Washington Square). Daddy is called daddy (this daddy actually Crews's uncle), no caps. There's a familiarity with the reader here, a comfortable intimacy. We're kin as we read.

With all four of these writers, we feel ourselves in their presences immediately, even in paragraphs plucked from the middles of things. This authorial presence is like the stage presence of an accomplished actor or other performer: The artist comes on stage and captures the attention of everyone in the room with a mere smile, with a plain gesture, with an otherwise unremarkable nod of the head. And the crowd awaits her every move, every word.

When a writer—Burroughs, Johnson, Baker, Crews—comes on stage and within a few sentences has grabbed us, hooked us, called us in, made us ready to listen and listen more, we say that writer has *voice*.

EXERCISE TWO: *Back to the Letter*

Cut the salutation from the letter you wrote at the beginning of this chapter. Go ahead and cut the initial small talk—most letters have some. What's left? (If the answer is nothing, you might want to pick another correspondent to write to, and try again.) Read the remaining paragraphs out loud, as a kind of essay. What's the issue at hand? What's the dramatic center? Why did you pick the person you picked to write to?

I wanted you to make your letter before we discussed the exercise much, because I wanted you to write it truly, without trying to do a job of learning or analysis. It's not too late if you haven't written your letter yet. Go do it, now. Please.

Okay. Now that you have a letter in hand, here's the rationale: This is a *voice* exercise. I hope that while reading your letter aloud you noticed how powerful your writing is in it, how it has changed, how close your passion is to the surface, suddenly. Then again, I know how hard it is to really hear your own stuff. In my classes, this exercise always produces the best writing of the term up to the time I assign it, leads to better writing after. Really, always. If you haven't felt the power of your letter, find someone you trust (but not the person you addressed, please) and read it to him or her.

Why so powerful? When we address a particular person (think of Montaigne and his friend La Boétie), we know exactly who we are. We know what the other person, our reader, knows about us. We know what the other will find of interest. We know what will bore her. We know what we can leave out. We know what's important. We know what's vital and urgent, and we know what constitutes information dumping. And all this knowing gives us a clear, confident, authoritative voice.

To whom do you suppose Augusten Burroughs aims *Dry*? Or Joyce Johnson *Minor Characters*, or Nicholson Baker *U and I*, or Harry Crews *A Childhood*? We can't know without asking the writers, of course, but the answers you come up with might be of great help in thinking about your own writing. To whom do you really want to be talking?

THE GHOST OF THE WRITER'S PRESENT

Time is perhaps the most mysterious part of voice. I've already talked about the writer-at-her-desk. Let's call that layer of time in an essay or memoir the *writer's present*. In the writer's present, you can serenely look back on all aspects of your life. The voice the reader hears is you, now, operating with the benefit of hindsight, quietly contemplating even the worst disasters, commenting on them, offering analysis. This is the voice of your exposition, for the most part, the voice the reader most closely identifies as yours, as *you*.

But your scenes take place in time, back in the past. While the reader is reading about 1928, she's *in* 1928 (or '48 or '68 or '88). Let's call this the *story's present*. Now the voice your reader hears is the voice of the scene, a voice in a time, often the voice of the person you were at the time, a voice that's part of the action, sharing in its emotion. A good writer manages the two voices—past and present—makes conscious use of their differing powers: one voice presents, the other reflects.

A SAMPLE LETTER

Here's just a small part of a letter by Vicki Schwab, a talented graduate student I had some years ago at Ohio State. Note the clarity of the voice as it travels through time.

> Dear Aliah:
>
> The night your father died, Jim came for us and took us to the hospice. He walked with you hand in hand, back to where your father lay and watched you climb on the bed and felt you kiss him on his cold brow. He's so white, you remarked. Psychologists say that children of three do not understand death—its finality, its various aspects, but I know you did. One night, after a visit during which he tried to explain what was happening to his body, you cried hysterically for nearly an hour and I could not comfort you. I was afraid something in you might break.
>
> The night of your father's death, Jim recalled at the memorial service, you asked to return—by yourself this time—and Jim and you once again made the trip down the long hallway. He waited at the door while you scrambled once again onto your father's chest, kissed him once more and said goodbye out loud.
>
> Jim, who rarely cries, did at this moment of retelling.
>
> When you are older, I have a vintage bottle of red wine to give you—very expensive—which your father bought in honor of your birth. The bottle is wrapped in yellowing newspaper containing an article about how he was in trial in Cleveland and raced home to see you newly born.
>
> What wonderful gifts we've been given, you and I.

Needless to say, this letter, this try, is built in a deep cushion of layers. Written to a daughter too young to read it, perhaps for reading later on in her life, it is really a letter to the dead husband. The grief and all the anger of grief, the sorrow, the shock are motherly restrained, but all that emotion lends radiance to each sentence.

The voice is contained in the relationships here but also in the layers of time. Vicki scans a whole decade past but looks to the future.

To address the daughter is hopeful, is to address life. To address the husband would have been to address death. The voice of this passage is multiple, arrives in layers of time, of address, of emotion, of mystery.

EXERCISE THREE: *Finding a Public Voice*

Pick one of your exercises from earlier in this book, or any of your non-fiction writings. At the top, write "Dear _____," adding the name of the correspondent you used in exercise one of this chapter. How must what follows the new salutation change to accommodate this special listener?

Try aiming your prose at different correspondents. Who gets you closest to a voice you recognize as your own? Who lets you say what's on your mind? Let this person into the room as you write.

Who makes you cringe the most, censor yourself? Kick this person out of your writing room, forcibly. Write up a restraining order, if necessary. Call the cops.

WHO'S LISTENING?

Voice, of course, is inextricably tied with audience. If the first question is *who's talking?*, the second question has to be *who's listening?* If you're going to write about your experiences growing marijuana, how might your essay sound if written for *High Times*? How might it sound for *The Atlantic*? How might it sound for *State Police Monthly*? Conversely, if you're going to write about being a narcotics officer, how might your essay sound in front of different audiences? Easily, we see ourselves shifting tactics, shifting affect, shifting, shifting, shifting to accommodate possible listeners. But eventually—this is important—eventually, if you're going to be a writer and not a hack, you will want your voice to be the same for all listeners. Tone may shift, but voice will not. As in life, you will want to come to know who you are when you are on a page.

When I was nervous going to a party or a job interview back in high school, my mother would reassure me: "Just be yourself." The advice was good, but I'd walk around doubly flummoxed, trying to be cool and trying to figure out what *myself* meant. Who was I supposed to be? What self?

Selves, as it turns out, are awfully complicated. That's what Scott Russell Sanders means (as quoted in chapter five) when he says that for a writer "The *I* is a narrow gate." I'm a different person in important ways when I speak at some big university function than when I speak at my best friend's wedding, and both are different from the person I was when I sweet-talked my late, lamented dogs or barked at them. As a professor I'm different than as a son. I'll lampoon the alcoholic excesses of my college students at the same time I fondly remember the beer blasts of my own college days (or last week, come to think of it). I'll make fun of sappy musicals, then go home and watch *The Sound of Music* with my daughter, and happily. Which facets of this complicated me do I let into the stuff I'm writing?

Juxtaposing inconsistent or contrary parts of your personality with one another will make your writing jump.

EXERCISE FOUR: *"Against ..."*

One of my favorite essays is Phillip Lopate's "Against Joie de Vivre," from the book of the same name. In it, he complains about dinner parties and other expressions of sociability and examines his complicated responses to a whole range of life's supposed joys.

Let's go back to chapter four and the "On ..." exercises you've already done. Try changing the title to "Against ..."

"Against Justice"

"Against Love"

"Against Motherhood"

Who could be against these things? Just a try. Write a page or two. Tilt at windmills. See if you are able to arrive at more complicated insights by way of negation, and see if more complicated insights allow for a more complicated—and more human—you on the page.

EXERCISE FIVE: *Get Pissed on Paper*

What makes you mad? I mean, really steaming mad, mad enough to throw something, mad enough to shout, mad enough to, well, what do you do when you're mad?

Some people get very quiet.

The exercise is to write about something that makes you mad and to do your best to *sound* mad. Let it rip. No restraints. I've got friends who will say they are mad but sound quite calm. Come on, man—what are you trying to hide? Other people will immediately resort to cursing, which isn't a bad way to show fury. But try subtler approaches, too. Just be sure anyone reading will get the idea that you're spitting nickels (as a furious secretary once explained to me in a loud voice), that you are in a *rage*.

The idea is not only to communicate but to make your reader feel the emotion you feel. And not just the heat of the emotion but the emotion itself. And keep your usual punctuation and font and spacing—the communication of emotion should come through your words and sentences, not through typographical tricks.

EXERCISE SIX: *Okay, There Are Other Emotions, Too*

What makes you happy? Can you get joy on the page without once mentioning the word? Ecstasy? And so forth: Envy, Love, Fear, Excitement, Loathing, Pride. How might you get each onto the page such that a reader will pick it up, feel it?

Emotion is the soul of voice.

EXERCISE SEVEN: *Method Writing*

Actors have long used the Stanislavski Method, which is still taught at The Actors Studio in the West Village of New York City. Method acting, to oversimplify, is a matter of the actor remembering and really feeling intense emotion before performing a scene. So, if he's supposed to be overjoyed at news of a victory, he remembers and holds a time he felt overjoyed. His heart filled with that remembered joy, he begins to play his part.

I'd like to propose a kind of Stanislavski for essayists. Call it method writing. It's a matter of using remembered emotion to bring fresh emotion to the page. If you wish to write about your love of a particular kind of bird feeder, think first about your love for your husband, say, or your first steady date. Get that heady feeling in your breast, even writing a little about the beloved. Then switch to bird feeders.

It's easy to get silly with this one. But if you are going to write about bird feeders, do so passionately. And if bird feeders don't matter, don't write about them. If you don't care and care deeply, your reader certainly won't.

EXERCISE EIGHT: *Yelling in Public*

Part of the training of certain young Japanese businessmen has to do with shedding inhibition. These young executives have to go out into a crowded urban street and yell, at the top of their lungs, about how stupid they are. Probably you've seen film of them, red faces, open mouths, the crowds coursing past, staring.

Yes, this is your assignment. Go yell.

The idea is (1) to prove that nothing bad will happen to you if you show some extreme emotion and (2) to put you in a really embarrassing position so you won't be so embarrassed when it comes time to write passionately.

If you get arrested, well, then the idea is (3) to show that you shouldn't listen to everything I tell you.

EXERCISE NINE: *Imitations*

In your reading, you've come across some memorable voices. This is an old saw of an exercise but still worth doing: Rewrite a passage of your own in the style of one or more of your favorite writers. But let's change that old word *style* to *voice*. The *voice* of a favorite writer.

The idea on the surface is to force a close analysis of what makes voice. The quieter result of a lot of work in this area is an unleashing of elements of your own voice. For in imitating others you may find yourself.

I write the way I write because I am the kind of person I am. ... I am a woman and I write from that experience. I am a black woman and I write from that experience.

—Lucille Clifton

Slang. We all use it. And—especially in the story's present—it's not only okay to season your writing with it, but imperative to do so. A good ear for colloquial speech is one of the writer's basic tools. Slang (jive, jargon, lingo) subtly reveals not only personality but the person: age, occupation, regional affiliations. And our use of slang and other forms of vernacular speech grows and changes as we do, situates our writerly voices in times and places. Judicious use of the demotic also moves us away from false voices, voices picked up writing school essays, reading newspapers, trying to fit in.

The teenage 1980s valley girl in you might have said, "Gag me with a spoon!" And put a question mark after every assertion?

Your stoner college-age persona might have said, "Whoa, dude, that's some righteous bud!"

The parent in you might say "Choices, son, choices," and *toot* instead of *fart.*

The assignment, should you decide to accept it (we will disavow all knowledge of your existence): picture yourself in various eras and aspects of your life. Make a list of slang expressions and arcane jargon you used as a child, as a teen, as a worker in different environments, as a lover, as a parent, as whatever you've been and when. You might list definitions, too, just for the fun of it.

Now pull out any of your exercises or a piece you've been working on, and find places to add just one of the expressions on your list, then two, then three. What's the effect on your voice in the piece at hand? When is enough, enough?

Crunk?

EXERCISE ELEVEN: *The Ultimate Voice Exercise*

This is one of the hardest exercises I know, and one that can seem daunting. Ready? Voice (like so much of good writing) is a matter of practice. Your assignment is to do just that: for years on end, perhaps comparing one year's output to the next, watch your depth grow, your clarity, your acknowledgment of the complexities of the world. With luck (and hard work) you'll grow in other ways, too, over many years, and along with you your voice will grow: richer, more beautiful, more irritable, more meaningful, more complex, more entertaining, more you.

WELL, THAT'S ME

I'll end this chapter with Mindy Mallow-Dalmation's letter, but first let's look at a small excerpt from Gow Farris's letter, which he addressed simply to "Brother," and which he read to us with huge passion, losing himself (I mean losing part of himself: that censorious and angry editor) entirely. He read a little, then wept copiously while we waited—we were rapt—and then he read some more, lost in the sentences, and not one joke, not one self-trashing aside, not one insult fired at me. When he finished he looked up a little startled and said, "Well, that's me." And it had been. Nobody laughed at the self-dismissive joke he was trying to make. It was as if we'd seen a picture of Gow's thoughts, his most private and most lyrical mind in action. For the first time we'd seen the whole man. He said later he'd never written anything better in his life, never in forty years in the newspaper business. Maybe so, maybe so. I can only reproduce a little, by his permission:

> Dear Brother:
>
> You know exactly what I have done with my days because you have been with me all along. I have got you in my mind a couple years older than I am with a beard and hair white as mine now. I have given you a life past death and you have aged past eighteen right along with me, and you have been contrary mostly always and full of advice which I have taken or not taken. One thing you said (*you* said it, even though dead) was, *Do not marry Eloise*. But I did marry Eloise, as you well know. Remember that river pilot in *Heart of Darkness* that opens the window on the boat no matter Marlow's warning and takes a spear through his chest? Brother, Marlow has to throw his shoes away, the blood is so bad.

And then there was Mindy Mallow-Dalmation, who'd gone along in our college semester writing very beautiful sentences but, in the end, fairly empty pages. Always there was a kind of foreground of insistence that nothing she might write was going to be of any importance. She hid from the reader, she hid from herself, the *person* wasn't there on the page, just a kind of wise-guy affability, a leather-jacket carapace, nose rings galore. But we all knew she'd been through some stuff, hilarious as she was. There had been that offhand mention of heroin usage, for one thing. The *person* was certainly there in the classroom. Her amused commentary on the work of her classmates was studded with unguarded phrases like, "When I was in rehab," and "Juvey will do that to you," and "I don't mean to put the razor to your neck." There was fire in the woman, unvanquished fire, but there was also pain, and a very quiet sorrow.

One day, she came to see me in my office, all heated up despite herself: "I didn't do the assignment because the assignment was stupid." To that I had no reply. We held a long silence. She broke it, looking past me to my office window and all the students out on the back quad enjoying the spring sun at Ohio State. "Also, because I was having one of my crying weekends."

The next day, she was unusually quiet in class. But when her turn came, she had her assignment ready, and she read her letter, and it was clear that her letter had let her let herself arrive. It was the first writing we'd heard from Mindy herself, and not by the persona she'd constructed to bring to college on her state funding, the one constructed to get her through college unseen:

Dear Mindy,

I think of you in the middle of every night. In other quiet times too, like driving. Because all you needed was the front yard. Blue-hair Barbie, that puddle in front of Me-Mom's. Your fantasy was to make the doll swim down a river to someplace safe. Or when Me-Mom wasn't watching, you climbed that cracked-tar telephone pole. Those spikes they had for the men to climb. Went up there just to look down the length of the wires that could kill you. You were a bird, the wind was in your feathers. Mommy was a place you could fly. I know you didn't expect your life to turn out like this. You were supposed to be a princess. Even better than a princess. And what can I say other than I'm sorry for what I did to you.

Love, Mindy

CHAPTER SEVEN

FINDING THE FACTS

*I just feel fortunate to live in a world with so much
disinformation at my fingertips.*

—P.C. Vey

Research. The very word sends my bedeviled undergraduates groaning into the nearest pub. They want to avoid research because they see themselves lost on the Internet, staring at a computer screen for days at a time, or hunched in the dusty stacks of the good old library, looking for ever drier facts, boring themselves into oblivion in preparation for writing a paper guaranteed to bore their teachers, in turn, and guaranteed to go unread forever after.

I understand why they're wary at just the sound of the word, and why you might be, too.

But let's get one thing straight: research is a creative process. And just like other creative processes, research gets hampered when we close down its possibilities, narrow too much our definitions. Research doesn't only happen in the library. And assembling facts and quotes on cards in advance of writing, as I was taught in high school and attempted to do in college, just seems nuts to me now.

Well, research papers are research papers, and they have their own mysteries. But you and I, we're engaged in making true stories. The subject is always going to be in some way ourselves. We're searching. So everything we've done so far in this book—every exercise—is research of one kind or another, though I've assiduously avoided the word.

Our mapmaking has been research: What do I remember? Our "On ..." exercises, too: What do I think? Our scenemaking is research, of course: Where have I been? Who was there? How did it look and sound? Work on voice is investigative, too: How do I feel? All leading to Montaigne's question: "What do I know?"

It's all an investigation. And with any luck our investigations have begun to lead us to the subjects we want to write about. Further, all this searching has begun to make it clear what's missing. What do we not know? Often the difference between quite good and publishable is the very stuff that research will produce, stuff you did not and could not predict finding, stuff you didn't know you needed.

By now you've got a subject. You've had at least one and probably quite a few ideas take off. Pages are accumulating. Perhaps you have a draft of an essay. Perhaps you have drafts of many essays. Perhaps some are advanced drafts. This is the perfect time to try some formal research, time to start reaching outside your mind. If we're going to operate in John McPhee's "literature of fact," we better have the facts. Facts give us authority and accuracy, clarity and (believe it or not) heart.

Okay, you've loafed and invited your soul. Now it's time for the legwork. Which, if you love your subject (as you must), will be deeply and profoundly pleasurable, a treasure hunt with guaranteed riches at the end.

The question for this chapter is this: What do others know?

The Library, Still Number One

If you're a college student, you've got the college library at your disposal, and with the Internet and other network connections, the place is effectively open 24/7. If you're not a college student, no problem: most colleges and university libraries will let community people and traveling writers sign in as guest scholars. Some big schools have dozens of libraries, collections and services built over years by specialists to accommodate sophisticated and specialized needs. Corporations sometimes make their unique (not to say eccentric) collections available to the public. Historical societies, museums of all kinds, churches, planetariums, government bureaus, all of them may have libraries, from basic to comprehensive in scope, all with a particular controlling interest. And of course, for students and independent writers alike, there's the public library, with its very different collections and missions. All of these resources are increasingly interconnected via the Internet and via interlibrary-loan programs, so much so that access to one library can mean access to the whole universe of research scholarship, which is good news for the memoirist, the essayist, the literary journalist.

Unlike the old days (and by this I mean, like, not that long ago), now you can chat with librarians online, search card catalogues online, and find journal articles and books using online library resources such as *Academic Search Premier* and *JSTOR* and hundreds of others that specialize in various disciplines. While the Internet can't replace the library experience, it can certainly cut down the amount of time you need to wander aimlessly through the stacks. (Although, come to think of it, this was some of the most romantic time I spent in my college years. ...) You can compile a whole list of sources before you even get to the building. Then, you can do a precision attack on the stacks with the librarian right there to help you—perhaps even the person you e-mailed or (virtually) chatted with before your visit.

But you don't absolutely need the Web, and you shouldn't solely depend on it: the library is still there, and it's still the best.

I keep thinking of the grumpy reference man at the Biological Sciences Library at Columbia University back when I was a grad student there. I made the mistake of asking him where the men's room was. He scowled and grimaced and pointed: *Get the hell out of here!* I found the bathroom on my own. When I came back in I saw a fellow grad student and sat beside her. I don't know why Mr. Librarian got so upset; the young woman and I were certainly talking about biological issues.

A couple of days later I was back. The guy remembered me all right. He pointedly ignored me as I slunk to his throne behind the reference desk. But now I had a question: How do I find information on the dust glands of great blue herons? (I was writing my first book, working on a chapter about a heron I'd spent an intimate morning's fishing with in Florida.) The librarian's eyebrows rose. His hooded eyes blinked, grew warm. All was forgiven. I wanted information and information was what he had. We marched about the library, comrades in arms, finding everything there was. He made calls for me to other libraries; he loaded my arms with books; he visited me with further information at my table, sent me three notes in subsequent weeks, helped me research further chapters. He made me an expert on herons and other things—I read what he found for me—and this new knowledge informed my book, though I used perhaps one percent of it and never mentioned the dust glands of herons.

EXERCISE ONE: *The Good Old Library*

Let's not make this too hard. Simply pick a subject that's come up in your writing of late. It might be as general as art or dogs or rivers or melons. It might be more specific: Michelangelo or Boston terriers or the Hudson or Catawbas.

Schedule a specific block of time, perhaps one you can manage every week (but don't steal writing time). An hour's fine, two hours will get you some depth, more won't hurt. Maybe you'll go after dinner or around lunch (with the meal as a break) or before that Audubon meeting downtown. Or how about scheduling library time and a movie? Library time and handball? Library time then a beer with the gang? Can you work this into your weekly schedule?

Anyway. The important thing for this exercise is to have a subject in mind and time to do it justice.

Go in with an empty notebook; come out with a full one and a stack of books to skim and explore (and sometimes fully read) in the week ahead.

You'll have gotten the important facts (for your essay about canoeing with your family when you were little): that the Hudson River is born in Lake Tear of the Clouds in the Adirondacks, that it's 315 miles long, named after Henry Hudson, 1,440 feet wide at its widest, named the North River down by Manhattan, and so forth (quite endlessly—later you'll choose what to use). But you'll also have a pertinent quote from Washington Irving and know who the mayor of Newburgh was the year your grandfather lived there and that (surprise, surprise) your grandfather was mentioned by that mayor in a speech banning dogs from trolleys.

And perhaps your essay will take a turn.

 *A library is thought in cold storage.*
                                    —*Herbert Samuel*

KRISTEN MINES THE MICROFILM

As one of his daunting assignments for Bibliography and Research Methods, a graduate class at the University of North Texas, Kristen Keckler's professor required her to track down book reviews for a work of her choice. She tells the story, and offers an assignment:

> I chose Lucy Grealy's memoir, *Autobiography of a Face*, pub-
> lished in 1994. Grealy writes about her experience with jaw
> cancer as a child, as well as the natures of illness, truth and
> beauty, love, and identity. I was working on this project at
> home, using the UNT library's databases, and realized that
> the book was too "old" to have all the reviews I needed avail-
> able online (a serious drawback of online research—older
> materials just aren't always available). I had to go to the
> library. I'll admit, I was a little pissy about the whole thing. I
> was busy! But I needed this particular review, so I trudged
> over to Willis Library. Remember those enormous old micro-
> film machines? I had to first locate the correct roll of film,
> *New York Times*, September 25, 1994, in a big dusty file
> cabinet. After I fastened the film into the grooves, I used the
> knob to manually scroll through the pages, sometimes whir-
> ring at top speed, sometimes pausing to goof off and read
> a couple lines of some unrelated article. When I found the
> review, the moment of satisfaction was particularly intense.
> You really do feel like a writer, a real researcher, sitting at
> those old dinosaurs. I fed it my copycard and printed out
> the review.
>
>   Now, my professor's assignment centered around the idea
> of "reception," how reviewers received the book in comparison
> to how everyday readers responded to it. Determining recep-
> tion also involves bigger questions, like what kind of world
> did this work enter into? A memoir that involves a devastating

hurricane in the 1980s might find a different reception if published a year prior to Hurricane Katrina, for example, rather than a year after.

I finally read the review, interested to see what the reviewer had focused on. Did she mention the scene in the basement of the hospital, the one with the lab animals? Did she mention Grealy's brilliant symbolism, lyrical writing? I was approaching the assignment from a critic's perspective and a writer's perspective, but not from a researcher's perspective. Not really. That is, not until I noticed the review printed on the same page as Grealy's: *Prozac Nation*. I had never read the book, but had, of course, heard of it. I read this review too, which was less than the stellar review afforded to Grealy. Then it hit me, the real significance of the *Prozac Nation* review. This was 1994. These two books, side by side in the bookstores! And though, nowadays, psychiatric pharmaceuticals are the focus of our Starbucks coffee talk, in 1994, *Prozac Nation* was exposing a society that was not only medicating itself, but taking topics once considered private into the public sphere. This world had watched Donahue and Oprah throughout the 1980s, and had recently—1991— graduated to Jerry Springer. And there was Grealy, in the middle of all that, writing about something physical, something medical, but also something deeply private and psychological, as well.

While searching for the review, I paused to skim an article about the Major League Baseball strike—the 1994 World Series, canceled! Now I realized that this "goofing off" was all a part of the assignment. The baseball information, though not directly relevant, did help put the year and month into a larger perspective. People who were reading about Grealy's book that day were also reading about *Prozac Nation* and mourning the World Series. Imagine what I would have discovered had I really taken the time to look.

If the *New York Times* review had been conveniently attached to my library's Web site, I would have missed out on my own moment of reception.

EXERCISE TWO: *A Focused Library Excursion*

Now that you've been to the library and sniffed around, checked out books and other materials about orb-weaving spiders, let's talk about another research trip, one in which you aren't looking for any and all information on spider webs but for a single, important piece of information.

Identify a person you'd like to know more about, someone who's an important character in one of your previous exercises or finished essays, and identify one piece of information you'd like to find, something that will require some serious digging. Here are a few generic ideas. You'll come up with your own by simply following your curiosity.

1. Your grandmother's wedding or engagement announcement, as it was originally published
2. Your uncle's obituary
3. An article mentioning your father's military or other such service
4. An article mentioning your sister's athletic accomplishments in high school or college

Your uncle's obituary might tell you stuff you already know through other sources. But look harder. Who else died that week? What was happening in the world? What were the types of things mentioned in obituaries back in, say, 1973? Did the obituary leave out any important information? (Why wasn't your father mentioned? Was that an oversight, a misprint, or was it intentional?) What other details stand out?

Start writing, using any new information or details you've discovered as your prompt. Perhaps your paragraphs will start off wondering why your dad was excluded from your uncle's obituary, but eventually turn into an essay about family feuds more than about your uncle. Or maybe the uncle in the obituary wasn't anything like the uncle you knew, and the contrast will put some fire under your discussion of the man.

THE INTERNET

The Internet's main function has become commerce, selling things. Another function, often tangled with the first, is the sharing of information. Realize that all Web sites are not created equal. Anyone—from the United States

Supreme Court to the Marilyn Manson fan club, from the Museum of Modern Art to a porn star selling gift baskets—*anyone at all* can have a Web site, and often you will need to wade through rivers of unsorted rubbish to get what you're after. Of course, this is a good thing, free speech at its finest and most technologically advanced.

But.

A good library's main function is the organized storage of information and literature. Unlike the stuff you find on the Internet, library resources have been vetted by a responsible intelligence operating inside a professional culture aloof from markets, skeptical of scams, disdainful of misinformation (accidental errors), vigilant about disinformation (the manipulation of facts to fit an ideology or other fell purpose, nothing accidental about it), wary of censorship. All of which tend to insure a certain credibility, accountability. For many subjects, Internet information only goes back as far as the *advent* of the Internet, late 1980s. Looking over the hits you get on a given subject, you'll get the feeling that no one thought much about, say, spiders, before those years. The library's holdings go back further, unto centuries, and have been organized, all the background noise filtered out—decades and decades of impassioned work.

But isn't it wonderful to type your keywords—spider, bites, deadly—into Google and see what a random word-pattern search combined with advertising plugs turns up? Some of it clearly credible information, such as a juried article in *Nature* about the particular enzymes in spider venom, an article that comes with an extensive bibliography, plenty more articles and scientists and experiments to chase down. Next, a whole page devoted to the killing of spiders: what chemicals work best; why chemicals are the best way to go; why all spiders must die; how spiders enter your ear and take over your thinking, make you want to date Jodie Foster. And then spidermanthemovie.net, half an hour there, cool interactive stuff. And, finally, maybe, you'll find a high-school kid's Web site of awesome spiders he's photographed all over the world, page after page of them, with lots of his notes and observations, facts all undocumented, identifications hard to verify, some experiences seeming farfetched (did a black widow actually turn on the faucet in his motel in Yuma?).

Really, you have to decide what kind of information you want. If you're working on an essay about your interest in the spiders of literature, you need the literature, and the Internet can help you find references in the scores. If you're working on an essay cataloging all the spiders in your house and their habits and possible threat to humans in order to get past a phobia and then write an essay, you need the science. If you're looking for photos of spiders because you want to physically describe one that was your constant companion in your childhood backyard in Micronesia, that high-school kid's photo Web site might be most helpful to you, and just what you need. You don't need the spider-hater's site, you don't need Spider-Man; yet, both will be interesting, and either might lead to some unexpected turn or metaphor in an essay or to a new idea altogether.

The Internet is just the world passing around notes in a classroom.
—Jon Stewart

EXERCISE THREE: *The Half-Hour Year*

Here's something fun for the Internet. Pull up one of your scenes or essays or exercises, one that's about finished. What year or years does the essay cover? What year marks the present of your memoir?

Now, set a stove timer or cell-phone alarm clock or hourglass for thirty minutes (or maybe forty-five, max, if you're slow on the keyboard). The time limit is just to keep you from spending the next eight hours online—seven and a half hours of which you could be *writing*!

OK, here's the assignment: Simply use the Internet (in any way you see fit, including search engines, library databases, corporate networks) to compile a quirky list of events from your year, things you find interesting or surprising or curious. Who made the news? What brand of car had a snazzy new model? Who had the number-one hit on Billboard's Top 40? What were the disasters? Who was in the White House, and what was he saying? What were the top movies? Follow your nose through 1967, say, or 1991.

Now look back at your memoir or essay or scene, and make a point of weaving the *era* into your paragraphs. Let the facts of the day help establish a sense of time and place more concrete than your memory has allowed. Let the world of your selected year help provide a context for your scenes, your discussions. Let new knowledge of the era lead to new ideas for your writing.

Public Records

Let's say you want to write about your great-grandfather's crazy life. Let's say it was so unconventional that no one talked about him much. Let's say that all those who remember the old bird are dead and gone, too. How might you track him down?

All kinds of records are carefully kept and carefully stored (and sometimes carefully concealed) by government, big and small. I'm indebted to investigative reporter Cheryl Reed Stricharchuk for some of the following ideas:

1. Property records at a county recording office might tell you which houses Grandpa owned, when he moved, and will give dollar values, as well.

2. Court records may turn up divorces, marriages, name changes, deaths, civil suits, criminal trials.

3. Probate records will show deaths and inheritances, the latter sometimes in fascinating detail.

4. Police records (available at county clerks' offices and at police department records divisions) will give voluminous information on convictions, arrests, even detailed reports from detectives' investigations.

Grandpa!

And there are myriad other public records: corporation and incorporation records at the Secretary of State's office, annual Securities and Exchange Commission reports, nonprofit corporation reports, campaign contributions, loan records, minutes of meetings, transcripts of speeches, health inspections, driving records, on and on.

Some of my more intrepid students have used the Freedom of Information Act (www.usdoj.gov/oip/) to get incredible material about activist parents, for example, or public figures. One student got hold of his own FBI file from the 1960s after prolonged, deathly dull, and daunting interchanges with bureaucrats. The file had startlingly minute and private information, all he needed to complete his memoir of his noble and quiet and patriotic work against the Vietnam War. His research led to his new project: a book about the FBI and privacy.

Several of my students over the years have looked into public records to investigate adoption—their own. One young woman, a marvelous writer named

Beth Lindsmith, received via fax a yearbook photo of her newly discovered birth mother. (Beth wrote the slow appearance of the photo through the fax machine as a kind of birth—nice.) She'd spent a year looking for any image. An interested school librarian had gone to the trouble for her. Beth's essay, in the end, was about her decision *not* to contact her birth mother.

Part of the research, when it comes to public records, is finding out which agency or library or bureau or office holds the paper or microfilm you want to get your hands on. Phone calls and visits to town and state offices do wonders. Often, the most daunting task turns out to be simple, and the simple-seeming one turns out to be nearly impossible. The point is that the information is out there for those willing to look. And sometimes the search becomes the story.

EXERCISE FOUR: *Getting Started With Public Records*

Which of your many subjects could use light from a little public information? Perhaps it will be something as simple as the exact address of your childhood home. Perhaps something as complicated as the number of farms in your home county the year of your birth. Perhaps hidden family information could be brought to light. (One student's mother said she had never married the student's father; the father said she had indeed.) Where to look for the truth?

The first step is to recognize the need for the information. This recognition is more complex than it may seem. A story may be quite good without any extra searching. But remember what I said at the beginning of this chapter: often the difference between quite good and publishable is the very stuff that research will produce, stuff you did not and could not predict finding, stuff you didn't know you needed. It's not hard to write your way around a missing fact, but be assured that readers will notice any vagueness, will crave the extra level of information and revelation that your research will bring.

The second step is to pinpoint where any search should start. What's the nature of the information you want? Where would it be kept? Whom to call? Whom to write? Whom to fax? Where to look on the Internet?

The third step, always the hardest, is to actually look. Make the phone call, flip through the file, befriend the librarian, create the necessary accounts on Web sites, harangue the clerk (whose first answer, by the way, will always be "No").

The exercise? Come up with something you really do want to know, something that will open up one of your scenes or memoirs or personal essays, something about one of your people, something about yourself (a woman in one of my classes was from Swaziland, and she didn't know the year or town of her birth), and then go in person or online to the appropriate office and find the facts. Follow your nose and instincts until you discover all you started out to find. But be open to surprises; be willing to go down information paths you didn't expect to find; let people who want to help, help. Don't let people who want to get in the way, get in the way.

The idea here isn't to become a famous librarian; the idea for now is just to get a little practice and get over the natural fear of musty files and chilly bureaucrats imposing Web site regulations. Challenge yourself; take the dare. And listen, it's not like I'm asking you to bungee jump off the Space Needle in Seattle. Doing that, you might get arrested, mangled, even killed. What's the worst that's going to happen in your search for information? Someone might frown at you? Failure isn't deadly in this game. It's not even permanent. But success in research, now that's as exhilarating as any number of bungee jumps.

PRIVATE RECORDS

Too often on research missions I overlook the obvious: photographs, journals, letters, scrapbooks, and so on, my own belongings and those of people who are willing to cooperate, friends and family. Photographs are particularly helpful, adding detail to scene, correcting memory, providing clues to personality, restoring lost faces.

My grandfather kept all of his date books, sixty years of little leather-bound calendars. After his death in 1970, I had a chance to look through them. They weren't terribly interesting for the most part, just the usual daily appointments set out in cryptic fashion. But just for fun, I looked up my mom's birthday, July 17, 1926. Grandfather's only note: "Mother has disappointed me with another girl." That led me to look up all seven of Mom's siblings: the boys were red-letter days, the girls like funerals. Perhaps I was onto something, some cryptic clue about my mother's personality, and through her, perhaps, a clue about my own.

People keep all kinds of stuff—I know I do. What can the stuff overflowing my file cabinets tell me about subjects I'm in the course of writing about?

EXERCISE FIVE: *Archaeology*

Dig and sift through your own records or those of family members available to you, looking for information pertinent to an essay or memoir you hope to write or have already started, or just to find ideas. What checks were you writing in July of 1992? What doctor's bills were coming in? Get out that box of photos, find that shot of the old family farm (and remember that most of the people in your true stories have similar boxes and are dying to show someone).

Poor Janet Bellweather: Looking through old credit-card statements for clues as to the date of a certain trip to Europe, she discovered that, in fact, she'd never gone—her airline tickets had been refunded in full. Her memory of the trip was *manufactured*. Somewhere back in the vaults of her mind she well knew this, but with her lies to others (she didn't want anyone to know she'd had a panic attack) she'd convinced herself, too.

But that made for a good, honest essay.

FACE-TO-FACE RESEARCH

Much has been written in journalism texts about the art of the interview. Basically, I've found that interviewing for journalism is a matter of fooling your subject into revealing herself, perhaps in ways she'll wish later she hadn't. People love to talk, especially about themselves. Note-taking, the tape recorder, the endless questions, all are flattering, hard to resist.

But for the memoirist, interviewing is a more delicate tool. Your subjects aren't politicians, for example, who are used to public life and tough questions. Your subjects aren't hapless and immediate victims of accident or disaster. Your subjects aren't experts you have approached for facts and figures. Your subjects, in fact, are very often well known to you, very often relatives, sometimes even your mother. And Mom isn't going to be flattered by any voice recorder.

Further, your story may be one no one particularly wants brought up, much less written about. In many cases, you'll prefer not to have all the advice or censure that comes flooding in when a project becomes public property. Certain kinds of people will withdraw. Other types will try to control what's said about them, sometimes in unpleasant ways.

Then again, and more likely, everyone may get excited about your project and want to be part of it: Uncle John calling to tell the old sunk-canoe story one more time, Dad sending over a typist, your college roommate unloading a U-Haul of photos in your driveway.

I mean, there are a million good reasons *not* to go to the people of your story and ask questions. But if a couple of questions will make the story better, all those reasons must be swept aside.

Interviewing even the friendliest witness takes a lot of nerve; you will be going past the small talk. But risk is what good writing's all about, no?

EXERCISE SIX: *Interview Somebody Safe*

Pick a person who appears in one of your drafts. Your sister, perhaps, or your current spouse, someone who's on your side, someone who's going to be glad to be mentioned. Make it a formal interview, with prepared questions. Use a voice recorder, but take notes, too. Transcribe the interview as quickly afterward as possible; immediately is best. (E-mail interviews are probably too easily controlled by your subject—too much time to ponder answers, erect defenses.)

With your notes in hand, your transcript to back them up, go to the draft and revise. How does the interview fit in? What must be changed? What parts get strengthened? How does your character grow in depth? Especially important: Can you use any quotations from the conversation to give your character her own voice?

EXERCISE SEVEN: *Interview a Stranger*

Again, pick a scene or draft of a memoir or other work-in-progress. To whom could you go for more information to add depth and light and exactitude? If you are writing about your house, could you find the architect who designed it? The builder who built it? A former occupant? The landlord? If you're writing about your time in the Navy, could you interview someone who was brass then? A historian who has written about the battle you lived through? An expert on ships?

The exercise is to interview at least one person for each work-in-progress.

Use the Internet to find likely interviewees, even e-mail addresses and phone numbers. Be polite and clear at first contact: this is who I am; this what I'm doing; this is what I want from you. Nervous is okay. Nervy, not so good. Never forget the interviewee is doing you a favor. Suggest a meeting; it's easier to make a round nonfiction character from someone you've spent time with, and you never know who will take a place in your work. Ask if your subject knows other people who might be of interest.

If your story is about your alcoholic brother, a suicide, could you interview a counselor, an addiction researcher, an ex-alcoholic, a rescued suicide? (In *The Perfect Storm*, an impressive work of literary journalism about a boat lost in a terrible storm at sea, Sebastian Junger uses a brilliant device along these lines. In order to talk about what it must have felt like to drown—six men were lost at sea, could not be interviewed—Junger talked to a fisherman who had all but drowned in similar circumstances, used those insights to imagine what must have happened to his lost subjects.)

If you're writing about the pleasures of cooking—even a personal account—could you interview the chef at a favorite restaurant? The farmer who grew your acorn squash? The manufacturer of your favorite knife? People like to talk about what they do, and the more they like what they do, the more they want to talk. And people, with their opinions, their quirks, their voices, give your writing something to push against.

Make interviews a regular part of your nonfiction writing process.

EXERCISE EIGHT: *Interview Yourself*

For each of my books, publishers have asked me to write a self-interview, a question-and-answer session with an imaginary reporter, quotes and information they could use for publicity purposes. First time around I was very serious about it, softball questions, sober answers. More recently I've taken to goofing around, for example getting in arguments with the interviewer over politics—I imagined Ann Coulter across the desk—and parrying her insults about my work. She hated all my books, especially the one in hand, which was *Temple Stream*, attacked it from every angle. The strategy worked in that it exorcised my self-doubt (at least to some extent), anticipated reviewer quibbles, and made the project more fun. It also generated much more lively quotes for the publicists to make use of, even if they thought I was weird.

The exercise: Type up an interview with yourself in which you talk about your writing, perhaps particularly your most current project. Might be fun to do the interview twice, once with a friendly interlocutor, once with a meanie. The idea is to learn a few things you don't already know and to find unexpected ways to say what needs to get said. Imagine that the story of your trip to China is big news—*Inquiring Minds Want to Know*—and ask appropriate questions.

Better yet, picture yourself across from Barbara Walters in your living room. What kinds of questions is she going to ask? How will you handle the tough questions about your divorce, say, or that skeleton in your broom closet? Where will the heartwarming moments be? Where are the shockers? What will everyone be talking about tomorrow morning?

EXERCISE NINE: *Get Someone to Interview You*

A variation on the self-interview is to have a friend interview you. You might do this reciprocally with a fellow writer, using digital voice recorders or just an old cassette deck. Give your interviewer the latest draft of your latest work, and let the interview focus on that material. When the talk's over, transcribe the recording (or transcribe for your partner and exchange transcripts).

The questions your interviewer asks are important: they let you know the kinds of things your readers will be interested in, let you know what's missing from your draft. Your answers are important, too, and will let you begin to articulate thinking that you haven't yet managed to say in your pages.

EXERCISE TEN: *The Impossible Interview*

Some people, you just can't talk to: the bad guys in your life, someone dead, former lovers, unsympathetic family members. In these cases, it can be helpful to make up an interview. What questions would you like to ask? Well, go ahead and ask them, and then supply the answers you think your subject would give.

Certainly, don't start to believe the interview is real. No quotations from it, of course. But use it to examine your own projections, your own role in relationships. Use it to discover the issue at hand. Use it to develop material.

Or use it to prepare yourself for a scary interview. Ask the questions on paper first, answer them yourself. Then go to your subject. What comes off as expected? Where are the surprises? What exactly was your own role in making the interview scary?

Knowledge is of two kinds. We know a subject ourselves, or we know where we can find information upon it.
—*Samuel Johnson*

NAMING IS KNOWING

Janet Bellweather wrote the following sentence as part of a scene depicting a violent spanking she got as a kid: "I stood alongside some flowers and watched as Grandpa closed the gate." Now, the soft spot in that sentence is the flowers. What kind of flowers are we talking about? Tall ones? Short ones? Dead ones? She fixed things up with a few well-chosen adjectives: "I stood behind some big, blue flowers ...."

But I sent her on a hunt: find the name of those flowers.

The task wasn't going to be hard for her, she announced: she remembered the flowers well enough to recognize them if she saw them. Why, if it weren't midwinter she could drive around and find some right now.

Nothing happened for months. Then in May, flower time, Janet went home to her folks' small New England town for a visit, drove past what had been her Grandpa's yard several times, then walked past, feeling like a stalker. Flowers galore, but not the one she was thinking of. At her mother's, Janet popped the question: "You know those big blue flowers?" Her mother had no interest in plants but recalled that Janet's grandfather had made something of a hobby of horticulture: every plant in his yard was some kind of trophy, grumble, grumble.

At the little library in town, Janet went through flower books till she found it: no question, the flower was a hydrangea. But the photos all showed white flowers or flowers tinged pink. The librarian knew the rest: hydrangeas bloom blue in certain soils, soils that happen to be endemic to the area Janet grew up in. And now Janet had this sentence: "I hid amid the big, blue flowers of Grandpa's prize hydrangea and watched as he closed the gate."

Driving back to the city, Janet spied a tree nursery just off the highway. Next exit, she pulled off, a few minutes for research. The nursery was in full swing: Easter lilies, saplings, perennials in flats. She asked one of the older nurserymen to see hydrangeas. Well, they were in a back greenhouse, wouldn't bloom until August, at the earliest. More often September.

Janet motored home and went about her life and was happy to have this sentence: "I stood behind the rare, blue flowers of Grandpa's prize hydrangea— it was September—and watched as he closed the gate."

Only later did the problem hit her: What had she been doing at Grandpa's in September? (And only later did she edit out the awkward dash phrase.) Why hadn't she been in school?

Now she had a question her mother could answer. A long phone call led to the revelation that after Janet's drifter father had left the family (this much Janet had known about), Mom had got so upset she'd been unable to care for Janet or her sister and had left them at Grandpa's for two months. That's all. But it was two months during which Janet was spanked too often and too brutally in a fenced-in yard with blue-blooming hydrangeas, two months Janet had misplaced and partially forgotten, a forgetfulness that stayed part of her life.

Janet's essay took a turn. And before she was finished, she (and the essay) knew a few important things about her relationships with men and the bubbling anger that plagued her days.

EXERCISE ELEVEN: *Naming*

Look for a vague spot in one of your drafts, some little bit of generic information: "a tree" (what kind of tree?); "our old car" (what make and model and year?); "the stream" (what was it named?); "the birds that flew around the pier" (what kind of birds?).

Do what it takes to properly name a tree, a piece of hardware, a street, a town, a school, a neighbor. Use databases and encyclopedias and dictionaries and phone calls and catalogs and Mapquest and nature guides. Try typing a flower description into Google Images—sometimes the right photo comes up: presto!

Get that name.

Even the smallest exactitude can lead to greater revelation.

NEED AN EXCUSE FOR TRAVEL?

Travel is a spectacular research tool. You're writing about your Peace Corps stint twenty years past? Go back to Guatemala. You're working on an essay about your heritage? Go visit that little town in Russia. Your essay is about craven American culture? Travel the land, or go study other cultures for comparison, firsthand.

Almost any essay could benefit from a trip somewhere. And the writer benefits, as well. You might travel to interview someone. You might travel to see an author's grave. You might visit an old neighborhood to see how it's changed. Or just take off: let the essay ideas arrive as you go.

EXERCISE TWELVE: *Travel*

Plan it now. An hour, a day, a weekend, a week—what's needed for the essay at hand? Really go someplace, whatever it takes, and make a point of taking notes along with your photos.

 *I know [...] how little I have researched, and what slender pretensions are mine.*

　　　　　　　　　—Horace Walpole

TALK

Too many writers (I among them) are shy about their subjects. "Too hard to explain," I always hear myself muttering. I wish I wouldn't, because so often a conversation on my subject has given me great ideas, helped me focus my argument, helped me learn what's needed. This is different from the formal interviewing above, in that your interlocutor isn't necessarily thinking of you as a writer, and certainly not thinking of your talk as an exercise.

I don't mean for you to go out and talk about your writing project as writing project—many writers find that this dilutes their work—I just want you to entertain conversations on the subject about which you mean to write. You don't have to (and probably shouldn't) reveal that you're writing anything. Just ask the question: "Do you think it's possible to feel compassion anymore?" Or make a provocative statement: "The Internet is nothing but a conduit for pornography."

In the right company, you'll get what you're looking for: new ideas, new facts, new angles, new people to talk to, antithesis for your thesis, challenges to your thinking, occasionally a pithy quote.

EXERCISE THIRTEEN: *Talk*

That's it: Talk to someone. Preferably someone smart. Tell her about your essay or not; maybe tell her what you're thinking about your subject. Then listen. Later, take notes. (This is good practice for when the time comes to talk to editors, as well.)

Or, bring up your subject at the next dinner party during one of those silences when forks clink and throats get cleared.

Or, just before the cotton gets stuffed in your mouth, ask your dentist what he thinks of insurance companies, if that's what you're writing about.

The idea is to reach out a little, to talk in advance and in person to a select few of your potential readers.

READING

General reading, unattached to a project at hand, is probably the best way to provision "the well-stocked mind" Elizabeth Hardwick has said an essayist must cultivate. If you read every day, your head gets filled with good lines from great books, with snatches of information from magazine articles, with examples of the perfect way to say it from any number of sources: novels, biographies, poems, collections of letters, plays and even screenplays, translations, textbooks (science, economics, philosophy, undertaking), and, of course, essays.

EXERCISE FOURTEEN: *Reading as Research*

This is one of those continuing exercises, for a lifetime, in three parts, with part three offering the grand challenge: (1) Read a lot; (2) take notes on your reading and keep records; (3) organize those notes and records in a way useful to your writing.

I know you already read a lot, because you've surely taken exercise two back in chapter one to heart. And probably you already take notes on your reading in some form. I write a lot in the end papers of most books while I'm reading. I write little notes on scraps of paper and transcribe quotations. I fill up notebooks.

Then I lose track of all of it.

I want to get organized, so I'm asking *you* to get organized. What's *that* all about? Still, I have advice: label a stack of folders (real or virtual) with various subjects you intend to write about in the next couple of years—Intelligence of Pigs. Aggravation. Chocolate As an Aphrodisiac. And then, as you bump into the odd fact or quotation or observation or article or photograph, you have a place to put it.

Another system is more random: folders with categories of all kinds—Love, Gardening, Dogs, Parents, Skunk Cabbage. The trouble is, the categories just keep going and going, and it becomes difficult to know where to put an item about, say, keeping your beloved dogs out of your parents' skunk cabbage garden.

The great challenge of this exercise is not so much to create a system, but to keep that system alive year after year by using it.

RESEARCH NIGHT

By now you've scheduled writing time and reading time. How about scheduling a research night? Say, every Tuesday. Head down to the library with a list of needs, or hop on the Internet with a purpose, or call a couple of people who know things you don't, making good use of the hour or hours allotted. Over time you'll get good at (and stop being shy or lazy about) finding out what you want to know and what your essays must know if they are to succeed.

CHAPTER EIGHT

METAPHOR AND MEANING

*Interviewer: What is the symbolic significance
of the birds in so many of your sex scenes—the
white bird that flies out of the gondola ...?
Hemingway (shouting): You think you can do
any better?*

—*The Paris Review Interviews, I*

When I say "I can relate" to a writer of memoir or to an essayist, I'm talking about a metaphorical process. Empathy is what I'm speaking of, the comparison between my experience and the writer's, the discovery that what has moved the writer moves me or that what has amazed the writer amazes me.

Additionally, the reader shares two names with the writer: *I* and *me*. And though the process of identification is largely subconscious, a powerful connection between reader and writer is forged in the continual invocation of self that is the first person.

The second-person address of your letter assignment from chapter six can be powerful in a similar subconscious way. There's that *you* you're talking to so passionately, and, of course, the reader feels himself standing in for the person addressed: *you* equals *me*.

EXERCISE ONE: *I and I Vibration, Yeah (Positive)*

Go to a favorite writer, someone writing nonfiction with a strong voice, a strong *I*. Terry Tempest Williams is a good example, or James Baldwin or Augusten Burroughs.

Pick a favorite passage, and read it aloud. Then pick another; read it, too. Do this by yourself; you're not putting on a show. The exercise is to feel the *I* in the work, to let yourself be that *I* for the length of the pages you read, to consciously experience what is normally unconscious, to be the writer's *I* while being your own *I*, to feel what's different, to feel what's the same.

The point of this admittedly nutty behavior is to get a feeling for the power of that little word, how it invites a comparison of nothing less, really, than souls. The point is to get a sense of how universal a set of clothes the word *I* and the concept *I* really is. The point of the exercise is to wear some other writer's *I* so as to better understand your own writerly *I*, the first step in understanding why someone else, some stranger, some reader out there, would want to read about your life.

(The cryptic title of this exercise is a line from a Bob Marley song, "Positive Vibration." In Jamaican English, "I and I" can mean "me and you" and also "me and my friends.")

METAPHOR, THE SOURCE OF ALL MEANING

Let's talk some more about metaphor in general terms before we turn to the specifics of using metaphor as a tool in the making of memoir and essays, before we turn back to gathering awareness of the power of metaphor in our own writing. Language, after all, is the basic tool of any memoirist or essayist, and metaphor, as we shall see, is the elemental condition of language. It's time to add a new layer of understanding to your use of language, a new tool to your box of writerly skills and talents. A deeper and more complex understanding of metaphor than you now enjoy will enrich your relationship with language, put you in greater control of its use.

So let's back up a little farther, all the way back to high school: English teachers forever have been saying, "A simile is a comparison using *like* or *as*, and a metaphor is a comparison not using *like* or *as*." That's simple and plain, but it's not quite right. I'll buy the old definition for a simile, but a metaphor—wow!—a metaphor is something enormously greater than allowed for by Mr. Bottomlifter back in ninth grade. First of all, a simile is just a *kind* of metaphor. A symbol is a *kind* of metaphor (and curiously, something more, as well: the thing itself). An analogy is a *kind* of metaphor.

Metaphor is big, and gets bigger the more you think about it. Metaphor, in fact, is the source of all meaning.

Yes, metaphor is a comparison. But that's saying a lot, given that comparison is the basic gesture of the human mind: closer, farther; lighter, darker; bigger, smaller; safe, dangerous; then, now. The extension of such elemental, dichotomous comparisons is the foundation of language, which in turn is the foundation of conscious thought.

EXERCISE TWO: *A Mind Like a Steel Trap*

A steel trap is one of those devices used in cartoons to capture Elmer Fudd and in life to capture fur-bearing animals. A steel trap is a pair of tempered-steel crescents joined by a powerful spring triggered by a round plate of steel. When an animal steps on this plate—*wham!*—his leg is caught, often broken, awful. The trap is staked to the ground at the end of a stout chain so a captured animal can't wander off.

Okay. A mind like a steel trap. What's the metaphor here? Let's see. You're so smart you hold on to an idea while it thrashes around and finally chews its leg off to escape, leaving you with only the leg of a thought and a bloody legacy of brutality? Or, as the comedian Steven Wright says, "I've got a mind like a steel trap: rusty and illegal in thirty-seven states."

Okay, okay, the assignment: In a long paragraph, compare the workings of your mind to something—anything—else. (Anything, that is, but a steel trap.) Don't be afraid to write the obvious; in my classes, everyone thinks her idea is the obvious one, but never in twenty years has a single class of mine produced two metaphors the same.

To get the sentences flowing, extend the comparison—the metaphor—as far as you can, to the very absurd edges of correlation.

In the steel trap cliché above, I immediately went to the ridiculous. But I left out a couple of things. If your mind is like a steel trap, what is the spring? What is the steel plate that triggers the release mechanism? If animals are ideas and minds are traps, do minds destroy ideas? Do ideas have lives separate from minds? Do ideas roam the wilderness? What are the furs of ideas? And tell me this: Who is the trapper running the trap line? What's the chain? What's the stake?

Here's a little Wallace Stevens (from his poem "Thirteen Ways of Looking at a Blackbird") to get you on your way.

> I was of three minds,
> Like a tree
> In which there are three blackbirds.

UNDERSTANDING METAPHOR

Before we get back to writing, let's consider some of the many forms metaphor takes. Think, for example, about those troublesome analogies on the SAT test. You know, *x* is to *y* as *xx* is to *yy*.

Here, let's do one. Fill in the blank: train is to track as airplane is to ___. Most would say *sky*.

Each element of an analogy is called an analog. In the above example, train is the analog for airplane, track is the analog for sky. All are comparisons not using *like* or *as*, by the way, and certainly metaphorical. And in this example (as in most) magical. Think of it: Our minds easily and completely accept the idea that dense, heavy bars of extruded steel manufactured by humans are similar to—analogous to—the sky. Which is air.

Kenneth Burke, in his challenging book *A Grammar of Motives*, says that metaphor "brings out the thisness of a that." Aristotle speaks of the way metaphor helps us understand the unknown or slightly known by comparing it to what's known.

Symbol, Image, Simile, Motif

Stop signs are metaphors in that they are symbols. Symbols are objects, generally, and are themselves, but also stand in for something, *mean* something else, something greater than themselves and not always inherent in themselves.

We've come to agree that a red octagon (my father claims they used to be yellow) with the following white shapes on it—S, T, O, P—will mean something particular. In practical terms, it means law-abiding types will put right feet on brake pedals till the motion of their vehicles is entirely arrested. The sign is a command to make your vehicle's status an analog for a word meaning, a meaning that is itself an analog for a condition in nature—stoppedness. But the sign is also something real: a piece of metal or wood on a stick or on the wall in a college dorm room. (Put it back, dudes!) It's a nonliterary symbol in that it is precise, stands for one thing only: *stop*.

The Nike swoosh is a symbol in the same way. The swoosh isn't the company. The swoosh isn't a sneaker. The swoosh merely invites us to consider the company, to compare the swoosh to what we know of the company. Swoosh does not equal Nike; swoosh only represents Nike, and this representation is a form of metaphorical comparison. But the swoosh is not so much a thing as is a stop sign or a duck. I mean, yes, it does have reality in that sometimes it's a grouping of threads or a thin layer of ink or a gathering of pixels on TV. But that's not much reality, less than you and I have even on our worst days. Still, it's a symbol, moving toward the literary, as it can mean more than Nike, can stand for a life devoted to sport, for example, or for the money exchanged in an endorsement deal.

Most words are symbols, most language metaphorical. (Or, actually, if you believe Jacques Derrida, all words are metaphorical. It would take a PhD in English to explain, and I happen to have one right here—Jennifer Cognard-Black, who was a graduate student at Ohio State when I was there, and is now an assistant professor at St. Mary's College of Maryland: "Give me an instance of language that isn't a representation. Even articles are metaphorical—although they don't stand in for a real-world thing or action, they do stand in for an idea or concept; *a, an, the,* and conjunctions—*and, but, for*—have no meaning in and of themselves.")

These letters—T, R, E, E—aren't a tree, though they make me think of one. And my thinking of a tree (I can see one clearly in my head, right now) isn't a tree, either. (Buddhists would say that even the *tree* isn't a tree; it is an illusion.) I've a conception in my mind that I compare to the great plants outside my window and both of which I compare to those four letters above and to a sound I can make with my lips. The sound isn't the plant or the letters or the conception, but yet another point along the *tree* continuum. When I use the word to invoke a particular oak tree in, say, a scene that includes the tree, a scene that is about my father's strength, as well, the word means both the tree itself, but also refers to my father and to his strength, but not in a precise way: some readers may think of the rigidity of oak wood, its tendency to break in high wind; others may think of the way dead oak leaves hang on through whole winters before letting go, giving way to the new. This oak tree is a fully literary symbol.

If I point to the comparison, saying, "My dad is like that oak tree," I'm making our symbol into a simile, not quite trusting the reader to make the leap himself. And while readers should always get your trust, they do seem to need help here and there. If the comparison is important to your purposes, it's often best to make it overt. Subtlety isn't overrated, but it can leave certain readers behind. How many do you want to keep? Not all readers are metaphorical thinkers, not at all.

And literal thinkers can drive you crazy.

If I say, "That oak tree is my dad," a literalist could put me on the stand, point a finger, and accurately accuse me of lying.

But, your honor! I didn't mean it *literally*! I'm making a simple metaphor, the boldest kind of comparison. And metaphor is a *figurative* kind of honesty. It's what we mean when we talk about emotional honesty, isn't it? That by making associations, comparison, contrasts, I am explaining how I feel about a person, place, or thing.

I'm not lying after all.

How complicated is the truth!

My father is a tree.

The sky is steel.

In *Perrine's Sound and Sense*, authors Thomas Arp and Greg Johnson, updating Perrine himself, grapple with definitions of our terms and come up with the following:

> Image, metaphor, and symbol shade into each other and are sometimes difficult to distinguish. In general, however, an image means only what it is; the figurative term in metaphor means something other than what it is, and a symbol means what it is and something more, too. A symbol, that is, functions literally and figuratively at the same time.

They go on to make a useful distinction between literary and nonliterary symbols: Literary symbols are imprecise. Though a writer may have a precise sense of the meaning of a given symbol, say a white bird in a Hemingway sex scene, much room is left for the reader to assign her own meanings, even if it enrages the author.

Kristen Keckler gives an example of the symbol at work, with some analysis:

> Perhaps you are writing an essay about your mother, who was a wonderful woman, a knitting freak as well as a gossip, the marathon runner of all gossips. In many parts of the essay, you show Ma with her knitting needles, working on some project. She knitted when she was bored, stressed, angry, joyful, depressed. She knitted in that big brown leather recliner, the kind with a magazine pocket on the side. Those needles were a drummer's drumsticks, an Empress's porcelain chopsticks. You *remember* that when your father was in the hospital, near death, Mama knitted you the crowning glory of all sweaters, her first perfect cowl neck, with yarn so vibrant, yellow and turquoise and greens, it was like sunshine in a forest of ocean. And though it was a masterpiece, you looked horrible in it—you are too busty for that style and have black hair and brown eyes, not the best colors for you. Of course, you wore it anyway.
>
> Your mother is a real person, but not a symbol, no. A good person, the best, but still, she's just Ma. Her knitting needles, now we have something. They exist in the essay as real, tangible, physical objects, themselves. But they also carry metaphorical weight, so they are a symbol. Perhaps they simply symbolize knitting, or perhaps it goes deeper, and they symbolize your mother's ability to cope, or even to weave a good story, keep the gossip colorful and flowing.
>
> The sweater is another symbol, perhaps of her love for you, her need to stay positive during your father's health crisis—thus the lively colors—or perhaps it's a symbol of her denial: notice that imprecision. That the needles were "porcelain chopsticks" is basic metaphor (no lo mein in this essay), one that shows both the utility and value of the knitting needles to Mom.
>
> And the big brown leather recliner? That's an image. Just a chair, something for mom to sit in. And of course Mom's an Empress, no argument there.

Now, here's an example of symbol from Lucy Grealy's *Autobiography of a Face*, a book about much more than a health catastrophe. At the age of nine, Grealy was diagnosed with a rare form of cancer. Doctors had to remove part of her jaw. The little girl (who would grow up to be a writer, then die young), spends a lot of time in the hospital, where she befriends other sick children. One Sunday, the kids convince a candy striper to take them to see the animals they've heard are housed in the hospital's basement. Grealy writes:

> The wall directly across from the door was filled with cages of white mice, and to our right was an entire wall of cats, cage after cage stacked upon each other. Most were tabbies. I'd never seen so many cats in one place, and yet it was eerily silent. They crouched in their cages and stared at us, every single one of them, as we filled up the room. As we got closer, some of them came up to the bars of their cages and rubbed, opening their mouths soundlessly. Years later I learned that it is not uncommon to cut the vocal chords of laboratory cats, especially if there are a lot of them. [...] A number of the cats had matchbox-size rectangles with electrical wires implanted in their skulls. The skin on their shaved scalps was crusty and red where it joined the metal.

The animals, especially the cats, clearly function as symbols: They are real animals with figurative associations. The animals can represent a number of things. Like the children, they have been cut into, operated on, altered. Also like the children, the animals are confined, separated from their natural environments, prevented from roaming outdoors. The cats and their silence convey a sort of involuntary censorship, like the children who do not yet have the language to explain or understand their illnesses and who do not have a voice, or choice, in their own medical care.

Grealy makes sure we understand the weight of these symbols, when, at the end of the scene, she writes:

> When asked where we'd been, our candy striper replied casually that we'd gone for a walk, and not one of us said anything to the contrary. Sooner or later we all have to learn the words with which to name our own private losses, but then we just stood there in front of the nurses' desk, speechless.

This silence becomes a recurring theme throughout Grealy's illness and treatment; her mother urges her not to cry when she is in pain, or to express any emotion at all; her father avoids talking about the situation altogether. Animals, too, become a reoccurring symbol (and because of the recurrence, a *motif*) throughout the memoir. Grealy writes about animals of all kinds, from the birthday party ponies she handled at her first job, to her childhood pets (gerbils, cats, dogs, and horse) to plastic animal figurines. With each new animal, Grealy's symbolic associations build, making the overall work more and more complex, richer, more meaningful.

ETYMOLOGY, METAPHOR, AND THE WRITER

Etymology, the study of the origin and development of words, amounts to the study of a long record of meaning shifts along metaphorical paths. To be a student of etymology is to have subtle layers of meaning at your command as you write. Probably, you've perused *The Oxford English Dictionary* from time to time. It's a fine tool for the amateur etymologist. In a standard American dictionary, definitions are listed and numbered from most used to least used, from major meaning to minor. The *OED*, by contrast, is a historical dictionary. Its definitions are numbered from oldest to newest, and there's a lot of fun in there, a lot of useful knowledge, the fullest meaning and nuance of every word laid out before you.

Here, by way of example, is something I just learned in the *OED*: The Romans used a stone sledge called a *tribulum* to grind and crush corn down to meal. When Christians came along, they found their torment at the hands of their Roman oppressors to be like what happened to corn under the stone. *Tribulation* is the resulting English word.

Metaphor is often hidden in this manner, hidden in the words we use every day, lost in the etymological shuffle. We still know that *discard* is something that happens in a game of gin, but at the same time we freely talk about discarding unwanted objects that aren't playing-cards: a broken couch, an old dress, a page of manuscript. We even discard notions. The comparison we are making to the move in a card game is largely forgotten. A pedagogue, now a teacher, was once a slave—what's the etymological story behind *that* comparison-then-meaning-shift (and how far have we really shifted)? See the *OED*. A *gossip* was a godparent, the person who knew the story behind the closed gates of the neighbor's castle. Comparison extended the word meaning to anyone who knew and told secrets. Simple words, too, arrived at their present-day meanings through comparison-driven meaning shifts: *corn*, for example, referred at first to any hard particle. To *inspire* was to breathe life into (generally God's job).

The ancient Greek meaning of *metaphor* is to carry over. We carry meaning over from one object or analog to the next.

METAPHOR IN DAILY LIFE

Once you start looking, you'll see metaphor at work everywhere. Headlines, for example, are full of obvious metaphorical usage: "On the Front Lines in Battling Electronic Invader"; "War Rages On"; "Police Chief Escapes Suspension"; "U.S. Senate Race Is the Crown Jewel of Tuesday's Balloting"; "Devotees Sing Praises of the Swiss Army Knife on Its 100th Birthday."

Some of the metaphors in the examples above are lost metaphors or dead metaphors. We've used them so much we forget their sources. But still, can't you see that police chief hanging suspended under a bridge? Or a bunch of knife lovers singing in a chorus: "*Oh how we love (how we love) our Swiss Army knives!*" Or Senators Kennedy and Inhofe in gym clothes and sweatbands running a foot race?

And speaking of politicians, they're very good at making use of symbols. The date 9/11/2001 will always be a symbol of tragedy, of course, and a reminder of the events of a certain day. But what else? That literary imprecision comes into play immediately. The phrase "9/11" carries multiple meanings operating in multiple contexts. A good rhetorician makes use of the doubt, speaks in generalities that leave his meanings open, leave room for a range of sympathetic interpretations so broad that few listeners will disagree with whatever proposal the phrase is attached to.

And the expressions we John and Jane Q. Public commonly use (so commonly, in fact, that most are clichés—used so much and for so long that their luster and humor and grace are gone) are largely metaphor of the *simile* persuasion: strong as an ox; built like a brick shithouse; dead as a doornail (a doornail is that plate under the knocker, banged to death by visitors); rich as Croesus (he was the last king of Lydia, sixth century B.C., and rich as Bill Gates); life ain't all beer and Skittles (as my father used to say). Some unimaginative speakers compare absolutely everything to one thing: hot as hell, fat as hell, happy as hell, clean as hell. Don't do this in your writing if you want like hell to delight readers. Spend the time it takes to come up with something new: happy as a hammer? Have fun, go outside the cracker box—you can always edit later.

Kids are great makers of metaphor, great believers in metaphorical magic: *I'm an airplane! Chili is barf! The car is a space shuttle!* Adults lose a lot of that natural ability as they gain the practical view: *Chili is not barf, sweetheart; sit down and eat.*

But we writers can't afford to grow up, at least not as regards language, because the connections and relationships and comparisons we see in the world are the connections and relationships and comparisons that make our writing sing and jump and play, that make our work appealing to readers, who love nothing more than to remake the connections and comparisons we've made.

Readers are rhinoceroses!

EXERCISE THREE: *Metaphor Watch*

Spend the next few days and weeks paying attention to the overriding influence of metaphor in human consciousness and daily life. What implied comparisons live in each corner of existence? How do these comparisons turn up in your work?

Is a co-worker a bitch? A prick? Is your boss cutting costs? Are you on the front lines in the battle against computer viruses? Is your writing circle turning into an encounter group? Is the Cold War dead? Is there a presidential race in progress? Have you driven by a mesa lately (*mesa* is Spanish for table, of course, and a mesa a flat-topped mountain)? Is your latest project an uphill fight? Are you working like a head with your chicken cut off? Is love a red, red rose? (Watch for thorns.)

MAKING USE OF METAPHOR

All this talk of metaphor and comparison has been fairly abstract. Let's start to think about how to get metaphor into your work. On the sentence level, this will be a conscious effort to use more colorful and intense comparison to illuminate what's not known, to explain the unfamiliar, to say what's hard to say. And why do you want to make this effort? Because the conscious use of metaphor and metaphorical strategies will make your writing more powerful, more resonant, more illuminating, more psychological. Metaphor, skillfully applied, adds layers of meaning—subtle layers that you control and that will please readers without their always knowing why.

Here's poet Howard Nemerov, in his essay "On Metaphor":

> While I am thinking about metaphor, a flock of purple finches arrives on the lawn. Since I haven't seen these birds for some years, I am only fairly sure of their being, in fact, purple finches, so I get down *Peterson's Field Guide* and read his description: "Male: about size of House Sparrow, rosy-red, brightest on head and rump." That checks quite well, but his next remark, "a sparrow dipped in raspberry juice," is decisive: it fits. I look out the window again, and now I know that I am seeing purple finches.

EXERCISE FOUR:
The Old Chinese Restaurant Menu Exercise

This one comes from my days as a grad student, when I taught a course called "Logic and Rhetoric." We new teachers passed around all our best exercises and used one another's freely (some dated from decades past), so I'm not quite sure whom to credit for this, but be assured: I stole it. Here goes:

COLUMN A	COLUMN B
Divorce	Pitchfork
Health	Leaf
Childhood	Danish
Truth	Pond
Science	Balloon
Desire	Shampoo
Music	Cleat
Jealousy	Mailbox
Madness	Perfume
Victory	Air
Inspiration	Kiss

Take one item from column A, one from column B. Write a comparison—a paragraph or two—beginning with the simplest statement of your metaphor. For example: divorce is a mailbox. Then go on to examine and elaborate the points of comparison.

After a certain number of sentences, the comparison is bound to grow strained. At that point, start a new paragraph that examines the inadequacies of the comparison.

A variation is to make verbs out of the words in column B. Start your exercise, for instance, with the following high exposition: music kisses. Or how about: madness perfumes?

The point is to get started actually using metaphorical strategies at the sentence level. Of course you can (and should) make up your own words for columns A and B.

Poetry provides the one permissible way of saying one thing and meaning another.

—Robert Frost

EXERCISE FIVE: *Poetry Scramble*

Let's take a few minutes to consult the poets. They, perhaps, know how to use figurative language better than anyone older than about seven, and they have a lot to teach us when we go to write nonfiction. Sometimes, in fact, I wonder why a beautifully written essay or memoir couldn't be called a poem.

The answer might be: because, generally speaking, poetry is about the art of compression. Most poems contain so few words that these words and images must function on several levels, to conjure a number of feelings and associations. Poems are great little multitaskers. If you don't currently read poetry, try to sprinkle a few poems into your reading time. (Careful, they bite.) Reading poetry will help sharpen your metaphorical sense, help you appreciate the power in a single image, the nature of symbols.

Take your time. Find a few good poems, ones you like (from an anthology, a favorite poet, a literary magazine, an e-zine, an old college text). The poems should be from several authors, and should span the centuries, with a healthy representation from living poets, contemporary minds. If you don't own any poetry collections or anthologies, this is a great excuse to buy some, or peruse the shelves of your local library. There are also some really wonderful Web sites that cover the wide range of expression in verse, but don't get lost—we need you here.

Start by just reading individual poems, preferably out loud, preferably multiple times, maybe with friends. Take time to understand the words, appreciate the sense of the poem. Then, poem by poem, pick out the similes and metaphors you find compelling. Write these out, collect them, till you have a list of at least ten to enjoy, memorize, internalize.

Now, scramble the metaphors. That is, take the first part of one comparison and fuse it to the second part of another. Feel free to adapt or streamline grammar and wording as you see fit. The idea is to think about just how wild a metaphor can get and still hold meaning. Are any of the new metaphors and similes as fresh, even fresher than the originals? Do meanings shift? Would you regard some of your inversions as usable tropes (a trope is an instance of figurative language)? Which are so bizarre as to be useless?

Example: The following metaphors appeared in the collections *Walking the Black Cat* and *Hotel Insomnia,* both by Charles Simic.

1. "the city, that winter, like an opera house on fire"
2. "I was a winter fly on a ceiling"
3. "The night birds, like children who won't come to dinner"
4. "Your undergarments and mine, sent flying around the room, like a storm of white feathers"
5. "Sleeplessness, you're like a pawnshop, open late on a street of failing businesses"
6. "Titanic on the screen, like a birthday cake sinking"
7. "The pages I turned sounded like wings"
8. "With the two of us riding the long flame, like a coach into the sunset"
9. "quiet as a bread crumb"
10. "Death's an early riser."

And here are a few scrambles:

1. Sleeplessness, you are like a child who won't come to dinner.
2. The night birds were quiet as bread crumbs.
3. The city, that winter, quiet as a bread crumb.
4. Your undergarments and mine, like a birthday cake sinking.
5. The pages I turned sounded like a storm of white feathers.
6. Titanic on the screen, like a coach into the sunset.
7. I was like a pawn shop, open late, on a street of failing businesses.
8. Death is a winter fly on a ceiling.

ADUMBRATION

Let's think about some more sophisticated ways to get conscious control of metaphor in our writing.

Like foreshadowing, *adumbration* means to suggest beforehand. But adumbration signifies a vaguer kind of foreshadowing, more sketchy, more cloudy. The root word in there is *umbra*, Latin for shade (and don't forget that one meaning of shade is ghost). I like to use the word adumbration to talk about those instances in which meaning attaches to objects that appear in scenes (this is something like what T.S. Eliot called "the objective correlative"). If a character lights a cigarette after sex, the next cigarette—even if puffed in a grocery store—will remind us a little of sex. (Advertisers, of course, bank on this.) If a character shakes hands to make a sinister deal, the next handshake in that piece will carry some whiff of the sinister. The first handshake adumbrates; the second handshake delivers. If a character who is angelically good has red hair, the next head of red hair we see will carry a feeling of goodness.

I had a student years ago in New York who wrote an intensely moving memoir of her father. In the first scene of the essay, she shows us the man throwing a stove down the basement stairs. It's a horrific vision—drunken, enraged man tearing the stove from its moorings with bestial strength and throwing it down the basement stairs, right in front of his children. Note that the stove is only itself at the start of the memoir, just sitting there, waiting for a match. But through the various juxtapositions of character and event that storytelling adds, it quickly becomes a symbol.

In a much later scene of the unfinished essay, readers see the writer's newest boyfriend. He's leaning against the stove in her kitchen, affably drinking a beer. The presence of that stove—the word itself now carrying all the weight of scene one—makes us question the affability of the new boyfriend, makes us wonder: has the writer chosen the wrong man? The stove alone does the trick. The writer doesn't have to say more.

What interested me most about this stove image is that when I pointed it out, the writer looked at me sharply, revealed. She was worried about this new guy's drinking but hadn't wanted to say anything about it at all in her essay. Wanted, in fact, to hide it from the reader. But of all the dozens and scores of places her new boyfriend has leaned and sucked a beer, she picked a *stove*.

Our writer went home to revise and came back a week later with a new draft. She'd gotten so excited about the stove image that she now had stoves in every scene. She'd all but renamed her boyfriend Stove Ovenworth.

Restraint, dear writer. One repetition is enough. Maybe two.

Our writer's next revision restored the delicate adumbration of the single stove repetition—beautiful. Also, she added just a few words of description to make the second vision of the stove a couple of notches more intense—beautiful, beautiful. And now, her essay was about her real fear of falling into the trap her mother had fallen into: alcoholic father, alcoholic husband.

In *This Boy's Life*, Tobias Wolff tells the true story of his childhood and adolescent years under the reluctant wing of a bad-news stepfather named Dwight, in a town called Concrete (an oppressive name, speaking of metaphors). What follows is from one of their first encounters:

> Dwight drove in a sullen reverie. When I spoke he answered curtly, or not at all. Now and then his expression changed, and he grunted as if to claim some point of argument. He kept a Camel burning on his lower lip. Just the other side of Concrete he pulled the car hard to the left and hit a beaver that was crossing the road. Dwight said he had swerved to miss the beaver, but that wasn't true. He had gone out of his way to run over it. He stopped the car on the shoulder of the road and backed up to where the beaver lay.
>
> We got out and looked at it. I saw no blood. The beaver was on its back with its eyes open and its curved yellow teeth bared. Dwight prodded it with his foot.

"Dead," he said.

It was dead all right.

"Pick it up," Dwight told me. He opened the trunk of the car and said, "Pick it up. We'll skin the sucker out when we get home."

I wanted to do what Dwight expected me to do, but I couldn't.

I stood where I was and stared at the beaver.

The poor beaver in this passage is only itself at first—a large rodent crossing a road—but in juxtaposition to Dwight, it quickly becomes an emblem of a step-father's cruelty. And when it turns up again, festering and wasted in Dwight's attic (along with a huge basket of chestnuts that carry their own meaning), the full profligate force of that cruelty hits us with a sick thud. And the beaver needn't be mentioned after that to continue to have its power. When Dwight brings home a dog—normally a blessed event in a boy's life—we know a lot about how to read the gesture, and we understand our hero's dread.

The truth is, anything from your days that you pick as a prop for memoir—beaver or stove or chestnut or hubcap—or anyplace you choose as a setting, may have some useful meaning hidden in it. Sometimes it takes a reader to point out the metaphorical stuff. Other times it just takes time for your own clearest vision to arrive. Sometimes, however, the discovery of meaning, of metaphor, is a matter of conscious reading, conscious investigation, conscious searching through the attics of your imagination, and a conscious, writerly effort to make use of all you've got. Very often, a certain symbol, carried through even a book-length memoir, becomes the heart of the story.

Remember our discussion of *The Glass Castle*, by Jeannette Walls, back in chapter five? The title of that book is taken from her disturbed father's dreamy plan to build a glass castle. He even drew up blueprints for the thing. The fantasy of the castle is both real and unreal. The blueprints are real enough. But the whole takes on more and more meaning as it keeps reappearing through the book, the father's dream more and more unreal, young Jeannette growing more and more disillusioned. One imagines the writer waking in the middle of some tossing night and realizing she had her title.

EXERCISE SIX: *Tweaking Up the Adumbration*

Here's an exercise to try as you revise any of your memoirs or essays or articles. Look for objects or places that have taken on meanings from your most dramatic scenes, then use those objects or places again somewhere in the essay to make use of the reader's unconscious associations. It's not as hard as it sounds.

Say you've got a scene dramatizing your engagement to be married. Say the big question was popped under an enormous, spreading tree. What happens if you introduce another enormous, spreading tree, perhaps in a later scene of chaos or strife?

In many cases, this exercise (and some of the others in this chapter) will make you realize that you have no enormous, spreading trees in your work at all, that in order to have objects to take on metaphorical significance, you need to have objects around in the first place.

Exercise Seven: *Making It New*

Here's an exercise quoted directly from novelist, story writer, anthologist, and critic John Clayton:

> Anaïs Nin says, "It is the function of art to renew our perceptions. What we are familiar with we cease to see. The writer shakes up the familiar scene, and as if by magic, we see a new meaning in it."

Take a familiar scene (perhaps from one of your earlier exercises), and make us see it in a new way. For example, see a liaison between a man and a woman as a military engagement; see a business deal as a dance.

TRUSTING YOUR PRECONSCIOUS MIND

The juiciest metaphors, the most fitting symbols, the largest meanings, the universal threads arrive most often entirely on their own. You as writer work and work to make a clear story clearer; your reader—absolutely because of the clarity you've finally achieved—sees something larger than your story, something as large as all of life. She sees meaning. She sees connections. She makes the grand comparison.

Simple examples include student stories of mountain climbing, a subject I've encountered frequently when teaching at conferences out west. In one memorable one, our young writer tells us about a time he decided to make the final ascent of a Utah peak when he knew a winter storm was coming. His bull-headedness nearly killed him, but he did make his goal. He held up his hand in class: missing fingers.

He offered to take off his shoes.

We said, "Nah."

The mountain might be seen as life, the bullheadedness as a particular aspect of the human spirit. The missing fingers? The price, perhaps, of hubris. What if, the class asked, the writer went back to his draft thinking in those grand terms? He might wreck everything, the class answered, making such an image too obvious, might steer the whole essay toward the hackneyed. But he might—ever so subtly—find a way to make use of the big stuff, find a way to understand his own essay, and so find a way to bring understanding to his readers.

In a much later draft, our mountain climber included a long section about his failed marriage. His actions as a climber became analogs for his actions as a husband. The mountain became the wife, the wife a mountain. The writer showed himself to be too much the conqueror, too little humble before great forces (nature, femininity). The essay showed the writer to himself, made him his own reader, taught him enough to bring a real close to the piece, to fill it with meaning, even wisdom.

Gow Farris—good old Gow—struggled and struggled to write about his brother. But now that Gow had broken into scenes, it wasn't hard to bring the dead man to life. The trouble was all the emotion. Gow couldn't read the stuff aloud, and sometimes at his keyboard he'd cry till he had to get up and do something else. Someone in our class suggested he *not* get up but sit tight with his emotion, write about *something else.*

And so he turned back to his project of the story of his reporting career, some days working on that, some days working on the memoir of his brother.

Quickly, it became apparent that Gow's story of himself as reporter in-volved scene after scene with another man. Gow and his succession of bosses. Gow and President Johnson. Gow and the guy at the next desk. Gow and an un-dercover police officer. One of Gow's classmates said, "It's like you were always looking for a brother."

Gow grumbled at that, but within a day he was glowing. He'd discov-ered over a glass of beer that his two stories were one, that one informed the other. It was true: all of his relationships with men his whole adult life were failed searches for the lost brother. Gow was on his way to writing something important, not only about himself but about men, and not only about men but about the human condition.

Juxtapositions, he'd discovered, can make meaning soar.

EXERCISE SEVEN: *Juxtaposition*

Please pick at random five or six scenes you've written over the last several months. Take them straight out of larger pieces, whether these pieces are finished or not.

Now, one at a time (one a day, perhaps), splice a scene—something like your first ski trip—into whatever you're writing now. You've been writing about the death of your great-aunt, and now—page break—there's a ski scene.

The challenge of this exercise is to make seemingly unrelated scenes work together. What has skiing to say about death? What do Aunt Lurlene's doilies have to say about skiing? Write your way out of the problem. Of course, some juxtapositions won't yield anything but silliness.

But some will bring inspiration, God's breath.

If toast always lands butter-side down, and cats always land on their feet, what happens if you strap toast on the back of a cat and drop it?
—Steven Wright

EXERCISE EIGHT:
Make Conscious Use of Symbolic or Figurative Language

Pretty simple: Working with several of your essays or memoirs, arbitrarily and forcibly try to put a metaphor or simile on every page, work an object into every scene. Give us a conversation, then tell us what it was like. Show us a man, then compare him to something, anything. Bring on the weather, and tell us what the rain was like in some fresh way. Put that squirrel skull your brother gave you at Christmas on the table. You'll generally get results that will fit into one of two labeled baskets: FAILURE and SUCCESS. Some in the failure basket can be rescued, perhaps. Some in the success basket won't turn out to belong there. But even if it's one out of ten tries that result in a usable language, you're ahead.

Two lessons here.

1. It's okay to fail.
2. Inspiration sometimes comes as the result of hard work.

EXERCISE NINE: *Create a Motif*

Have a look at a memoir or essay you're working on, with an eye to figurative and symbolic language. What elements in your pages could be considered symbols? What kinds of metaphorical comparisons do you make? What are your most memorable images? How are these figures spaced in the work at hand? Are there clear relationships between them? Or are they all over the place? Try bringing these important features into some kind of cohesion, spacing them more or less regularly through the work. Further, try getting them to "rhyme" with one another, that is, to have something clear to do with each other, something thematic, like Lucy Grealy's animals. Then make an effort to draw these themes through the length of the work, filling gaps where you've gone pages without, trimming here and there where you've packed things too full.

If you're finding nothing to work with, go back to exercise eight.

DO NOT GO GENTLE INTO THAT GOOD NIGHT

People afraid or wary of their own unconscious or preconscious minds tend also to be wary of any discussion of metaphor. Lots of my students like to shout at me the amusing old saw, "Sometimes a cigar is just a cigar!" True, true. Don't go overboard in your search for figurative truth.

But don't go underboard, either. When a cigar is just a cigar, there's not much for the writer in search of meaning to go on. Sometimes, dear writer, a cigar is a village in France!

CHAPTER NINE
SAYING IT RIGHT

One day the Nouns were clustered in the street.
An Adjective walked by, with her dark beauty. The
Nouns were struck, moved, changed. The next day
a Verb drove up, and created the Sentence.

—Kenneth Koch

In college and in the years just after college, I sang and played keyboards in good bar bands, one after the next. In one, we were stuck with a drummer I'll call Ditch. Ditch was nearly seven feet tall, but no basketball coach had ever convinced him to play. He had a sharp wit and a cold eye, would pull up late for practice on his Harley, pull up late for gigs in his monster van, all our equipment trapped inside. He'd be at fault, but angry at the rest of us.

Ditch's drumming was unlike him, lush and gentle, very full. But we were a rhythm-and-blues band, spare and loud. Ditch didn't leave a lot of room to think, filled every pause, killed the drama of every silence with a flourish, flattened the dynamics. The places where we wanted to get loud he couldn't come with us: too many notes to play them very hard. Or to play them very softly, either. But our music—the stuff we'd agreed we wanted to play—needed those highs and lows. We wanted Ditch to whack that snare drum sharply. We wanted gaps of silence. We wanted *dynamics*.

Jack, our fearless lead guitarist, brought up the subject with Ditch at every practice and before every gig. Ditch got testy, rageful. His eyes were dark slits. He'd spent years learning all that stuff. All the adornment was his *style*, and we could pretty well jam our complaints up our noses. But he didn't say noses. And he didn't stop there.

We needed a new drummer, hard to find. When we did find one, the problem was going to be protecting him from Ditch. The problem, in fact, was going to be protecting *ourselves* from Ditch, with his history of violence. Sneaky Jack figured it out: we break up, wait a month, take a new name, and reform with a new guy in Ditch's place.

Maybe two weeks before this uncourageous plan was to be implemented, Ditch did something unheard of: he showed up early for a gig. Frat house at Cornell. He slammed his kit together at the back of the makeshift stage, got out his sticks, gave himself a sound check, popping each of his forty percussion pieces in an amazing unbroken roll, thirty seconds of subtle rumblings and cymbal crashes, the usual. But then he shouted in animal pain, a frightening wail, and wailing he leapt to his feet, suddenly berserk, kicking cymbals out of his way, knocking his huge bass drums into a stairwell, breaking the heads of his timbales and tom-toms with the pointed stand of his seat, flinging snare drums through the open window into the dark frat-house yard, then kicking the rest of it all around the room, scaring us shitless (but delighting the frat boys, who were already drunk).

Turned out Ditch's dangerous (and definitely desirable) girlfriend, Cheetah, had run off with someone from the Attica Free Men, a motorcycle club associated with the eponymous upstate prison. We had to play in ten minutes. Fearless Jack the guitar man led old Ditch outside, and there, in the middle of the sweeping frat-house driveway, dressed him down, and whatever it was Jack said, it got Ditch back in the room, just as the busload of young women from Wells College arrived, dressed to the nines, giggling.

Ditch, darkly sulking, set up one bass drum, one snare, one hi-hat, one ride cymbal. All those other drums and cymbals represented the excesses of love somehow, and in any case he'd damaged them beyond immediate usefulness. Without them, his usual lush style got boiled down to solitary hits on single drums. He was pissed, and he played hard—those single, spare hits let him do so. He was pissed, and Cheetah wasn't there, and some other biker was caressing her tattooed shoulders.

He'd never played so well and the band was electrified by his focus and we'd never played so well and the frat boys had never heard anything like it in their broken mansion and the Wells College women danced and stripped out of layers of fancy sweaty clothes and we played hours extra, roaring into the night.

From then on, Jack made sure he pissed Ditch off before every gig. Pissing Ditch off wasn't hard. You just told him you'd seen Cheetah at Micawber's with Attica Ken.

By the time Ditch got over her, maybe three months, four, he was a new drummer. I played with him for years.

EXERCISE ONE: *Forget About Style*

In this exercise you are to throw a fit—perhaps you're furious because of the latest round of rejection slips, a stupid reading from a friend, Cheetah run off with Ken—*throw a fit* and kick the pieces of your style kit around the frat house while the drunken brothers yell. Break the bass drum of your punctuation with the pedal of your adjectives. Ram your stout verb sticks through your adverbial tom-toms. Nix prolixity. Fling cymbals out the windows; listen to the crash.

The best kit is the essential kit.

Hit it hard when you're hitting, but don't be afraid of silence.

As for style: just get mad and stay that way.

THE NEXT STEP

Writing is all about language, and writing in English is all about the English language. Mastery of its many nuances and subtleties and often arbitrary rules is a lifetime proposition. Words and sentences and paragraphs are endlessly adaptable, always plastic. It's up to writers—you and me—to discover strategies that produce clarity, motion, density, rhythm, precision, texture, urgency, all the things that in the end can add up to beauty.

Now, most of us have come to writing because of a facility with words. This facility was noticed by our teachers early on, and we've been told for years by various authorities—from parents to teachers to bosses to friends—that we are good writers. Some of us have even had editors give the thumbs up. Okay, we're good. We've got a way with words. But we want to be, well, *great*. What's next?

I'm not going to dwell here on the rudiments, really. All that's been well covered in other places, in books that are accessible to you already, probably right on the shelf above your desk, certainly at your library or bookstore, grammar handbooks and usage dictionaries, thesauruses and spellers. Instead, let me pull some fairly abstract words from my earlier sentences: clarity, motion, density, rhythm, precision, texture, urgency.

These are difficult topics to talk about. They tend to interweave, each fading into the provinces of the next. But with some discussion, I hope to help you further plumb the differences between merely competent writing and *big* writing, writing that rocks the hippopotamus.

Clarity

If writing isn't clear, it's nothing. If readers have to guess at your meaning, only some will guess right. Leave nothing to chance, dear writer. Your authority lies in your control of the language.

Under the heading of clarity come most of the rules of grammar. Those commas you're not quite sure how to use have been given jobs by a consensus of good writers over many years. Learn how to put them to work. Those semicolons and colons you avoid so assiduously—and those dashes—divide your thought into discrete and functional blocks of meaning. Mechanics, my friend: You've got to know the basics (for example, how does one punctuate around parentheses?). Usage? Good usage is a matter of knowing the difference between *that* and *which*, *further* and *farther*, *principle* and *principal*, *its* and *it's*, and knowing—never guessing—about pronoun cases: *he* and *him*, *who* and *whom*, *me* and *mine* ("... between you and I ... ," says Donald Trump, in a full-page ad decrying today's educational standards). Word choice is everything. If you say *accept* when you mean *except*, *allusion* when you mean *illusion*, you lose your reader every time.

Do you know how modifiers work? Apostrophes? Do you understand predication? Subordination? Can you recognize an independent clause? If not, you'll have a raging hippopotamus of a time with commas. (In the first edition of this book I said you'd have a hell of a time with commas, but after revising the previous chapter, I know hell's not much of a metaphor. And there was this ridiculous hippo hanging around from the previous section ....)

Many of us, even with our fine facility in language, answer the questions above with sheepish negatives. Many of us do our grammar by ear. All of us need to do the work of checking our intuitions against the conventions of grammar, punctuation, and mechanics—the rules.

It's fun to be a little fussy.

It's also fun to break the rules.

Which are mere conventions. Groups of smart people have agreed on these conventions over many years. There's no natural law that says one way or the other is correct. But if we can all agree what an ellipsis should do, or how to use a semicolon, we'll have an easier time getting our ideas across clearly. Why fight it? If you're going to be unconventional, why not in your content rather than in your grammar and mechanics?

The only rule, really, is clarity. If you can be clear using fragments, use fragments. If you can be clear with no quotation marks in your dialogue, cool. If you can be clear using not one mark of punctuation, go for it. If you want to spell like a second grader, fine. But if I'm your editor, get ready to argue with me. Sometimes you'll win, especially if you know what you're talking about, if you know the rules you're flouting, if there's method in your rebellion.

Exercise Two: *Time to Become an Expert*

For this exercise, you simply buy books, or look for language Web sites, and then you use them. I own, like, twenty-two grammar handbooks, because I teach and edit (and, okay, because I get them in the mail constantly for free). You only need one, really, though owning more than one helps you see that even the experts aren't always in agreement in matters of style, usage, grammar, and mechanics. If you're on a budget, college-town bookstores generally have a great supply of used handbooks. A kindly professor may have old desk copies to give away. And more and more, the Internet gives you access to all you need to know for free, and instantaneously (though you can't always be sure who's behind the information you're getting—might be someone out of touch with current thinking, someone with an axe to grind, someone a little crazy).

Handbooks are perfect toilet reading: small sections that you can read quickly, no fear you'll drop your laptop in the can. Read these books as daily entertainment. You'll find your most cherished ideas about commas, say, are not entirely correct. You'll learn how to use a word you've had wrong since you were fourteen. Also, you'll be affirmed in all the stuff you do know how to do, and you'll learn the names of the things you do so well intuitively: here as everywhere, naming is knowing. Next time you see an error in the newspaper, name it, using your handbook.

Along with the grammar handbook, buy a dictionary. And not one of those dollar college editions from guys on the street. And not just the speller in your computer's memory. Invest in a fat book that provides etymologies (the unabridged *Random House Dictionary of the English Language* is excellent and affordable, though no match for the multivolume *Oxford English Dictionary*, which is a writer's dream and dear to those of us who understand its value; consult it online by subscription or in the library for free). Read your dictionary for fun, not just for spelling; go in there with a flashlight and find magnificent words, learn their histories, use them in conversation. (My mother used to tell me what her mother told her: "Use a word ten times and it's yours.") The best strategy is to look up words as you do your daily reading. Of course you'll want to look up all the words you don't know, but it's smart to look up the words you do know, too. I'm constantly surprised by shades of meaning I've been missing. Sometimes I'm chagrined to learn I've been using a given word wrong for years!

H.W. Fowler's *Modern English Usage* is antiquated in many charming ways, but Fowler is still funny. He's also endlessly interesting, always persnickety and wise. He collects a dozen examples for every point he makes, quoting authors when they're right and when they're wrong, praising them or making fun. He's got eight pages on *that* and *which* alone. (Note that most handbooks have at least a small usage section, with advice on commonly misused words and expressions.) *That* and *which*. Good example. Are you using them correctly? Can you say why you use which of the words when?

A thesaurus is very useful for getting that word off the tip of your mind, but sometimes it can be a little dangerous. I had a student who liked to use the thesaurus to dress up his prose, mistaking the listings under familiar words as exact synonyms: "I marched on Washington to bring a message to Congress" becomes "The self paraded on the first president so as to transport a bulletin to intercourse." I love my computer thesaurus—that list of alternative choices arrives in seconds, helps me widen my standard vocabulary, helps me remember words I know well but seldom use. But no thesaurus can make the decision on word choice alone: that's up to you and your dictionary, and the extra time you take with every word and every phrase will mark you as a writer to reckon with.

Handbooks, dictionaries, and usage manuals aren't books to sit down and read in an afternoon. But they are not books to use only as needed, either. They're books to peruse a little every day as part of our work.

And that perusal, gentle writer, is your assignment, ongoing.

There was an old legend among late, lamented (by me) typesetters that went: "Set type as long as you can hold your breath without getting blue in the face. Then put in a comma. When you yawn, put in a semi-colon. When you clear your throat, put in a period. When you want to sneeze, that's time for a paragraph."

—Campbell Geeslin

Exercise Three: *A Toddler's Game*

Remember those toys, the ones that teach toddlers about shapes? Square block in the square hole, round in the round, star in the star. You were amazed and satisfied when the fit was right. Or maybe you were like me, always hammering the star into the circle with a toy bus.

Let's think of punctuation as having shapes and sentences as having holes to fit those shapes. Every sentence is a kid's game; your challenge is to use each distinct shape to best fit a particular tone and idea, to shake up your syntax. Do you think hard about punctuation as you type or scribble away? Probably not—sentences happen quickly, almost automatically. The assignment here is to slow down and *consciously* make use of all the punctuation at your command. (Return to exercise two in this chapter if your command is a little thin.)

Now that you've internalized so much of the punctuation and the parts of speech in your grammar handbooks, it's time to make use of what you've learned, to expand your normal style and syntax. So, pull out a favorite scene or passage from your recent writing. And let's fit shapes into holes. That is, let's revise some sentences.

No hammering allowed—that's for later.

Your existing sentences (and paragraphs) are your holes. Here are your shapes (use your handbook if you need definitions):

1. An em-dash pair
2. An introductory clause using a gerund (watch out for faulty predication)
3. A subordinating conjunction to start a sentence
4. One simple sentence
5. A semicolon, used correctly
6. One compound sentence
7. One compound-complex sentence
8. One fragment
9. One set of parentheses
10. One colon
11. One set of quotation marks, properly punctuated
12. One set of single quotation marks inside double quotation marks
13. One hyphen
14. A single em-dash
15. An exclamation point
16. Italics for emphasis

Of course, you will have already fulfilled several of these categories. And one sentence may fulfill several by itself. But be sure to consider how you order your shapes, reworking and rearranging when necessary. Perhaps you decided to use the simple sentence and then the fragment midway—at a tense moment in your narrative—or wanted to start with a descriptive compound-complex sentence, a sentence like a tangle of snakes and monkeys, chutes and ladders.

The object is to use all sixteen shapes above, always altering your sentences and paragraphs to accept the blocks at hand, to put knew knowledge into purposeful practice, to import new strategies into your sub-conscious and from there into your future automatic sentence making.

And to have a little fun along the way.

Claire and Me

In the interest of clarity, let's look at an example of student work (this one I'll make anonymous at the student's request).

> Jane and Claire and me stood to our feet, drunkly. She went straight to the car to get the box of books. It was parked outside under a tree at college, the berries had stained the windshield like bruises. They were important to us. She came back with them and Jane said "Now is the time to read the mystery quote". Falling open to our certain page, we read it out loud.

Without feeling superior (since we all make mistakes), let's get out our handbooks and name the problems above. Okay, you can feel superior if you want to, but at least don't be mean. Our writer needs our help, our compassion, just as we ourselves need writing help and writing compassion from time to time. Most of our disdain comes from insecurity anyway, is really aimed inward.

Jane and Claire and me. The writer is subject of this sentence, along with her college friends. The problem is pronoun case. The proper case is *I*, of course (though there're plenty of times when voice demands just such usage).

Stood to our feet. What else can you stand to? Perhaps *struggled* for *stood*, or some other verb that gets it exactly right—*tottered*? Apparently the protagonists here are *drunkly*. Where would you send this writer to check her adverbs?

She went straight. Which she? This is a pronoun-reference problem. (Often these are more subtle than the one we have here; check your pronouns carefully.) *Went* isn't much of a verb to describe an intoxicated young woman rushing outdoors. (Is she stumbling down some stairs? Into snow? What exactly?)

To the car. What car? Whose? What kind? How much might a writer slip in here?

It was parked. What was parked? The box of books? Another pronoun reference mystery. The books are the first referent the reader comes up with (at subconscious speed) before switching to the correct referent. *It* is a pronoun of particularly pesky vagueness. I'd check every *it* you ever use for clear reference, and I'd check to see how often you use that little word. I've discovered it in my own rough drafts five, six, seven times in a single paragraph, with references flying every which way.

Under a tree at college. Wouldn't hurt to name the tree, especially given the berries (what berries?) that follow. Mulberry tree, is my guess. College? What college? Are we at college? Was that a dorm room we were in? Name the school, and you solve all kinds of problems: location, setting, class and success level of protagonists, and so forth.

Stained the windshield like bruises. Our writer is reaching for a nice metaphor here, but it's a faulty analogy; the wording here says that bruises cause stains. That's not quite right. And did you find the comma splice? Do you know what a comma splice is? Back to exercise two!

They were important to us. Again, pronoun reference. Does *they* refer to bruises? To boxes? To books? To what? The reader, of course, can figure it out, but to do so she's got to leave her dream. And most readers will resent even momentary confusion, especially if confusion keeps coming.

"Now is the time to read the mystery quote". Is our writer in control of quotation? Where do final periods and commas go when you have quotation marks? (In American usage, always inside.) How about question marks? Colons? The rules are clear and easy to find; read up in your handbook, and carefully examine dialogue by good writers. (Parentheses have their own conventional punctuation with a logic different from that of quotation marks: again, read up. Even if you think you know, read up! I'm continually surprised by what I have wrong, or have forgotten. I'll bet you've found an error or two in this here book.)

Falling open to our certain page, we read it out loud. Faulty predication, for one thing: This says that *we* fell open, not a book. (And by the way, what book is it?) Notice the vague *it* here.

I could say more about this passage, lots more, even as short as it is, but suffice it to say it's not clear. And despite a pretty interesting story lurking there behind the fuzz, as reader, I'm about to give up, move onto something clearer.

MOTION

The notion of motion is mighty metaphorical, but let's give it a shake.

Motion is about verbs, of course, and it's about voice (eschew the passive!). It's about transitions between sentences and paragraphs and sections, but it's about something else, too, something less concrete. Say you're on a ship: always you feel its connection with the living ocean. Prose without motion is like a ship in dry dock: no connection with the great sea that is our language.

Prose is like a shark: if it quits moving, it's dead. Prose is like a relationship: if it quits growing, it becomes stifling. Prose is like sex: it's better if you move.

Prose should be made of movement the way a symphony is: *allegro, andante, cantabile.* Prose should change before our eyes, like Proteus, from this form to that.

Let's examine for motion the opening paragraphs of "Giving Good Weight," the title essay from the collection *Giving Good Weight* by John McPhee:

> You people come into the market—the Greenmarket, in the open air under the downpouring sun—and you slit the tomatoes with your fingernails. With your thumbs, you excavate the cheese. You choose your stringbeans one at a time. You pulp the nectarines and rape the sweet corn. You are something wonderful, you are—people of the city—and we, who are almost without exception strangers here, are as absorbed with you as you seem to be with the numbers on our hanging scales.
>
> "Does every sink grow on your farm?"
>
> "Yes, Ma'am."
>
> "It's marvelous. Absolutely every sink?"
>
> "Some things we get from neighbors up the road."
>
> "You don't have no avocados, do you?"
>
> "Avocados don't grow in New York State."
>
> "Butter beans?"
>
> "They're a Southern crop."
>
> "Who baked this bread?"
>
> "My mother. A dollar twenty-five for the cinnamon. Ninety-five cents for the rye."
>
> "I can't eat rye bread anymore. I like it very much, but it gives me a headache."
>
> Short, born abroad, and with dark hair and quick eyes, the woman who likes rye bread comes regularly to the Brooklyn Greenmarket, at Flatbush and Atlantic. I have seen her as well at the Fifty-ninth Street Greenmarket, in Manhattan. There is abundant evidence that she likes to eat. She must have endured some spectacular hangovers from all that rye.

Look at all the movement here. We start in the voice of a kind of everyman market person observing the hordes of city folk and move through the quickly shifting voices of the market to an authorial voice—the voice of McPhee, who has seen the rye-bread woman around. We slip from city to country and back again, taking both points of view. We slit and excavate and pulp and rape. And we move to surprising places—women allergic to rye bread (she's from *abroad*, too), for example. We leap from Brooklyn to Manhattan. I like the prodigious flow of information in this short opening—already I know stuff I didn't know before, already McPhee is challenging my preconceptions.

Movement is the sense of going somewhere as we read. It's easy to say, "Use better verbs." I say it to students all the time. But what I'm saying now is, "Make it *all* a verb." ("God is a verb," Reverend Mullendore said once in church—I puzzled over that one for years as a teen.)

The motion of your stuff puts the reader in motion, too. Maybe that's what we mean when we say a story *moved* us.

EXERCISE FOUR: *Get Moving*

Picture a schematic chart of a great river. First you'd observe the flow to the sea, a big arrow, after that hundreds of smaller arrows indicating eddies and currents and boils and inversions. Always, part of the water is flowing upstream, part is flowing to the river bottom, part is flowing right, part is flowing left.

The exercise is to chart the movement of a more-or-less finished piece of your work, an essay or memoir or other true story.

On a large piece of paper, draw the sea. Label this with some appropriate word or phrase. This will be harder than it sounds. To what ocean is your essay flowing, anyway? The grandest terms will do: Reader Satisfaction. Truth. Also, the most prosaic: The story of my first job.

Now for your sentences: Where does each fit in the flow toward your sea? Do any of your eddies threaten to become whirlpools? The point is to help you recognize what's flat in your writing, to isolate the stuff that only moves one way: downhill. And sometimes you'll find that a piece isn't moving at all; it's caught behind a dam (usually of personality—yours) and growing stagnant.

DENSITY

Sentences are a little like purses: they come in various sizes and can hold a little or a lot. Meaning is a bit like money: the more the better, in most cases. And if your purse can only hold so many bills, you might as well make them large-denomination bills, right?

Here's a first sentence from a student essay:

> My mother walked to the kitchen table and placed the scissors normally kept in her sewing basket on the table.

Let's try to add some density to this perfectly acceptable opening sentence, get it doing all the work it can do—characterization, scene building, setting, poetry, and so forth—without making it any longer. Right now, it's twenty words.

First, I'd like to get rid of the double use of the word *table*. This will free up some space for further meaning. But which *table* will I cut? That will depend on other changes. For example, I want to get rid of the passive "normally kept in her sewing basket." I want to do something about the bland verbs: walked, placed (*kept* will go when we fix the passive construction). As reader, I want to finish reading this first sentence having some clues about Mom's character, her age in the present of the sentence—the daughter's age, too.

I'll take some liberties here and add meanings and attributes wholly fictional for the sake of example. Only the actual writer of the original sentence could do the real work here.

> Momsy blundered into the kitchen, slammed the sewing-basket scissors into my place mat.

Not great, but an improvement. Best of all, it's only thirteen words. We've got seven words to play with as we get the thing back up to twenty.

> Momsy blundered in, stabbed my place mat with her sewing-basket scissors; they quivered, as I did, in the trailer's new silence.

Okay, it's twenty-one words, but now we have a name for mom, a sense of her character, a sense of her life. We've lost nothing in the way of meaning. We managed to get rid of both tables—where else would a place mat be? We dropped the explanation about the sewing basket, without losing its image, and kept the sense that the kid's in trouble for using Momsy's scissors. We've mentioned the trailer, and with it managed to give the socioeconomic condition here. We've given the reader a picture of the child, too: she's quivering.

How much can you get into a sentence? How much can you get into every sentence?

This is what density is all about.

EXERCISE FIVE: *Density*

For this exercise, I want you to consider the first sentence of one of your "finished" works of creative nonfiction. Take a half hour or more (really—set a timer if necessary—you're working out, after all; be a tough trainer) and play with getting as much as possible into that sentence, while keeping it at the same or near-same word count as the original. When that's done, go to the next sentence. What must change? And keep going, all the way to the last sentence of your piece.

As a variation, try boiling your first paragraph down to one sentence.

And keep in mind it's possible to boil things down too far: Once I made maple syrup so thick it wouldn't pour. And I've made sentences massive as lead ingots. Neither result was much good.

RHYTHM

A drum beating one note continuously, regularly, becomes either unbearably irritating, or recedes into background noise. Even a complex beat, endlessly repeated, recedes.

Rhythm in prose is a matter not so much of prosodic mathematics (iambs, tetrameter, syllabic feet)—though once again naming is knowing—but a matter of ear. And the question is, do you have an ear? A sense of rhythm is a cultural sense, a sense of tradition. Do your sentences pick up the cadences of childhood rhymes? Of marching bands? Of biblical phrasing? Of television scripts? Of the squad room? Of a preacher's repetition? Or, are our writing-rhythms always and only variations on the beating of a human heart (perhaps the one we listened to so comfortably in the womb)?

Variety, as in all things, is key. Too many new writers rely on a single rhythmic strategy, or none at all, letting the words fall where they may, so long as things are grammatical. Rhythm, of course, is one of the components of voice. Rhythm assumes a spoken discourse, sentences designed to be heard, and not just seen.

Time to go to the masters, once again. Try reading the following passages out loud, listening for the music here, listening for the ways the writers control the beat, listening especially for the differences.

Truman Capote makes use of a variety of rhythms in his opening to "Hand-carved Coffins: A Nonfiction Account of an American Crime," from his collection *Music for Chameleons*:

> March, 1975.
>
> A town in a small Western state. A focus for the many large farms and cattle-raising ranches surrounding it, the town, with a population of less than ten thousand, supports twelve churches and two restaurants. A movie house, though it has not shown a movie in ten years, still stands stark and cheerless on Main Street. There once was a hotel, too; but that has also been closed, and nowadays the only place a traveler can find shelter is the Prairie Motel.

The opening phrases here are blunt. The sentence fragments cut the rhythm short—shorter, that is, than our ears expect. This chopping isolates the fragments' beats from the beats of the full sentences that follow. But Capote doesn't allow those longer sentences to flow, either. He breaks them with commas, a semicolon, with subordination, interruption, and apposition. This is the vocal rhythm of someone with bad news to tell: hesitant, throat-clearing, yet resolute. And note that each of the last words in these sentences ends with a tongue-stopping (and beat-stopping) *T*, except the last sentence, with its motel, whose *T* echoes the earlier stops, but trails into the "el" sound, enough to carry the music forward into a new paragraph. Capote wants the delivery halting, but not so halting that the reader stops and turns elsewhere. Note that you can't read this paragraph in a joyful rush.

The next passage is from Doris Lessing's memoir "Impertinent Daughters":

> Modern-minded John William McVeagh, proud of his clever daughter, was thinking of university for her, but was confronted with a rebellious girl who said she wanted to be a nurse. He was horrified, utterly overthrown. Middle-class girls did not become nurses, and he didn't want to hear anything about Florence Nightingale. Any Skivvy could be a nurse, and if you become one, do not darken my door! Very well, said Emily Maude, and went off to the old Royal Free Hospital to begin her training. It was hard: conditions were bad, the pay was low, but she did well, and when she brilliantly passed her

finals, her father was prepared to forgive her. She had done it all on her own, without him.

This one you could sing. Note the alliteration that opens the paragraph: "Modern-minded ... McVeagh." Note the long opening sentence, its singsong rush. Note, too, how hard the sentence lands on the word *nurse*, which turns out to be the critical word of the passage (an instance of rhythm providing meaning). Note the tongue pleasure of the phrase "utterly overthrown." I want to say it again and again. And why does Lessing use Emily's middle name ("Very well, said Emily Maude, and went off ...") when she hasn't used it earlier and doesn't use it later? Why else but rhythm? And listen to the rhythm of this series: "conditions were bad, the pay was low, but she did well." The repetitions in structure here give the sentence the sound of a folk tale, very nearly a folk song.

In the next passage, Annie Dillard purposefully plays with biblical rhythm, even conflates it with the rhythms of childhood song. The passage, in which she gives a child's misinterpretation of what goes on in Sunday school, is from her memoir of intellectual awakening, *An American Childhood*:

> James and John, the sons of Zebedee, he made them fishers of men. And he came to the Lake of Gennesaret, and he came to Capernaum. And he withdrew in a boat. And a certain man went down from Jerusalem to Jericho. See it here on the map? Down. He went down, and fell among thieves.
>
> And the swine jumped over the cliff.
>
> And the voice cried, Samuel, Samuel. And the wakened boy Samuel answered, Here am I. And at last he said, Speak.
>
> Hear O Israel, the Lord is one.
>
> And Peter said, I know him not; I know him not; I know him not. And the rich young ruler said, What must I do? And the woman wiped his feet with her hair. And he said, Who touched me?
>
> And he said, Verily, verily, verily, verily; life is not a dream. Let this cup pass from me. If it be thy will, of course, only if it be thy will.

There's plenty to say about this passage, of course, but I'd better stick to rhythm. Along with the doggerel rhythms of childhood songs, note the use of rhyme and repetition to create rhythm. Normally, of course, good writers avoid repetition hoping to make full use of the richness of English, avoid obvious rhyme to avoid sounding childish, but here Dillard makes it plain that repetition and rhyme can make music of our words. A name repeated, he-said/she-said tag lines repeated, whole phrases repeated, all are rhythmic techniques. Dillard makes a joke of repetition in the end, but there are lessons here. Dillard crafts a joyful rush. How different in every way from Capote's dirge-like opening, from Lessing's little drum-song, yet all three appropriate to their subjects and intentions.

Rhythm should be attended to in each sentence we write, in each paragraph, but there is a rhythm of paragraphs, as well, a rhythm of sections in an essay, a rhythm of chapters in a book, and all of it ought to be in your control as you write.

EXERCISE SIX: *Tap Your Feet*

Pull out the work of a favorite writer, and read it listening and feeling for rhythm and rhythms. Tap your feet as you read out loud. Look for repeated words or phrases that set up a beat. Listen for sentences that rise, for sentences that fall. Where does the prose stop? What kinds of words create pauses? What kinds flow? How do paragraph lengths fit into the music of the work? Is there a visual rhythm? Can you sing any lines?

Then pull out another author, and do it again. What accounts for the changes you hear in rhythm?

Finally, pull out your own draft, and read the same way. Are you satisfied? Can you get more music in there? More of a beat? More aural surprises? More variety? Do you start most sentences with the subject? Do you always subordinate in the same way? Do you avoid alliteration, repetition? Does every paragraph end on a rising note, or falling? Does every sentence have about the same number of beats, every paragraph the same number of sentences?

Shake it up, baby!

PRECISION

Precision is a matter of getting everything right, from names to weights to dates to ages to sizes to hues. Precision is also a matter of excellent grammar and usage, which we've discussed. But, as always, there's more to it.

Precision is honesty. Precision will not allow self-deceit (or the writer's deception of others). Precision means filling in the blanks, staring down our defenses, checking every fact, even when it's easier not to. Precision means knowing what our essays are about. Precision means that, like a good surgeon, we know where and when to cut, when to sew. Precision admits to limitations: we can't know everything, and we say so.

When vision is precise, clarity results, and thence beauty.

Let's go to the page:

> We met in the winter months, not surprisingly in a bar. Brenda
> was beautiful and tall and I knew right away we'd be good for
> each other. I asked her home or she asked me, I can't remem-
> ber, but home we went, talking all the way, and then we made
> love the first time, not knowing, of course, that almost fifty
> years later we'd have been married, divorced, reunited twice,
> broken up twice, but talking on the phone again.

Not bad writing. Grammatical, clean, romantic. Still, I asked the writer—Gow Farris—to do some work: precision. Leave nothing vague, I coaxed. Precision's in the details. Gow said he meant it to sound nostalgic, not exact.

"It's just an exercise," I said.

"If you're about to tell me to relax, don't," Gow said, interrupting me. "You always tell everyone to relax!"

Anyway, here's what he came back with, an hour later, no research:

> Brenda Leavenworth (this is not her real name, Professor)
> and I met February 8th, 1950, during a record cold wave.
> Minus 38 degrees that night and just the two of us and
> Frankie (the bartender) at the Pine Tavern on the lake road.
> Brenda was freezing at home and so came out wearing four
> sweaters and a raccoon coat owned by her boyfriend, an
> acquaintance of mine named Tom Dell. You couldn't see any
> woman under all that clothing but I'd seen her before and
> knew she wasn't only tall. Her eyes were brown and her hair
> blond with roots showing and she was twenty-two years old.
> Frank let her sit at the bar and the three of us drank heavily
> (not exact enough for you? Okay:) Three of us drank shots
> of bar whiskey and bottles of beer (I don't know what kind of

beer, professor, so give me an F). At 12:47 A.M. she aimed her eyes at me and said: I ain't walking home. I said she could come to my place, but I wasn't driving up Tom Dell's driveway or anywhere near it. At my house we drank more and kissed on the couch with all the lights off till the sun came up. At that point I had maybe twelve layers of clothes off her, leaving one or two more to go. And this is as much as I'm likely to tell anybody. Exactly 48 years, five months, and three days later, I called her on the phone. Two nights ago, to be exact.

I always loved Gow's parenthetical commentary. Our sparring seemed merely the expression of the sparring that must have gone on inside his head as he tried to get his story to come out. And, oh, I wish you could have seen his reaction when I asked him to shorten the revision back to the length of the original paragraph!

Exercise Seven: *Vagueness Patrol*

Once again, I'm going to ask you to examine a "finished" draft. Starting at the beginning, look for vague constructions: *"about* seven years," "a grocery store," "a *good-looking* man," "a *good-size* dog," "*late* at night." And so on. Do everything you can and whatever it takes to bring precision to your constructions without greatly increasing the length of a passage.

Gow, in his revision, also brings precision to his observations: Brenda wasn't beautiful, exactly, but appealed to him. They "made love" that night in the old sense, certainly—flirting, making out—but not in the new sense: no actual sexual intercourse. "I knew right away we'd be good for each other." Really? Gow dumps that as too imprecise to even fix. And, rather than hiding behind vagueness, he just comes out and announces that he's going to plead privacy.

The point of the exercise is to teach yourself to see as your reader sees: what's clear in your memory is opaque to your reader unless the language is direct, the details exact, the truth out there in front, including the truth of reticence or other shyness. And every "finished" draft can benefit from a reading for precision.

TEXTURE

I don't mind cross-country skiing across a frozen lake; in fact, I love the speed and squeak of snow on deep ice. You can get a real cadence going, zoom smoothly along as the hills ahead grow larger and the hills behind retreat. Hours can pass as you cover the miles; your mind wanders the earth like a beatnik seeking the Buddha.

But I much prefer actual terrain: peaks and dales, bumps and flats, a grand and natural mix to give the pleasures of variety—chances to rest, chances to puff, hard skiing, easy skiing, views, canyons, sounds, a hundred kinds of trees, lots of smells, emotions unavailable on the lake (is that a moose?), a hill to go flailing down, a patch of ice, my big dog Wally (R.I.P. April 2, 2006) standing right in my way around a blind corner as I roar downhill—oomph.

Texture in writing is like terrain in cross-country skiing. You surprise your reader with shifts of speed, unanticipated layers of meaning, curious images, unexpected feelings, startling word choice, shifting moods as your paragraphs flip past.

Certainly, writing can get over-textured (Annie Dillard sometimes gets accused of just this)—too steep, too icy, too many rocks in the path—the reader isn't up to the challenge and falls down, gives up. Over-texture is a trap for some new writers. But the writing of most new writers goes the other way: one note, one direction, one layer, one mood. It's like skiing on that frozen lake—not entirely without its pleasures, but monotonous, the destination always clearly in view, the colors uniform, the trip rewarding only in terms of distance covered.

Tim Rushford, primarily a fiction writer, decided to try something different and took my memoir course in Vermont. He wrote about his twin younger brothers, pests who used to wake him when he wanted to sleep in. Here's his line, which comes smack in the middle of a pretty straightforward paragraph:

> And then the twins marched in and pissed in the soup of
> my sleep.

Oh, man, we workshoppers argued about that line. Everyone in the group had marked it. Some thought it was terrific. Some wanted it cut right now: horrid! Tim himself said he had cut it and restored it and cut it and restored it probably twenty times, deciding in the end to hear what we, his readers, had to say. We said a lot, and never agreed. I had hated the line at first, but my feeling after the discussion was: keep it. If it gets that much attention from good readers—keep it. And keep writing lines like that till you start making lines just as outrageous that no one wants to cut. Practice, practice, practice, that's what I've got to say.

EXERCISE EIGHT: *Peeing in the Soup of Your Sleepy Prose*

Again, get out a "finished" draft. In each paragraph, add a line that feels wild to you, one you'd never in a million years put in that place. The wildness can come in content or punctuation or mood or language or what have you. Just let 'er rip. Be a different writer, just for that moment. Use second person suddenly, or an absurd metaphor. Use a ten-syllable word, then use it again. Admit to a craving for horseradish even as you write. Be gross, if gross is not your norm (or be polite if it is). Or throw in a description of the Grand Canyon for no reason. Anything, whatever, go for it. Don't examine the fit, not yet.

And don't edit the lines away, but print out a draft with all of them in place. Find a reader, or wait a couple of weeks and read it yourself. What can you use? What new directions are suggested, both for your essay and for you as a writer?

Texture arrives with the practice I mentioned above, with confidence, with the acquisition of a voice. The idea of this exercise is to speed up the process, even if just a little.

URGENCY

If it doesn't matter, why write it? If it doesn't matter deeply, and right now, why read it?

The best prose gives off a sense of inevitability: this had to be written, and written this way. There's nothing extra; even the ramblings seem vital; there's something at stake. The idea is important, the event was momentous, the love was alive. I'm not saying only write about car crashes and presidential impeachments, just that when you write about the migratory paths of snails you make bloody sure your prose is alive and breathing—as you are—that when you write about images of lizards in Coleridge you never relax, never repeat yourself, never sound like a tour bus driver on the ten-thousandth run.

EXERCISE NINE: *You Could Start This Thing Anywhere*

If you're at all like me, you put a lot of time into your first paragraphs. You want to launch your memoir or essay with klieg lights and a marching band, you want to catch your reader, you want to inspire yourself. That first paragraph, you write it over and over, this way and that; you juggle words; you rebuild sentences; you get that thing just right.

The exercise is to flip through a "finished" draft of a memoir or essay to a random place—pick a paragraph and start to read as if this were the start of your true story or essay. How would the paragraph you choose have to change to be a first paragraph?

Go ahead and make the changes.

And do the same for every paragraph: urgency.

EXERCISE TEN: *A Poem of Your Prose*

Pull out yet another "finished" draft of an essay. Select a block of it—a page, a section—and make a free-verse poem out of that section. This you can do even if you have no experience with poetry (although if you don't know what free verse is, you might want to look into it before you start).

To get your work into lines, to have line breaks and enjambments that make sense, to put stanzas together, you have to think of the shapes of the words and their relationships, and not just meanings. You might have to pare away a great deal to get rhythm; you might have to add things to get clarity, shuffle words to get texture, interlayer phrases to get density, alter structure to get urgency, invent verbs to get motion.

When you're satisfied (or fully frustrated) with your poem, wait a couple of weeks, then convert the poem back into prose—without consulting the original text of your essay.

There.

So, first get one thing right—one thing that you really want to say. It's like a seed crystal; you can build on it, even if it's just one sentence.
                                                    —*Ian Frazier*

When I first moved to New York City for my twelve years there (the eighties, basically, plus a little on each end), I was amazed by the beauty of nights spent on the stoop, bottles of beer, a couple of friends to laugh with cheap. I was amazed by the Hudson River piers, abandoned pilings, the tide in and out, guys fishing for striped bass, people looking to kill you. I was amazed by the music, the late nights, the synchronized stop lights, the scope of the food, the variety of people. I was amazed by the old *Village Voice*, a weekly newspaper of culture and hip, behind-the-scenes news. I was so amazed that I actually decided to enter their short-short science-fiction contest. The rules: exactly 250 words of science fiction, not one word more or less. Prize was $1,000, more at the time than six full months rent and beer and cigarettes.

I worked with feverish hope (delusions of grandeur, really). My story was about an annoying scientist on a distant planet whose pet plant pushes him into an otherworldly pond where he's eaten by another plant, friend of the first one. Whatever. Getting the original draft of 1,500 words down to exactly and only 250 was an exercise in narrative necessity: cut, cut, cut; yow, yow, yow. But it worked. I mean, I got the story cut down. I didn't win the prize. I remained poor. It was beer on stoops all winter, bigger and bigger coats.

The exercise: Tell a true story in exactly 250 words. Not one word more or less, please. You may use an earlier try and simply cut it down to size. Pay attention to the kinds of words and sentences (and even paragraphs) that can go, the kind that can stay.

LEARNING TO FINISH

Slowly, I've come to see that when I'm finished with a piece, I've really just begun. It's a matter of trudging the extra steps—no oxygen mask, toes frozen—to get to the top of the mountain. It's the tough stuff, and it's the place where real writers leave the hobbyists behind. Not that there's anything wrong with hobbyists; writing makes a great pastime.

But you're an ambitious writer. You've got a polished draft. You've figured out what you're going to say. You've made your scenes. Your characters are doing their jobs. You know exactly where your true story, your essay, is going to go, because it's there already. Your structure is in place. The arc of your narrative is so firm it could stand at the confluence of the Missouri and the Mississippi rivers in St. Louis. Your ideas are out front. Your images are clear as ice sculptures.

Time to go back in. Time to read more closely than ever. Time to fearlessly open up paragraphs already sealed, time to knock sentences over their heads, time to get the language just exactly right so there's no question you've got the basics of beauty alive in every corner of your essay: clarity, motion, density, rhythm, precision, texture, urgency.

The wolves are howling.

CHAPTER TEN

BUILDING A BUILDING

*I don't believe the writer should know too much
where he's going. If he does, he runs into old
man blueprint.*

—James Thurber

When I think of structure in creative nonfiction, I see an enormous old farm in Maine, 1972. I'm there with my friends Bob Meyer and Michael Levine, trying to get ideas for Mike's cabin, miles away. A group of hippies (that's what they call themselves), part of the back-to-the-land movement (they don't actually know this), have bought this spectacular five-hundred-acre spread for next to nothing. In the course of the previous six years, individual members of the community have built themselves private houses, twenty of them by now. We get the grand tour. Variety: a geodesic dome straight from a Bucky Fuller kit; an enormous yurt, sod and timber; a Cape Cod saltbox, built from seventeenth-century drawings and home-sawn boards; two really wild tree houses, one with walkways through the canopy of the climax hardwood forest at the farm's fringes; a plain rectangular box (its owner eschewing adornment for spiritual reasons); a three-story tower, its first floor octagonal, second floor hexagonal, third floor round; a house made of stones from the farm's creek; a house made of free slabwood from the local mill; a house made of wine bottles set in mortar. It's thrilling, all these well-planned but eccentric places, all whimsical but suited to buggy summers and tough winters, all clear expressions of a builder's personality.

Likewise, there are no formulas in memoir, personal essay, or literary journalism (the three modes central to creative nonfiction). Each successful creative nonfiction work, whatever its genre, creates its own rules about structure and offers its own vision of what a memoir or essay or article can be. This new vision, certainly, may spring from models, may modify common forms or mix elements of several subgenres, but in the end, the right form for your material should be as individual as you, as quirky or straight, as mysterious or matter-of-fact.

FINDING YOUR FORM

It's time to start thinking about completing a true story or an essay or an article or a piece or a chapter or a section—a try. (Any of those labels will do; you choose.)

Back in chapter two, I used the analogy of a stone wall: you've been piling up rocks with nice shapes and heft, various sizes, various shades of color, some rough, some smooth, some nearly round, some more blocky—all the fragments and exercises and tries and odd paragraphs and even full drafts you've been writing. How many pages have you got? I hope a great many. (If you've been skimming along in this book, doing an exercise here and an exercise there, that's fine, but probably now it's time to go back and really make some writing.) My theory is that it's best to have your materials before you start to build.

How to fashion the stone wall? And what kind will it be? How high? What shape? What length? Will it be primarily decorative? Will it serve a function? Is it part of a castle or only a cairn?

EXERCISE ONE: *Arbitrary Structure*

We'll get to more elaborate approaches shortly, but now—especially if you haven't already got an essay in mind—I'd like you to try one of the most productive drafting techniques I know. Let's call it arbitrary structure.

Take your response to the map exercise (way back in chapter two), attach it with a page break to your response to the "On ..." exercise of chapter four. To these attach your letter exercise from chapter six (without salutation and sign-off, and sans small talk). To these add three or four more fragments—characters, places, ideas that somehow feel right to you. Keep mixing and matching until you have ten or fifteen pages arbitrarily tacked together.

Don't labor over the selection much; if you've been working steadily in this book or on your own for a week or a month or a year, it's you yourself—your consciousness, your concerns, your consistency of interest—that will supply the needed connections and common threads.

Oh, and some hard work: The assignment at hand is to form the once-random pieces of your effort into a personal essay. As you battle to make the connections necessary and perhaps as you write new material to fill gaps, what you are doing is coming up with an original structure in a genre that isn't big on conformity.

SOME DEFINITIONS

You'll find, I think, that a large part of getting your story or idea down on paper is finding the shape it wants to take. The beauty of the essay, or one of the beauties at any rate, is its ever-elastic form. Structure arises as an organizing response to specific material. What works for one subject—same writer—may not work for the next subject. And what works for one writer may not work for another.

Some definitions of familiar forms (or form categories, i.e., subgenres), in no particular order:

Memoir

Memoir is a rendering of lived life, as filtered through memory and the wider net of the needs of narrative. Memoir just tells the story, no explicit thesis here. Memoir examines a life, a self, and does so through a period of time, say early childhood or the month you spent with Grandpa in France. Like novels and short stories, memoirs tend to operate in time and space, tend to have a story arc, rising action leading to a climax, a balance of scene and summary. A reflective voice might tell the story, might analyze events, but it tends to stay in the background, tends to let the action do the work. Research can support the storytelling, but the point isn't a display of facts or information. A memoir lays out the evidence of a life, lets the reader make the conclusions. The mode ranges from pure, plain storytelling to more reflective storytelling. Some memoirs get so reflective and analytical that they move close to and overlap with the personal essay. A few pages, a book, a few volumes, memoir is an expansible form. Examples of book-length memoir: *The Kiss,* by Kathryn Harrison; *The Glass Castle,* by Jeannette Walls; *Minor Characters,* by Joyce Johnson. (See appendix D for an extended list of books in this and all the following categories.)

Personal Essay

A personal essay is a conversation with the reader, an informed mixture of personality, wisdom, facts, and storytelling. A personal essay examines a subject outside the self, but through the lens of self. The subject may *be* the self, but the self is treated as evidence for an argument. Passages of narrative often appear but generally get used as evidence in an inductive argument; given the evidence, the personal essay strives to say what's evident, to come to conclusions with which the reader may agree or disagree. An essay can wander through its subject, circle around it, get the long view and the short, always employing morsels of experience, knowledge, book learning, and personal history, all the stuff that rattles around in a writer's well-stocked mind. The writer's research supplies facts and figures, quotes and ideas, and augments previous knowledge, stories, ideas. Note the lack of form in this form: it's as open as free verse—and as difficult. Many personal essays extend into full-length books. Examples? *Great Plains*, by Ian Frazier; *The Silent Woman*, by Janet Malcolm; *U and I*, by Nicholson Baker.

Literary Journalism

Literary journalism is a big and varied category, but to be truly literary, an article must make elegant use of the tools of the novelist: scene, characters, drama, dialogue, plot. Very often, an *I* is present explicitly. Sometimes, as in *The Right Stuff*, by Tom Wolfe, the *I* is implicit in the language and approach. Sometimes, as in *Into the Wild*, by Jon Krakauer, the *I* emerges as the re-creating imagination. More often, the *I* is found at the center of the work, all biases embraced: John McPhee operates as an affable host, letting us know how he came to his subjects, having a drink with his guides. In the best work, the writer immerses herself in the story, living with her subjects, getting to know them well, observing and even sharing in their lives, always aware of the potential for exploitation (which I'll define as profit, literary or financial, at the expense of others). For her *Harper's* article "Nickel and Dimed" (later expanded into a terrific book), Barbara Ehrenreich lived only on the money she could make in the kinds of jobs unskilled American workers must take. It's a harrowing story, and you'll tip better after you read it.

Mosaic

A mosaic is an essay constructed entirely of discrete blocks of text, usually short and self-contained, that are ordered and juxtaposed without any particular attempt at transition one from the next. Mark Rudman's "Mosaic on Walking" takes this form: sixty-four blocks of text (some call these *crots*; my old Ohio State colleague Sebastian Knowles points out that *tesserae* would be more accurate) divided by page breaks. The whole of the piece is about thirty manuscript pages. Some sections are one sentence. Some are several sentences. Some are two paragraphs. The longest are roughly 250–300 words, about one typed page. Nick Flynn's *Another Bullshit Night in Suck City, a* poignant and funny memoir of his homeless father, is a mosaic of sorts, and book length.

Lyric Essay

A lyric essay is a kind of prose poem approached from the nonfiction side of the movable fence between genres. The term was first used by the brilliant nature writer and poet Sydney Lea to describe a hybrid mix of personal essay, mosaic, lyric poem, the aforementioned prose poem, and certainly memoir. A touch of fiction is not unusual, either. A lyric essay is short, often divided into multiple sections or strands (not to say stanzas), and makes use of all kinds of unconventional materials, from documents (say, a telephone bill) to lists of facts (everything on the shelves in a writer's office), to oddball quotation (Mickey Mantle's last words), to you name it. The writer doesn't necessarily draw the connections between his elements—he's often content to let juxtaposition speak for itself, leaves the reader to make associations on her own. The writer's attention is largely on language and expression rather than story or thesis; the point is to make art. Many fine poets are attracted to this form. Current practitioners include Albert Goldbarth, Ann Carson, John D'Agata, Michael Martone, Lia Purpura, our own Kristen Keckler, and many others.

Journals and Diaries

A journal is just that: a collection of dated entries that gather force by accretion of experience, always chronological. Many journals are meant from the start as public works (May Sarton's *At Seventy*, Sue Hubbell's *A Country Year*, Rick Bass's *Oil Notes*). Others are actual journals published posthumously (John Cheever's frank and beautiful *Journals*, Paul Gauguin's dreamy *Noa Noa*, George Dennison's anthropological and painful *Temple*, Edward Robb Ellis's obsessive *Diary of a Century*).

Nature Writing

Nature writing is as American as Emerson and Thoreau, and generally places an observing and appreciative consciousness out among the beauties and powers of the world. Nature writing is the personal essay with one foot in the woods. Or the formal essay with an environmental thesis. Or literary journalism with nature at the center. Scientists shine in this category, wedding good writing with special knowledge. More and more, of course, nature writing is elegy, and more and more of it will have to do with the accelerating effects of man-made pollution. Once again, the *I* plays a central role. Note that nature writing might appear as memoir, personal essay, or literary journalism. Certainly a mosaic upon nature would be ideal. Aldo Leopold's *Sand County Almanac* is a nature-writing classic and is in large part a journal.

Much of my own nonfiction falls into the category of nature writing. Other books include *Desert Solitaire*, by Edward Abbey (memoir); *Annals of the Former World*, by John McPhee (literary journalism); *A Country Year*, by Sue Hubbell (personal essay).

Literary Travel Writing

Literary travel writing is as British as gin, though Americans have done some terrific work in the form (and don't seem to mind a gin and tonic). Go to the Amazon in search of a lost tribe and exotic drugs, like Redmond O'Hanlon ("Amazon Adventure"), or attempt a circle trip around the entire shore of the Mediterranean, like Paul Theroux (*The Pillars of Hercules*). Tamer trips get immortalized, too: walks, drives, train rides, vacations in France. The structure is generally chronological, the shape of the essay or book the shape of the original trip, with the stoical traveler at the center of a ceaseless flow of minor characters, unexpected discomfort, carefully rendered scenery, and adventures and discoveries minor or major. One of the great challenges of the form is to move beyond the notebooks of the trip, another is to move beyond the newspaper travel page. Literary travel isn't about how much a given hotel costs; it's about the bigger picture, the feel of a place from politics to romance, from food to friendships. Once again, the *I* is at the center; once again, the form might be presented as memoir, journals, personal essay, or literary journalism.

Crossed Genres

Crossed genres actually account for most creative nonfiction. Memoir is often one of the parents of the handsome mutt that results: memoir and history, memoir and journalism, memoir and scholarly writing, memoir and book review, memoir and profile, memoir and polemic, memoir and instruction manual. Other crosses produce unusual volumes, hard to classify, fun to read: biography mixed with novel, cookbook mixed with personal essay, nature writing mixed with gardening manual, free verse mixed with formal essay, shopping list mixed with diatribe, literary criticism mixed with character assassination. The combinations are endless, usually multiple. Film and video, radio, blogs, podcasts—new technologies, new combinations—all hold distinct possibilities here. Most often, the cross isn't particularly apparent to the author, who's just being herself.

Experimental

Experimental nonfiction may stem from genre crossing or from the lyric essay, though often entirely new genres of writing (or not-writing) are invented. John Berger makes an essay entirely of photos, no text. Sidney Lea makes essays like extended prose poems, going more for sound and mood and emotion and image than idea or narrative. Deborah Sobeloff asks a couple of dozen people to tell her about a meal their fathers cooked for them and simply transcribes the answers, no context. One of my students is trying to write an essay entirely in text messages. Editors and teachers often look on this stuff with interest, but can't help themselves when it comes to revisions: "Make this more like what I know!" Some experimental writing is very difficult to enjoy—the experiment overtakes sense. Other innovative work, such as *Nola: A Memoir of Faith, Art, and Madness*, by Robin Hemley, provides narrative delight even while exploring experience in unfamiliar ways.

Hacking

Hack writing isn't a form but a trap. A lot of possible writing jobs fall into this category, though, so I think I'll include it here both as warning and definition. Hack writing, simply put, is writing for money in the way that contract killing is killing for money or prostitution is sex for money. You know you're hacking if you don't care about your subject, you obsess over word count, your paycheck never feels like enough, your paycheck is the only source of satisfaction in the work, you violate all your standards of language and seriousness, you violate other precepts, you say things in print that you don't believe, you know that if you were to drop dead you'd be quickly replaced and no one would miss you—there's always someone who could do the job as well and in the same way. Speech writing and ad writing often fall under this category, but fancier stuff can, too. Freelancing can be a gerbil wheel of ideas spun out for cash, diminishing returns. Then again, any writing for publication is good practice, and it's nice to be able to afford shoes when the wheel puts holes in your old ones!

EXERCISE TWO: *Mosaic*

I want you to try all the forms at some point (including hacking, I guess; as Voltaire says: "Once is science; twice is perversion"). Sometimes just doing it is the best way to discover one's strengths as a writer. And weaknesses.

But the exercise here is to try a mosaic. You've already got ample building blocks—I guess we'll call them tiles for this exercise. Try stringing a series together around a single subject. Food, say. Just quick, discrete blocks of text. No transitions allowed.

The idea is to experience no-form as form.

WHAT ABOUT OUTLINES?

I have finally figured out a way to use all the outlining skills I learned back in junior high school: do the outline last. Or almost last.

I'm not saying that outlining in advance can't work. In some cases it saves a lot of time and a lot of spelunking in blind tunnels and caverns. Journalist friends of mine (and I, when I'm playing the journalist role) will draw up outlines before writing (but certainly not before reporting, if they are honest at all; the reporting constitutes drafting, really, a stage of finding out what you want to say, finding out the truth).

Then again, I've found some amazing gems in the blind tunnels and caverns that outlines tend to keep me out of. Unlike traditional reporters or academics, writers of memoir and other creative nonfiction (this includes literary journalists) seldom know exactly what a piece of writing is going to be about before the writing starts. Even the most formal writers, outlines in hand, are often surprised by the direction a true story or essay ends up taking. The experienced among them are not afraid to throw the outline away or to make a new one.

Exercise Three: *The Good Old-Fashioned Outline*

Yes, an outline. But rather than trying to organize thoughts you don't yet have, try outlining a piece that's done, or nearly so.

Remember how to do it?

Start with the Roman numeral I. That's section one of whatever you've written. Then break your section one into subsections (all with titles), and break the subsections down into sub-subsections, numbered (and lettered) as follows: A, 1, a, i. That gives you five levels of meaning—or you can keep going with double lower-case letters. Some word-processing or office computer programs will set this all up for you, if you'd rather have the help.

To outline a piece of work already in existence is to see its form, its structure. Often you'll see blank places where more is needed, or find sections you can't seem to find a label for. More often, you'll see the way a certain section wanders into subcategories rarer and rarer, further and further from the trunk of the tree that is the essay.

Remember for this exercise that we're using the outline as a tool of form rather than a tool of preparation, an event of organization that takes place *after*, not before, the drafting.

Exercise Four: *Diagramming*

Diagramming can have the same effect as late-draft outlining, without imposing the tree shape of a formal outline.

Here's the exercise: Analyze the structure of several of your finished (or "finished") works. Pick an essay that works well, and pick one that you consider a failure. Can you diagram both? Which is easier to get a shape for? John McPhee has described the shape of his piece of literary journalism "Travels in Georgia" as a lower-case e. He starts in the middle of the story, circles back to an earlier point in the time frame, works his way back to the middle, then continues on to the end. Ladders, jagged mountains, snakes after eating, cell phones flipped open then closed, smoking chimneys—any shape might apply, and whatever shape you see will help you evaluate the work at hand.

Let me make a try with this book.

Okay. I've just closed my eyes for a few seconds and seen a staircase. Definitely a cliché, but useful: step-by-step instruction, with a steep incline. And seeing the book that way, if only for the moment, gives me a tool to go back and evaluate my success chapter by chapter. Is the incline really there? Are there any gaps in the stairs for readers to fall through?

CLASSICAL STRUCTURE

Hollywood screenwriters make much of classical three-act dramatic structure, and in fact, most screenplays and ultimately most movies follow the formula closely (and, as it turns out, most stories of all kinds, from jokes to cocktail anecdotes to *Moby-Dick*). If a script for a two-hour movie is one hundred twenty pages long, the first thirty will comprise Act I, the next sixty Act II, the final thirty Act III. Act I sets up the characters and story, gets things moving along, introduces the problem our character faces, only comes to a close after a "plot point" comes along, some big moment in the story that changes the direction of things. Act II follows that new direction, putting obstacles in the path of the main character, who seeks a solution to the problem introduced in Act I and complicated by the plot point. Act II ends after another "plot point," an even bigger moment in the story, a point of no return. Act III resolves the story, shows the change and growth of the main character, solves or accommodates the problem set up in Act I, offers a denouement, or "untying." And then the curtain falls.

Something about this structure seems to be innate, as if it arises from human nature. It's been used forever, mostly unconsciously, and can be found across cultures in all kinds of storytelling and drama: rising action, action rising even further, climax, falling action. Notice that even its definition forms an arc. Some scholars have compared the form to male sexual experience—a point to ponder, and well taken; is the ideal structure for a female writer something different? More enveloping? Less penetrative?

Anyway. In its simplest statement it's this: beginning, middle, and end. In a way, that's all you ever have to say about structure. Some short pieces might be seen as just ends, with the other acts implied, or just beginnings, or just middles. But every scene has a beginning, middle, and an end—every section, every paragraph, every sentence, really. Certainly every life.

Have you seen the movie *Million Dollar Baby*? If not, go rent it and watch it before you continue reading, because I'm going to give away the plot.

Okay. Clint Eastwood plays a crusty old boxing coach who operates out of his own failing gym. That's the set-up: action in a gym, character actors, the usual sidekick, nothing too promising for the old coach, except this one boxer who's on his way to the championship. He's dissatisfied with Clint's character's coaching. That's the problem, and it comes within the first ten minutes of the movie. There's also this woman who insists on coming to the gym and wants Clint to coach her. Forget it! He ain't gonna coach no dame!

But she keeps coming around and coming around. And then Clint's boxer *fires* him. Clint's at loose ends. One fine day, he watches her hitting the bag all wrong but with real heart, and bang, he changes his mind. That's plot point one. He's going to be her coach. He's going to make her a champ.

Act II is consumed with her development, her trajectory to the championship fight. Obstacles? You bet. She has to beat fighter after fighter, overcome obstacle after obstacle, that is, and she does, getting better and better at the sport along the way, finally getting the golden invitation to the championship, against a fighter known to be dirty, dangerous.

But she's got heart! She's going to win! We watch her dominate in the ring. She's a female Rocky! Boom, boom! So gratifying. Coach and boxer, soaring to new heights. End of round four, our fighter is walking back to her corner, all but triumphant, when the opponent cold-cocks her from behind. Our fighter falls, hitting her head on the stool in her corner, and *breaks her neck*. Plot point two. She's paralyzed. It's horrible. It's a point of no return.

In Act III, Clint doesn't abandon her, but spends all his time at the hospital. You almost think it's going to be a love story, and, well, it is in a way. He sees she's going to be more than unhappy in her new condition. She's never going to walk or talk again, much less box. He pulls the plug on her. That's the climax. Quickly thereafter, the action unwinds, and the film is over. Fade to credits.

Go see some movies. Use your watch. Plot point one should turn up at about a half hour. Plot point two an hour later. Read some novels. Can you find this structure in each chapter, each book? How symmetrical is its appearance in the work of various favorite authors? Read some memoirs: The structure will be there, whether out front or subtly. Open the book at about one-third. Open it at about two-thirds. Are big developments in the story nearby?

Read *The Kiss,* by Kathryn Harrison, an intelligent, disturbing, book-length memoir. In Act I, Kathryn is a college girl whose long-lost father has reappeared. That's the problem. She goes to see him. Upon their separation, he kisses her inappropriately, a soul kiss, if brief. That's plot-point one, which brings us very exactly to one-third of the narrative. The action has been turned around. Act II is all about our memoirist trying to deal with that kiss and the frequent appearances of the father, wanting more. At exactly two-thirds of the way through the page count—nothing approximate about it—the memoirist and her father have sex for the first time. Point of no return. The plot points are both perfectly organic to the main subject of the story; in fact, they *are* the story. Act III is all about Kathryn getting out from under the weight of the transgression, the climax coming when she says, in effect: No more!

EXERCISE FIVE: *Looking for Classical Structure*

This will be fun. Go in search of classical three-act structure. Start by examining narratives other than your own: TV shows, movies, the stories told at the water cooler (1. "Mr. Grumbly saw me eating at my desk. He said, 'What do you think you're doing?' 2. I said, 'Saving time?' He said, 'You're fired!' 3. I guess it's time to look for a job"). That arc is everyplace.

Now—and this is the exercise—look for it in your own work. If it's not already there in obvious ways, see if you can start to put it there, use it to analyze the effectiveness of your structure. Sometimes, you can't find any plot points at all. That's not good. Sometimes, you'll find that Act I is, say, 90 percent of the whole; Act II is 7 percent; Act III is 3 percent. Or that a given act is missing altogether, often Act III. Or that after the climax, after the story has been told complete, you still have twenty pages. Revise.

 *The artist is the one who never gets it right.*
—*Mose Allison*

EXERCISE SIX: *Somewhere, Over the Rainbow*

Pick an essay you want to work on. Draw an arc, preferably an enormous one, perhaps on a blackboard. The beginning of the essay is represented by the left terminus of the arc, the end at the right. Your rising action occupies the left half of the curve to roughly one-third, where something important should happen; continued rising action (through a series of setbacks or obstacles in your story) occupies the middle third of the arc, ending with something even more important happening. The story climax should come very near the right-hand terminus of your arc. That takes care of the narrative.

But exposition can fall along an arc, as well. And so can mood. And idea. And so can all the many layers of your essay, including meaning.

Plot the points of your arc for as many layers of your work as you can identify: individual characters, time frame, objects, events, subject, argument, motifs, and so forth. How much of any one category falls all to one side? How many items of structure find a start at the left but never make it to the right? How many characters fall only on one side of the arc? How much time is contained in each section? Where does, say, your father's Mercedes appear, if that Mercedes is an object important to your story? How many layers can you get to move all the way from left to right—rising, then falling?

EXERCISE SEVEN: *Another Way to See It*

I used index cards to write my English papers in high school. Mrs. Potts insisted. I got very elaborate, with color coding and fancy numbering systems, and got very neat, saving quotations, cataloguing facts and figures.

I use cards a different way now, as yet another way to make the abstract structure of an emerging essay (or book) more concrete. I don't use the cards exactly the same way twice: sometimes each section of an essay gets a color and a caption; sometimes each scene within a section gets its own card. Computer files work just as well, or sticky notes (real or virtual) or charts in chalk on sidewalks. You can take scissors to a manuscript, free the scenes and sections from their confines, rearrange, rethink.

But I like cards because I can juggle them easily, move scenes around, move characters, get a sense of structure before I begin, and then again after I've done some drafting. I don't want to get too organized too fast; I want to leave room for surprises. But when the time comes, there's nothing I love better than to see the shape of my essay laid out across my studio floor.

EXERCISE EIGHT: *A Stroll Through the Junkyard*

Sometimes to build a château at the end of the dream highway, you might have to borrow a few bricks from all the wreckage along the way. Often, we've said things right, long ago, but for whatever reasons, these morsels remain buried among the detritus. Why not take a long walk through your junkyard of exercises, essays, e-mails, stories, blogs, poems, and ponderings, all those pieces that didn't quite make wholes?

Choose a foul-weather day, or a day when your current project seems unbearable. Fix your favorite beverage, put on old clothes. Now, scour your computer files or your actual file cabinets for defunct or abandoned projects, dig up old notebooks and journals, print out memorable e-mails from your travels. Gather a big pile of boards and old doors, bathtubs and electric cable.

And start a brand new computer file, new notebook, or even a paper file-folder. Skim carefully through your old work extracting a few sentences, words, or images that stand out as well crafted, moving, evocative—a glass doorknob here, a pink toilet there. Try not to think about the overall merit of the piece. Instead, feel good about how far you've come. But dig. Be discriminating. Limit yourself to two or three objects per piece. If there's nothing valuable, back in the Dumpster it goes.

In Conclusion

Now, to give this chapter a false arc, a forced structure, a pair of tired bookends, I might go back to the old farm in Maine where I saw the fabulous and individual houses of back-to-the-land hippies. I might tell you the story of the cabin Bob and Mike and I built on Mike's land after that, and about the trouble we had with our girlfriends there—they didn't share our thrill at sleeping under the stars and cooking in the rain and living without money.

I could tell you about how when I moved back to Maine as a new college professor nearly twenty years later, one of my first thoughts was to go find that place. I perused maps till I found a town name I remembered, then inspected the blue shapes that represented water until I found the distinctive *W* shape of the pond we'd swum in, bathed in, drunk from.

I drove alone two hours, dreaming of the glorious castle we'd built, the hand-chinked logs, the hand-dug and free-poured cement pylons, the windows salvaged from a barn, the well we'd dug, the garden we'd grown, the fun we'd had, the trouble, too: pervert neighbor man, chopping accidents, too much drinking, a rumble with locals in a mill-town bar, the breakup of first Mike and his girl, then Bobby and his, then me and mine, the big snake I'd inadvertently slept on all the night of my twentieth birthday and found crushed flat beneath my sleeping bag next morning. We finished the cabin, slept in it maybe two nights, then headed back to college, hell of a summer.

None of us had ever returned, not yet.

Oh, the newly minted Professor Roorbach took a number of wrong turns on back roads, but then there was the familiar pond (was it really so small?), there was the dirt road (so steep?), there was the stone wall. I hiked in along our overgrown right-of-way, slower and slower steps, suddenly confronted with sorrow: lost youth, lost days, lost friends, lost idealism. The cabin was there, pitched by frost off two of its pilings, leaning dangerously, full of beer cans and painted with Satanist or romantic or pornographic graffiti, all the glass smashed, all the doors stove in, the roof gaping. The chimney at least was still glorious and gloriously eccentric. It was made from an assortment of groovy rocks we'd found on hikes—a chunk of quartz, a long shape of feldspar, a good and genuine fossil. We'd used thick mortar, and still impressed in it—just where the chimney narrowed—was my girl Annie's handprint.

Really, I should never have gone back.

CHAPTER ELEVEN
GETTING PUBLISHED

*Writing is a hard way to make a living, but a good
way to make a life.*

—*Doris Betts*

After many seasons of study and contemplation (sitting lotus on my hummock of rejection slips), after years of talking to and dealing with scores of editors (and after being an editor myself), I have discovered something momentous—nothing less, ladies and gentlemen, than the secret to getting published.

Are you ready?

Here it is: write something good.

That's it. Simple as that. Good writing. That's all an editor wants. And the fact that every editor is going to define that simple phrase in a different way is not a problem, not really. If you're making good writing—fresh, important, well-made, compelling, top-of-the-line stuff—someone out there is going to want to publish it.

As for the next question (and the really important one)—how to *make* good writing—the answer is practice. A good start would be back in chapter one, though I don't blame you if you turned to this chapter first.

Listen to me: Publication in, say, *The New Yorker*, is the equivalent of singing with the Metropolitan Opera. And the Met's singers—even the ones in the chorus—got there because of years of practice, years of voice exercises, years of rejection and invisibility, years of the well-intentioned doubts of friends and family, years of making luck happen, years of what adds up to something noble and underappreciated in our culture: apprenticeship. (See appendix C for my essay on the subject.)

Many of my adult students come to my workshops wanting to know how it's done; unfortunately, by *it* they mean publication, not writing. They want to publish, and they want to publish *now*. And new writers say the darndest things! "If *The Atlantic* doesn't take this essay, I'm going to burn it."

Get the matches out!

"I've rewritten this thing twice, and I'm getting sick and tired of it."

Twice? Wow! Here's your Pulitzer!

"People just don't understand my work."

Ah, poor thing, but isn't it a writer's job to make herself understood? As my late, grumpy mother used to growl to us kids when we'd whine and complain about the unfairness of life: "I feel for you, but I can't quite reach you."

APPRENTICESHIP

Good writing is, among many other things, an illusion. The primary illusion is of ease. We read a beautifully constructed book with pleasure and admiration, forgetting that the writer had to sit down day after day for a year or two years or more (often many more) to do the job. We forget—because it's the writer's job to make us forget—all the drafting, all the false starts, all the seamlessly incorporated suggestions and corrections of editors and other readers, all the self-doubt, all the projects started and never finished, all the manuscripts in drawers, all the learning, all the patience, all the writerly reading, all the study, all the practice: the apprenticeship. So we read the book and feel cowed. How'd she do this? And worse, we get the idea that we ought to be able to sit down and write a beauty on the first try. Should be easy: ten pages a day for thirty days is a book.

Good writing occurs not in bursts of inspiration (although inspiration can't hurt) but in time so slow it feels like geologic time. Ten thousand years is nothing, a moment. A million years is but a day. That some good writers write terrific drafts fast is a function of experience, of many years' hard work in preparation, and rarely of raw talent, though there's that, too, the bastards.

It's easy to get devotedly stuck to a single piece of writing—I've had students in my summer workshops tell me that the work they'd submitted had been workshopped fifteen times. I see student drafts that were written twenty years past. In these cases, learning has stopped. In these cases, writing has stopped. Instead of seeing that dead essay as a step toward the next and the next and the next (perhaps all on the same subject—the subject, at least, being very much alive), the dead essay becomes the end point, propped up on a morgue slab with unhelpful tubes still in its nose, reluctant writing teachers leaning over it like priests and morticians.

If you're that devoted to a single piece of writing, it will be very hard to hear criticism. I have been known to spend hours on a critique for a student. And nothing's more familiar or depressing than this response: "Oh, that's just what my other teachers said!"

New writers like this aren't listening. They are not honoring their own apprenticeships. They're shopping around for a teacher who'll say the work is good. And when that doesn't happen, they leave workshops furious: *Roorbach and his crowd are just as stupid as the last bunch.* And go on to blast the editors and magazines who reject their work: "*Tin House* publishes crap. It's just their friends they publish."

"It's all connections," people like to say.

Well, connections are helpful, but connections only help if the work is good.

Okay, you've gone to every writers conference in the universe, you've shaken hands with Annie Dillard, you've slept on Stephen King's lawn, you know every other writer in creation, and they love you and want to help you. Now make your move: write something good.

Luck is a fine thing for a writer, too, but take note: good writing creates luck. Good writing is the ultimate connection.

EXERCISE ONE: *Write Something Good*

Yes, write something good.

Preferably really good. As Donald Hall says, take all the time you wish. Ten years would not be unusual. Twenty is fine. If you're already eighty years old, don't worry, your life experience will surely speed things up. But the assignment is the same: write something good. When you've done so, bring your draft back and we'll talk about it.

HOMECOMING

Ah! You're back. Wow, we missed you. But you look great. Not a spare pound after all those years! And dreadlocks, that's awesome! Love the long white beard!

And what's this? A draft of something good. And man, it really is good. Let's go public with it—but not to editors, not quite yet.

EXERCISE TWO: *Going Public*

The Latin root of publish is *publicare*, which means "to make public." In that light, of course, it's possible for anyone to publish. The Internet is full of embarrassing stuff people want to make public. So are bathroom walls. One of the beauties of magazines and books and more and more Web sites is that they define a particular public, a particular group of readers that the editors feel they know the tastes and interests of.

For this exercise, please make ten copies of your finished draft. Pass these out to people you suspect are readers. Your boss. Your neighbor. Your bartender. Your tennis coach. Your pastor. That guy at the gas station who's always talking about books. Your dentist.

Your writing circle doesn't count for this exercise, by the way. They're accustomed to taking an editorial role, or perhaps a pedagogical role, often a competitive role. What we're looking for here is plain old readers, ten of them, who'll have your book at bedside, on the kitchen table, in their shelves.

There. You've published yourself.

Phase two is to try to engage each of your readers in a conversation about your work. This might be difficult. Not everyone will even read what you give him. Many people will be mystified. But if you've picked your readers with a little care—people who read other stuff, people who have literary points of reference—you'll get at least some response.

"Oh, pretty good," they'll say.

You boldly answer: "What did you like?"

"I liked the subject," they'll say.

You: "What did you end up thinking it was about?"

"I didn't get it," they'll say.

You: "Well, how much did you understand?"

"I just can't put my finger on it," they'll say.

You: "Let me tell you what I was trying to do."

And so forth, till you've got some information you can use. Of course, the interrogation above will take a lot of guts, depending on your reader, but some version of it will help you understand how you're being read and misread, where you are connecting, where you aren't.

Phase three is to go back to the work at hand and make it answer to your readers. Sometimes a small change or two clarifies some point of meaning and fixes everything. Sometimes, on the other hand, your lawn-mowing guy will have made you see a major flaw. And he'll have saved you from squandering your big chance with that editor you met at Bread Loaf.

Against Polishing

When I think of polishing, I always get the image of some poor slob (actually, myself) buffing and buffing his twelve-dollar shoes. When he's finished, those shoes will shine, all right, but they will still be twelve-dollar shoes.

Polish is insidious. You polish up your essay—put a finish on it—and the surface gets so bright you can't (and don't want to) delve beneath that surface. Your prose becomes reflective, a mirror. You see yourself in it. You actually begin to confuse the writing with yourself. And now there's no way to cut into that writing, no way to smash that veneer, no way to see clearly beneath it.

Polishing is a form of tinkering, and tinkering, for too many new writers, is what revision amounts to. You can spend days adjusting sentences in a first paragraph that ought to be cut altogether. You can spend months moving paragraphs around in a piece that ought to be shelved forever—honorably, of course—perhaps seen as a study for work to come.

Real revision—it's right there in the word—is re-*seeing*.

Exercise Three: *Seeing It Again*

F. Scott Fitzgerald wrote his editor, Maxwell Perkins, with news that *The Great Gatsby* was almost finished. Just one more step: he'd send it along just as soon as he'd rewritten it from memory. This, he felt, would give the work continuity, remove the seams where scenes and characters had been shuffled, removed, replaced, contribute to consistency of voice.

Your assignment is to re-write *The Great Gatsby* from memory. No. But can you imagine? The dedication? The confidence? The results were good, too, weren't they?

I'd start this one by taking a good, finished piece, and placing it in a drawer, or in a computer file directory labeled "resting" or "pause." Work on other things for two weeks, a month, or more.

Then, without referring to the original draft, write it anew, experimenting all the way. Try a radically different voice. Try retelling the big central scene from memory. Shift the position of the camera. Use more summary, or less. Yes, it's a lot of work, daunting to contemplate. But often that's the difference between writing that gets published and writing that doesn't: a lot of work. Often again, it's the person who works the hardest who has the most success.

When you've got a new pile of pages on the old theme, pull out the original draft. What can you use from your re-seeing?

GET OUT THE PRUNING HOOK

Cutting a manuscript is about the most painful thing you can do. Painful, that is, until you do it. Once a chunk of unneeded prose is gone, it's beautiful how fast you forget it. The trick is recognizing what's unneeded. Nothing's more annoying than the first time an editor chops a chunk out of your manuscript. Often, of course, it's the chunk you love most that goes, the sentence that everyone in your workshop praised, the paragraph that brings your mom to tears every time, the passage that contains your title. Working with an editor, though, however annoying, will help you begin to develop an editor's eye: an eye for the extraneous, the unneeded, the gratuitous, the filigree, the frosting, the decay.

An editor at a certain literary magazine once offered to accept an essay I'd submitted. One condition: They only had room for 5,000 words in the next issue, and the piece I'd submitted was 10,000 words long.

What would you do?

At first I was pretty whiny. That was half my essay! And the problem wasn't that the editor and his board didn't like it, just that they didn't have room.

I said no.

Middle of the night I woke up and reconsidered. That essay needed a home, badly. In fact, that essay was a wild child—it was going to be hard to place in the best of circumstances.

But they wanted me to cut it in *half.*

I did the deed.

The brutal chopping required quite a bit of rewriting, of reimagining, but in the end the essay did its job—the same job it had done when longer—with startling economy. And it didn't end up seeming thin, not at all. In fact, while its body was smaller, somehow its soul was bigger. While I cut, I kept thinking I'd restore the original one day for a collection. But now nearly twenty years have passed, and I find I love the cut version, find I can't even remember the original: rather than an assault on a finished product, the cut turned out to be the final step of drafting, and that step of drafting made the essay. I put it in my essay collection, *Into Woods.*

Later I met the editor at a conference and told him thanks, reminded him of our relationship. He said, "Oh, that old trick. We had all the room in the world, but we needed to get you to finish your essay."

EXERCISE FOUR: *Let's Just Suppose*

Pick a favorite draft, something complete and pleasing. Now, pretend the phone is ringing. It's the editor of your favorite magazine. "Love your piece," says she. "Want to publish it." She lets you bubble and enthuse for a few embarrassing minutes, then: "Too long," says she. "We can't publish it unless you cut it in half."

And that's the exercise: Cut your draft in half.

Remember, the original is always there for you to return to—no danger of its disappearing. Do the exercise in the spirit of experimentation. But don't be surprised if the results make you forget all the sentences you cut, forget them forever.

EXERCISE FIVE: *Clear-Cutting*

This is a variation on exercise four, above. Again, I'll ask you pull out a favorite draft. But this time, take it by the ear to a literate friend, perhaps another writer with whom you can exchange the favor of a severe cut.

This is an especially good exercise if you weren't able to get yourself to do the preceding exercise. I certainly understand if you couldn't. Our own work can start to seem inviolable. And this exercise isn't foolproof; even literate friends can be squirrelly about cutting sentences that have been labored over, paragraphs with neat turns of phrase. So be tough. Be arbitrary. Tell your friend that he must halve the word count for you. Yes, fully half must go. For the cutter, it's a fun exercise, a kind of puzzle: what can go without changing the argument, the meaning, the story?

When you have your cut manuscript back, type it up new, just the way your editor asked. Fair warning: You're not going to like it at first, not at all. But type it up as suggested. Next, without looking at your original (no cheating—if you can't remember the old way in the face of the new, that's a good sign that you're on to something), go to work on a revision.

Even if you do end up going back to all or part of your original version, you'll find lessons and suggestions in the cut. Also, you'll have worked with an editor, and that's good practice, too.

WHO WOULD WANT TO PUBLISH ME?

Okay. Now you've got a short nonfiction manuscript (we'll get to books shortly). You've examined the language of it; you've tried it on literate friends; you've cut everything that can be cut. The thing is good—really good. Finally, it's time to start thinking about publication. Where to start?

Most new writers, understandably, decide to start at the top. And why not? One or two out of a billion manuscripts are probably placed this way. *The Atlantic, The New Yorker, Harper's, The New York Times Magazine*—periodicals like these get thousands of submissions a week, tens of thousands a year; manila envelopes fill their hallways. But try. It's nice to have a high-class stack of rejection slips to get you started. And it's good to exorcise delusions of grandeur, if you've got them.

At the other end of the confidence spectrum is the writer who assumes *no one* will want her work, the talented writer who doesn't send anything out at all. But editors do need good work to fill their pages. And in the end, you can't get published if you don't get your stuff out there.

Given that, rejection is no disgrace. By the time most good writers start to publish work regularly, they've amassed many hundreds of rejection slips, in all shapes and sizes. Good manuscripts have been known to rack up dozens of rejections before finding a home. Good manuscripts have been known to never find a home (but I doubt many).

Don't go into the submissions game thinking you're going to make tons of money. In fact, don't go in thinking about money at all. This is art we're talking about, not a job. Your payoff will be an audience. If a check eventually turns up—small or large—well, that's just gravy.

A Tidy Chart

Overconfident, under-confident, there's really only one place to start when it comes to getting published: reading. Of course, you've been reading all along, reading your whole life. So think about it. What magazines and journals are your favorites? Who has published excerpts from your favorite books? A magazine that publishes work you love is more likely to be sympathetic to your work than a magazine that publishes work you can't fathom.

Avoid the amateur's error of sending out blind to magazines you've never heard of because they pay a little more or have interesting names or convenient submission dates. You need to be familiar with your target publications. You need to know that your work fits in with their format, their focus, their taste. You really need to like what they do.

EXERCISE SIX: *Another Library Mission*

Once again, I'm sending you to the library. But by now you've scheduled a regular library night, so this will be easy. Take a break from your other research one visit and use the time to peruse literary and other magazines. (Generally, the bigger the library, the bigger the collection.) We'll still try for the appropriate big, commercial magazines. But let's line up some backups.

The exercise is to find ten or twenty or more literary or other magazines that for whatever reason—layout, authors, apparent philosophy, genre balance, literary quality, good paper, gut instinct—you like. Make this an ongoing investigation, and over months and years you'll start to have a real knowledge of what's out there and who's publishing what. More importantly, you'll start to know where the kind of stuff you like is appearing.

Make a tidy chart. Or a sloppy one, if that's your style. List editors' names. List addresses. Put together a long catalog of magazines you like, with notes about the kinds of work each magazine seems to publish and which magazines seem right for specific manuscripts of your own.

EXERCISE SEVEN: *Volunteer*

Many little magazines and small publishers and reading series take on interns, a kind of formal apprenticeship with young people, usually recent college grads or college kids on summer break. Some of these positions pay a little, many pay nothing. If you can afford to take such a position, by all means do it—you'll learn so much about publishing that can be applied to your own search for publication. You may even find a profession.

For other writers, perhaps especially for people who've retired, there are also ample opportunities to simply volunteer, as manuscript screener, grant writer, office assistant, what have you. Take a look around, get on the Internet, ask everyone you see: What are the various literary enterprises in your area? Which ones need help and could use your free hours?

EXERCISE EIGHT: *Internet Night*

Most literary and other magazines have a Web site now, some of them even publishing solely on the Web. Take an evening and make a focused search for sites related to the magazines you found in the library, and for new sites, new ideas for putting your work forward.

SUBMITTING YOUR WORK

Probably you've already got your *Writer's Market,* or you've signed onto Writers Market.com and other helpful Web sites, so you know how to prepare your submission: simple cover letter; self-addressed, stamped envelope (SASE); manuscript clearly typed or printed out—no fancy fonts, no tiny fonts, no faint print—name and address on the manuscript. And that's it. Nothing else. No photographs, no long explanations, no so-so manuscripts (you know when your writing's not very good; people you trust—teachers, friends, classmates, and often you yourself—have told you so), no dumb jokes, no résumés, no large-denomination bills, no bullshit.

Kristen Keckler was an editor of the Katherine Anne Porter Prize contest at the University of North Texas Press, and she offers a parody of the all-too-common *awful* cover letter, addressing it to the famous editor of a fictitious literary magazine:

> Howdy, Frank!
>
> Allow me to introduce myself! Ron Spoolhead, at your service. After a successful career as a Veterinarian (large animal, they call me Dr. Thoroughbred), I've recently retired (except for some part-time consulting work—got to keep up with the wife's shoe habit) and devoted my life to writing (with time, of course, for a few holes of golf and trying to keep up with my six beautiful, sometimes mischievous, but always delightful grandkids).
>
> I'm enclosing a chapter of my memoir-in-progress, which chronicles the coming-of-age of a rural boy in Horntootersville, New York, one marked by the hardships of poverty, illness, and a hard drinking father and devoted mother.
>
> Although I've never read your magazine, I'm enclosing a chapter and think it's the perfect fit for "The Clever Metaphor," as I'm known in these parts for a clever phrase or two. (My motto: always leave them laughing.) I think you'll enjoy "The Trick of a Lifetime," a humorous rendering of a young man's (the young me!) adventures through magic; of the many surprises he pulls his hat includes casting a spell over the preacher's daughter, and eventually enjoying the marriage of luck, dedication, and promising never to disappear. My buddy and colleague, Dr. Feelers (I kid you not), you've probably heard about him. He's a renowned in the field of equine neurosurgery and an excellent writer (always has the ladies in tears with his speeches at the annual Equine Health Convention) and well, he believes the chapter is ready for the world.
>
> I have published various articles and stories in such fine magazines as "The Putter's Bogey," "Hoof and Fur," (the Official Newsletter of the Degenerative Equine Illness Asso-

ciation), and most recently, had a (quite persuasive) letter featured in my country club's monthly newsletter concerning the quality of salmon served in the clubhouse (I conducted thorough scientific research and thankfully, they have committed to purchase fish known for lower mercury content.) I am not enclosing a SASE, since I doubt you'll need it (wink!) and I will eagerly await to hear you're comments on my writing. I just know your magazine will be the magic wand (pardon the pun!) I've been waiting for.

Cheerio,

Dr. Ron

PS ... I am enclosing my business card for my part-time consulting business (providing medical opinions for prospective horse owners.) When you're ready to discuss my essay, I'm available on the cell listed, though I'd ask you to avoid calling me at home because I've been hiding my lit'ry efforts from the missus (not an easy task, nosy woman!) in hopes to surprise her with my acceptance. We'll also want to talk about eventual publication of my book. Hopefully in time for the holidays! Enjoy!

How many problems can you find with this letter? Though it may seem far-fetched, editors receive letters peppered with sentences like these all the time. First, you probably noticed that the tone is excessively chummy. Would you send a prospective attorney a letter like this? The editor is not your friend (unless, of course, he really is), will not laugh at your jokes, does not want to get to know you at this stage; he simply wants to determine if your work is appropriate for his magazine. "Howdy" and "Cheerio" are a no-no, but just as damaging are the phrases "think it's a perfect fit" and "think you'll enjoy" (or even, "hope you'll enjoy"). Telling an editor what to like reveals your insecurity. You sound like a waiter at a bad restaurant dropping a sloppy plate of beans: Enjoy!

What else do you see? The wordy and clichéd descriptions of both the memoir and essay are unnecessary, even mistrustful, as if the editor won't get what you're doing without your explanations. Best to let your work speak for itself.

How about the publication list? It's often helpful to list a few previous publications, if you have them, but only if they're relevant. Literary journals aren't likely to be interested in your successful forays into professional newsletters and trade publications. Letters to the editor just don't count. List a publication only if it's similar to the journal you're submitting to.

"Eagerly waiting for your reply" is needy and, again, mistrustful. Requesting the editor's comments is not only unrealistic but rude. These are incredibly busy people, often working volunteer hours. An editor will not take you more seriously if you claim you've devoted your life to writing—that should be a given—and though he probably loves kids, he doesn't need to hear about *your* grandkids (or if you're a kid yourself, what school you go to, what your parents do).

This letter is stuffed with grammatical errors—how many can you spot? A poorly written cover letter promises one thing: a poorly written submission. And a letter like this would most likely result in your pages hitting the rejection bin without a look. Can the editor do this? Of course he can, and he will. Can an underling do this? Yes, and very likely, your letter will first fall in the hands of a reader, very likely a college student or intern, someone smart and dedicated and overworked, desperate to find something wonderful to pass along.

So, let's say Ron's essay *is* really good. A veterinarian magician's memoir has some inherent interest, no? Okay, chances are that Ron's essay is as painful to read as his cover letter. But the point is that you, or Ron, shouldn't nix your chances before the essay is even out of the gate.

Your letter will be individual—there's no real formula to follow. But let's let Ron try again:

> Dear Mr. Bookly:
>
> Please consider "How to Saw a Horse in Half: Confessions of a Veterinarian Magician" for publication in *The Clever Metaphor*. And thanks for "Bait for a Shallow Stream," by Curt Razor, featured in your summer issue. I especially appreciated Razor's rendering of the Oregon landscape, the way it tempered the harsher vista of the author's addictions.
>
> This is a simultaneous submission, with your forbearance, and of course I will promptly notify you if I place it elsewhere. I've enclosed an SASE. Thank you for your time and consideration.
>
> Sincerely,
>
> Ronald Spoolhead

Ah, much better. This letter is concise and provides the editor with only the necessary information. Instead of boasting about himself, Ron demonstrates that he's familiar with *The Clever Metaphor*. His thoughtful impression of Curt Razor's piece asserts his authority as a quality reader. He thanks the editor and quickly wraps it up, using the same name that's on his piece—no nickname, no formal title. Oh, and notice the new title he's given his work. Much better. It gives the editor just a hint of what the piece will be about. Good titles can do a lot of hard work, quickly and subtly. And a good, modest, professional letter has at least put Ron in the running.

EXERCISE NINE: *Submit*

You've got a great piece of writing to show. And you've got a great list of magazines made up for that specific work: all the addresses, editors' names, submission windows. Time to start mailing.

I like to send things on a given day each month, whatever's come home to roost, whatever I've just finished. Regular first-class mail. Not a penny too much postage. Plain manila envelope, 9×12. A brand-new piece I'll send first to a dream publication. After a month—unlikely I will have heard back in that time—I send to another. After six months, I'll have put it out to six places, and will have probably begun to get some rejections back. I keep my spirits up knowing that it's already elsewhere, and come my monthly send date, it's going to be somewhere new again.

I keep a chart, cross off the magazines as the piece comes back: their loss. I'll keep going till the piece has been twenty places, thirty, forty. As long as I still believe in it, I keep it out there. Occasionally, I've done a mass mailing, but this invites depression: thirty envelopes out, wait six weeks, thirty envelopes back.

Some magazines don't appreciate simultaneous submissions. Fine, if they can get back to me quickly. One well-known publication kept a story of mine *two years* before rejecting it with an apologetic letter outlining the story's flaws and inviting resubmission. This was kind, and welcome, but I'd long since given up on them. Apparently they hadn't noticed my letter pulling the submission, hadn't noticed the piece in *The Atlantic*, hadn't noticed it in the O. Henry Prize anthology, hadn't noticed it in my Flannery O'Connor Award-winning book *Big Bend*, all of which happened in their long rejection cycle.

I'm sorry, but even for the kindest editor of the best literary magazine, I can't wait two years. I can't even wait six months. In my humble opinion, six weeks or two months is plenty of time if a magazine insists on exclusive submission. If they don't, if I can make multiple submissions with their permission, they can take as long as they like, as long as they need. For my part, I'll let them know if I manage to place the work elsewhere. That just seems like good business on both ends.

Remember—your work is good. Don't let rejection bring self-doubt. Luck is involved at every step of the process. When your essay comes home, brush it off, clean it up, make a new copy, write a new letter, and send it back out.

Ping-pong, my writer friend Bob Kimber once called it. You shoot a manuscript out, they shoot it back; you whack it back out there, it comes back. As long as you have done the honest work and know that what you're offering is good stuff, you have every reason to play the game. Don't get discouraged. Pip. Pop. Keep writing. Pip. Pop. Keep writing more and better. Pip. Pop. Retire any manuscript that time and experience begins to show you is inferior, but keep in the game a manuscript you know is good. Pop. Pip. Pip-Pop.

You may also have found magazines that accept e-mail submissions, or Web sites that only accept work via e-mail. The game is the same: ping-pong. But it's cheaper and much easier, if you've got the proper Internet skills.

Keep the work out there, in whatever form.

EXERCISE TEN: *Collect Rejection Slips*

No really, I'm serious: collect rejection slips. This will toughen you up. Learn that a rejection from one of the great magazines of the world (or from any magazine) is not an indictment of your work, not a message that you should hang your head and quit writing. It's just not. It's only a rejection. Your envelope may well have been opened by a college student interning for a summer, seen by no one else.

Start a file of rejection slips. I've got one several inches thick.

I love my rejection slips. I've even started thinking of what I'm doing when I submit manuscripts as *collecting* rejection slips. That way, I'm always successful.

If you get back personal letters, start a separate file of those: good bets for the future.

If you get an acceptance, wow! Have a party. Stay out all night.

Then in the morning, two fat aspirins and back to work.

Well, after several months we got the first copies of the book in the mail, and Mimi immediately grabbed one, took it to the bedroom, and read all afternoon. When she came out she looked appalled. "Well, what do you think?" I said to her, and she said, "It looks different in print." "That's what they always say," I told her.

—Russell Baker

PUBLISHING YOUR BOOK

Yes, when it comes to book publishing, you probably need an agent. And yes, agents are as hard to get as publishers, or harder. Again, there has been plenty written on the subject of getting published, and I'll assume you've read quite a bit of it. I wouldn't necessarily believe every word of what you find, especially if every word is negative, pessimistic, doom and gloom. Because fresh books do get sold, agents do connect with new writers, and editors do make offers on unagented books. If you haven't and want to, hie thee to a bookstore or library, get on the Internet; you'll have no trouble finding titles, sites, and blogs to help in your quest to add your title to the tens (and even hundreds) of thousands of books published each year in the United States alone.

Nonfiction by established writers on compelling subjects can often be sold on the basis of sample chapters. Sometimes, this sort of work can even be sold on the basis of an outline. Sometimes, on the basis of a conversation. If your last book was an international bestseller, you're good to go. If you know where the missing eighteen minutes of Nixon's White House tape are, you've got a book deal. If you were held captive by terrorists and your image was on TV for two months straight, knife to your throat, you've got a book deal. If you've slept with six presidents and four rock stars and have proof: deal, deal, deal. More prosaic stories will be harder to sell.

Dull writing about prosaic stories will be impossible to sell.

Most memoirs, and, in fact, most books of all descriptions from new writers, need to be completed before the placement campaign begins. Once you've got a good, solid manuscript, read by friends and fellow writers, extensively revised, brought to near-perfection, I'd suggest a letter-writing campaign. Again, you don't want to waste time with editors and agents who aren't going to have any interest in the kind of thing you're doing. One strategy is to find out who edited and who represented the books you like best, the books most like the book you intend to write, or have written. Probably, since you're a reader, you can name ten favorite books right off the top of your head. Well, not just favorite books, but favorite contemporary books. And not just contemporary, come to think of it, but recent books. *Very* recent is best. If you can't name ten recent titles that knocked you out or that in some way bear on your project, you'll need to do a little research. In a big library, there will be millions of titles covering a couple of centuries. The editor of *Walden* isn't going to be able to help you much, even if *Walden* is your favorite book.

But you know the kinds of writers you like. And if you list them to most librarians these days, you'll get a longer (and more informed) list back. Spend your library night with a stack of books around you—you're looking for authors new to you, titles new to you, and, in some cases, publishers new to you. You are looking for literary soul mates.

And go to readings. Most college writing programs have reading series. Go to every event—don't just attend when you know a writer's name. You'll find wonderful new voices, get to meet real people who are doing what you're doing, who've been where you want to go. Attend writers conferences—especially if you're living in an isolated area, or are long since out of school. The focus will be on writing—a good thing—but you'll also get a chance to meet editors, agents, and writers, find people who seem to be operating on your wavelength, make those connections people talk about. And connections in the end are about human relationships, nothing more or less.

Exercise Eleven: *Finding Ten Names*

Okay. I've got you at the library, or at your favorite bookstore, or on the Web. Narrow down a list of books to ten titles that have real affinity in scope, style, subject, ambition, and so forth, to your book or book idea. Don't limit the search in any other way. (One of my grad students, for example, wouldn't consider any publisher not located in New York City, at least not for the first two years of her search, but her project eventually found a prestigious Southern home.) Only two criteria: one, you like the book; two, it has some definite point of connection to your book.

Now comes the detective work: Who's the editor? You'll usually find him or her named by the author in the acknowledgments. Next question: Who's the agent?

If editor or agent or both are not listed in the acknowledgements, try the Internet. Do a search. See what you can find. If all else fails, get your nerve up and call the publisher. You'll get a receptionist. Ask: Who is the editor of such and such book? In a smaller place, the receptionist will know. In a bigger place, you'll be connected to layers of secretaries and assistants and mumbly apparatchiks, perhaps some publicity people, perhaps the guy from permissions, but eventually you'll find out. Next questions: Does that editor still work there? What's the address there? And finally: Who's that author's agent?

Do not call the editor. Do not call the agent. And I would say, at least for the moment, don't e-mail the agent or editor either. Those inboxes are jammed full. And even for the most jaded editor there's still nothing like a nice-looking business envelope with someone's name and address neatly typed, or, better yet, written in your warm, humble, human handwriting.

EXERCISE TWELVE: *Letter Campaign*

Now you've got the editors' names and the agents' names for ten terrific books, ten books all of which have some bearing on your own completed project or proposal. (And your own project is *good*. Of this, you are confident. If the project is a proposal for a book not yet written, you are confident that you have the ability to carry the project out and that you have the credentials to prove you can carry it out.)

Write up a description of the project. Get it in one paragraph—one smashing, fascinating, elegant, urgent, startling, fresh paragraph that not only presents the idea but shows what a terrific writer you are. Try this paragraph on a bunch of friends. Do they understand your project? Or do they end up with lots of off-the-mark questions? Keep writing until anyone who reads your letter looks up at you and says, "Wow! Where can I get this book?"

Only then, make neat and businesslike letters (called "query letters") containing your paragraph and the briefest introduction of yourself

("I'm a dentist with four kids. I write at night"). Do not lie. Do not stretch the truth. Do not say anything extra.

Add one more paragraph at the beginning, written with utmost sincerity and from the bottom of your heart, something like this: "I've just finished reading Acne Bonbon's *Life of a Chocolate Addict*. It's a terrific book—I can still see Acne trying to climb out of those chocolate vats in Switzerland. Your work on that book made me think you'd be interested in my book, *The Ice Cream Diaries*."

Or something. It needs to be true and real. Don't say you loved a book you didn't. Editors are extensively trained in the detection of crap.

End your query letter by offering to send along sample chapters or the complete manuscript, should the editor or agent wish.

Send a similar letter to as many editors and agents as you've found, as many as you want, really. Out of ten editors, three will not reply at all, five will send a form letter saying they only deal with agents, one or two will politely decline in a personal note. But maybe, just maybe, one might ask to see a sample chapter.

Bingo. You have been solicited.

If the first wave peters out, keep going. You can send your proposal to as many editors and agents as you wish until you get some real interest somewhere. The interest—however slight—of an editor can get you the interest of an agent. And if an editor gets interested enough to make an offer, plenty of agents out there will be glad to help you out in the contract process (for 10 or 15 percent—well earned—of any cash that comes in).

And if after fifty or a hundred letters you get no interest at all, don't despair. You've learned a few things, and that's a big part of the game. Don't curse the agents. Don't question the quality of the editors. Instead, question the quality of your project or the presentation you've made of it.

And always, always, keep writing, growing.

THE ULTIMATE ASSIGNMENT

Publication isn't, I know, the real goal of everyone reading this book. Some of you just want to get your stories down for your grandchildren to read, and for their children—a noble ambition. Documents like that are priceless in families. Some of you just want to get your story right for yourself. And that is noble, too. In the end, this is just what Janet Bellweather realized: her writing was meant for her own edification; she didn't really need or want an audience of readers. Some of you—like Janet—are going to be content with writing as a hobby. And that's good, an important fact to know about yourselves.

For others, publication is a kind of hunger, the hunger of ambition. I hope I've helped you see that the only helpful ambition is the ambition to write something good, something that will satisfy readers unknown to you in both predictable and unpredictable ways. If your ambition is about the work, the dream of publication won't eat at you, won't make a fool of you. When you finish something good, buy yourself a present. You are a success.

But really it's a great moment when I get a thick envelope in the mail—usually unexpected—and in it is a book or a well-made little literary magazine. I pull out the book and turn it over and over and suddenly recognize the name or the photo (or sometimes even the title); I inspect the magazine essay by story by poem by article till I find what I'm supposed to: a former student, now a friend, whose hard work has paid off.

Someone, in fact, has just sent me a copy of something called *The North Woods Quarterly*, a handsome little journal. It takes me a minute to find out why, but there it is, the leadoff essay: "Krock's Store." Gow Farris is on his way, age seventy. The first chapter of his book has found print. I'm glowing, man.

And this: an e-mail from Mindy Mallow-Dalmation—haven't heard from her in years. She's found an agent for her book, one of the top names in the business, and they're going out *big*. I can't wait to go buy the thing, maybe in a year or so. I'll show everyone I know, read it lovingly, put it on my shelf of books by former students (and, yes, by readers of this book), titles in the hundreds by now, presses large and small, successes every one, no matter what the sales, no matter what the reviews.

Let me know how *you* do.

I like to just make the film, not read the reviews, not follow the box office, put it away and make another film. And then make another film. I find that if you don't like the actual making of the film, you're lost, because that's all there is. The rest of it is too mercurial, and you don't get the pleasure you think you're going to get from the success.
—Woody Allen

EXERCISE THIRTEEN: *Live as a Writer*

Most writers lead double lives. While neighbors are sleeping or trimming the roses or shopping for sheets or taking a drive, we're sitting staring at computer screens or yellow pads. Why? (I'll let you answer that.)

The world of nonwriters conspires to make it difficult to protect writing time, difficult to daydream, difficult to find psychological space to create in, difficult to justify ourselves. (My unamusing neighbor in Maine loves to wag his finger at me and say, "Some of us have to work!")

Rejection is painful and constant. And publication, when it comes, turns out to be emotional and difficult—nothing like what we'd dreamed. Parents don't give us much credit for our successes, much less understand our failures. Children clamor for much-deserved attention of their own. Well-meaning friends say the stupidest things about our work, enemies scoff, certain colleagues seek to minimize our achievements.

Turns out that handling all this is a large part of what being a writer is about. A writer is someone who writes, it's true, but a writer is also someone with a large capacity for suffering. You'll want to cultivate that capacity. Stamina is a writer's first quality. But if you wake up one day and decide all the hours aren't worth it, if you wake up one day and decide never to try another essay again, if you wake up one day and realize writing for you is a hobby and not more—that's okay. No dishonor. Writing something good is very much harder than it looks. And writing makes a really satisfying, soulful hobby—especially if you have an audience of family, friends, and colleagues.

But some of you have a more public vision. Some of you are going to keep at it no matter what. And while you work, I hope you'll keep some things in mind: You don't need to be jealous of other writers. You will be, but you don't need to be. You don't need to feel envy (but you will, you will). Writing isn't a race, or if it is, it's only a race against time, against yourself. And writing isn't professional baseball. You're not trying to fight your way to the one starting position at third base for the Yankees. What you're pushing toward, growing toward, working toward is a place only you can occupy. It's a place waiting for you, and no one can usurp it; no one else can occupy it. All it takes to get there is your hard work.

Here's the final exercise, and it comes along with a fond farewell and best wishes for success: *Write.*

"Into Woods"

"Into Woods" was first published in April of 1993 by *Harper's Magazine*. My editor there was Colin Harrison, a smart guy, now a friend, who had till that time rejected a long parade of my stories and essays, sometimes with encouraging notes, but not always. He read the original draft I'd submitted of "Into Woods" (the working title was "Woods II") and made up his mind to argue for it to his colleagues. Fortunately for me, he prevailed. He phoned then and said, "We're going to publish your piece."

I gasped and giggled and tried to sound cool: "Wow."

"One thing," said Colin. "You have to finish it." He gave me nothing more than that to go on, only this: a deadline, one month hence.

And I sat down with the piece I'd thought quite finished and puzzled and groaned and read and tore my hair and reread till in the middle of a deep, tossing night, one week to go, I had an idea: My dad had just visited my new house in Maine, and we'd just rebuilt the garage. Though the material was fresh—only a couple of months past—it turned out to be what I needed to bring the story full circle.

Thanks, Colin.

—Bill Roorbach

Into Woods, by Bill Roorbach

In a dive near Stockbridge in the Berkshire Hills of Massachusetts, I nearly got clobbered by a big drunk who thought he'd detected an office fairy in the midst of the wild workingman's bar. He'd heard me talking to Mary Ann, the bartender, and I didn't talk right, so by way of a joke he said loudly to himself and to a pal and to the bar in general, "Who's this little fox? From Tanglewood or something?"

I, too, was drunk and said, "I am a plumber, more or less." I was thirty years old, was neither little nor a fox, had just come to work on the restoration of an inn, and was the foreman of the crew. But that seemed like the wrong answer, and too long in any case.

He snorted and said to everyone, "A more or less plumber," then appraised me further: "I say a hairdresser."

"I say a bank teller," his pal said.

I didn't mind being called a hairdresser, but a bank teller! Oh, I was drunk and so continued the conversation, smiling just enough to take the edge off: "Ah, fuck off."

"Cursing!" my tormentor cried, making fun of me. "Do they let you say swears at the girls' school?"

"Headmaster," someone said, nodding.

"French teacher," someone else.

"Guys ...," Mary Ann said, smelling a rumble.

"Plumber," I said.

"More or less," someone added.

"How'd you get your hands so clean?" my tormentor said.

"Lily water," someone said, coining a phrase.

My hands? They hadn't looked at my hands! I was very drunk, come to think of it, and so took it all good-naturedly, just riding the wave of conversation, knowing I wouldn't get punched out if I played it right, friendly and sardonic and nasty all at once. "My hands?"

My chief interlocutor showed me his palms, right in my face. "Work," he said, meaning that's where all the calluses and blackened creases and bent fingers and scars and scabs and cracks and general blackness and grime had come from.

I flipped my palms up too. He took my hands like a palm reader might, like your date in seventh grade might, almost tenderly, and looked closely: calluses and scabs and scars and darkened creases and an uncleanable blackness and grime. Nothing to rival his, but real.

"Hey," he said. "Buy you a beer?"

❊

My dad worked for Mobil Oil, took the train into New York every day early-early, before we five kids were up, got home at six-thirty every evening. We had dinner with him, then maybe some roughhousing before he went to bed at eight-thirty. Most Saturdays, and most Sundays after church, he worked around the house, and I mean he worked.

And the way to be with him if you wanted to be with him at all was to work beside him. He would put on a flannel shirt and old pants, and we'd paint the house or clean the gutters or mow the lawn or build a new walk or cut trees or turn the garden under or rake the leaves or construct a cold frame or make shelves or shovel snow or wash the driveway (*we washed the fucking driveway!*) or make a new bedroom or build a stone wall or install dimmers for the den lights or move the oil tank for no good reason or wire a 220 plug for the new dryer or put a sink in the basement for Mom or make picture frames or ... Jesus, you name it.

And my playtime was an imitation of that work. I loved tree forts, had about six around our two acres in Connecticut, one of them a major one, a two-story eyesore on the hill behind the house, built in three trees, triangular in all aspects. (When all her kids were long gone, spread all over the country, my mother had a chainsaw guy cut the whole mess down, trees and all.) I built cities in the sandbox, beautiful cities with sewers and churches and schools and houses and citizens and soldiers and *war*! And *floods*! And attacks by *giants*! I had a toolbox, too, a little red thing with kid-sized tools.

And in one of the eight or nine toolboxes I now affect there is a stubby green screwdriver that I remember clearly as being from that first red toolbox. And a miniature hacksaw (extremely handy) with "Billy" scratched on the handle, something I'd forgotten until one of my helpers on the Berkshires restoration pointed it out one day, having borrowed the little thing to reach into an impossible space in one of the eaves. Billy. Lily.

My father called me Willy when we worked, and at no other time. His hands were big and rough and wide, blue with bulgy veins. He could have been a workman easy if he wanted, and I knew it and told my friends so.

In my rich suburban high school in Connecticut we were nearly all of us college track, which meant you could take only two shop classes in your career there. First half of freshman year you could elect Industrial Arts, which was an overview: a month of Woods, a month of Metals, a month of Technical Drawing. Second semester, if you still wanted more, you went into Woods I, Metals I, etc.

I loved Woods. I loved hanging out with some of the rougher Italian kids, Tony DiCrescenzo and Bobby LaMotta and Tony Famigliani, all of them proud and pleased to be tracked away from college. I wanted to hang out with Tommy Lincoln and Vernon Porter and Roland Fish, the three black kids in my class, all of them quietly (maybe even secretly) tracked away from college. Wood shop was first period, and it was a wild class. Mr. Schtenck, our little alcoholic teacher, made no effort to control us and often left the shop for the entire period to sit in his car.

The rough kids used the finishing room to smoke pot, the storage room to snort coke. We all made bookshelves and workbenches and record racks and knickknack shelves and lamps and tables and guitar stands and frames for photos of our girls. The year was 1968, so we also made elaborate bongs and stash boxes and chillums and hollowed-out canes and chests with secret drawers. Wood shop (and along with it the very act of working with my hands) took on a countercultural glow, the warm aura of sedition, rebellion, independence, grace.

Sophomore year I signed up for Woods II, which was the advanced course. My guidance counselor, Miss Sanderson (a nice enough lady, very well-meaning, very empathetic—you could make her cry over your troubles every time if you played your cards right), thought I'd made an error on the electives form. "Only one elective a semester, William. Surely you'd like a writing course! Journalism! Or how about Occult Literature?"

"Woods II," I said, flipping my hair. I had to get parental permission to take Woods again and thought a little note with my mother's neat signature would be easy to snag, but it was not. "Why do you have to reinvent the wheel?" Mom said, one of her phrases, something of a non sequitur in this case, her meaning being *someone else will build the furniture*. Her next question was, "What kind of kids are in that class?"

Dumb kids, Mom. Mostly Italian kids and blacks and, of course, Alvin Dubronski (the class moron) and Jack Johnsen (the plumber's kid!) and me.

My dad thought it was fine, especially with the alternative being literature courses where who knew what kind of left-wing occult hippie double-talk Mrs. Morrisey would tell you!

So into the wood shop again, every day first period (if I wasn't late for school; by that time I was hitchhiking to avoid the uncool school bus). I was the only college-track kid taking Woods II, maybe the only college-track kid who had ever taken Woods II, though the other kids got to take it semester after semester. And I got peer-pressured into smoking pot in the finishing room and occasionally even into blowing coke in the storage room, always a sweet, nerve-jangling prelude to another round of boring college-track classes.

One day when I was in the storage room with my high-pressure peers, (and the two smartest kids in Woods II, maybe in school, both destined by their blackness for bad times in Vietnam) Roland and Tommy, fat Tony Famigliani stuck his head in the door: "The Stench is coming!" But Schtenck was already there, standing in the door. I saw my college-track life pass before my eyes.

"What are you little fuckers doing?"

"We're tasting coke, sir," Tommy said, the idiot, total honesty, as we'd all learned in Boy Scouts.

Florid Schtenck raised his eyebrows clear off his face and said, "Jesus Christ, boys, put it away—you want to get me canned?"

He never looked in the storage room again.

And later that year he stumbled and cut his finger off on the band saw. For two weeks then we had a substitute who made us file all our plans and actually checked them, stood beside us as we drilled holes in our wood or turned bowls on the lathes. It seemed an eternity before Schtenck came back and we could finally fill all the bong and hash-pipe and stash-box orders we'd been sitting on. *Sedition.*

The next year I took Woods II again, having secured special permission from the principal to go along with my parents' special permission and the special permission from Miss Sanderson. Senior year I signed up for the class once more—what the hell—but I don't think I ever got to school in time to attend.

❀

Somewhere in there I stopped being a willing volunteer for my father's list of chores. Now he had to *command* me to help with his corny weekend projects. I had better things to do, things in the woods with Lauren Bee or cruising-in-the-car things with some of the guys in my various garage bands—minor-league dope runs into the Village or actual gigs in actual bars in Port Chester, where the drinking age was eighteen and we could get away with it.

At home things were quiet. Except for my long hair, you wouldn't have noticed that a teen was testing his folks. I was good at talking to my elders, and good at hooking grades without working too hard—college track—and very, very good at staying out of trouble. I was on the student council. I helped with the student newspaper. I went to the homecoming rallies and proms and parades. I memorized the headlight patterns of the town police cars (I still get nervous around those big old Plymouth Furys), could smell a cop from miles away, leagues away, light-years. I had a plan for every eventuality and an escape route from every party.

Weeknights I'd turn in early, out to my room over the garage, wait for the main house to quiet down, then slip out into the night. I was caught only once, coming home about five in the morning with a friend named Melanie. Someone had called me after I'd left, and Dad couldn't find me. He was asleep in my bed when Melanie and I walked in. I was grounded, and here was the punishment: I had to spend the next four Saturdays and Sundays helping him build a playroom in the basement—drilling holes in the concrete for hours to anchor the sills for a Sheetrock wall, running cable for a hanging light over the bumper-pool table, slamming up paneling, churlishly working side by side with my dad and his distinctive smell, Aqua Velva mixed with cigarettes and Head & Shoulders and sweat.

❃

The college track barely got me to college. As part of my desultory rebellion I put off applying until well past all the deadlines, never lying to my folks, never lying to my guidance counselor, but showing all of them the forms ready to go, then just plain old not mailing them. My plan was to play rock and roll and maybe—if necessary—make money working as a carpenter or maybe drilling holes in concrete or maybe making furniture or bongs. Then Miss Sanderson got a list of our school's applicants from one of my supposed top choices, and I wasn't on it. Crisis April already, when most kids were hearing from Colby and Yale and Michigan and the U. of Hawaii.

My trusty guidance counselor got on the phone and found some schools that would look at a late application. She was crushed for me, so crushed she spared my parents the full brunt of my dereliction. At hastily arranged late interviews, admissions counselors never failed to ask why I'd taken Woods II *six semesters straight*. Finally I was accepted by one famously lame school, to which I resigned myself; then, at the last possible minute and by great good fortune, I was put on the waiting list at Ithaca College, where, on August 21, one week before school started, I was admitted into the freshman class.

❈

I never saw my father at work, and he never talked about his work, which I vaguely knew was Executive and had to do with Mobil Oil and was desky and involved meetings and much world travel and made us pretty rich. And because I'd never seen him at work, my natural adolescent impulse toward emulation had little to go on. What to imitate? How to surpass, destroy? What I saw of my valiant dad was his work around the house, and so, emulation gone awry, I set out to be a better home handyman than he'd ever be, the real thing, even, a tradesman.

Two dollars and fifty cents an hour was well known as great money, nearly double what I'd made stocking frozen foods at the A&P during high school. Two-fifty an hour was what truck drivers got, longshoremen, a full hundred rasbuckniks (my father's word) a week. I dropped out of Ithaca College in my junior year (just when most of my buddies were heading off for a year abroad), went back to Connecticut (not my hometown, God forbid, but one nearby), and went to work for an electrician.

Lawrence Berner was a former electrical engineer who'd thrown it all over at age sixty, a theory ace but a fairly clumsy worker, a guy who had actually tossed away everything and left the college track for good. Larry was British and Jewish and unconventional and very charming, all qualities that impressed me. Best of all, he was divorced, the first divorced person I'd ever seen up close. He was filthy of habit—decadent, disgusting (maybe not as bad as my friends at school, but Larry was *old*). He lived in his marital house, wife long gone, and had trashed the place—filled the garage with electrician junk, filled the kitchen with dirty pots and jars and cans and dishes, filled the refrigerator with his important papers (fireproof, he said), filled the bedroom with the most slathery skin magazines imaginable, filled the whole house with take-out cartons, TV-dinner tins, and his own filthy underwear. His living room seemed buried in death.

He paid me $2.50 an hour.

Working beside him (tradesmen often touch—four hands to pull the cable, four arms reaching into a small space, heads together to look into a service panel ... *hey, hold my legs while I lean out over this here abyss*), I'd feel sometimes like I was with my dad. It was Larry's thin hair, maybe, or the Aqua Velva and cigarettes, or just regular old transference. I spent every day beside this parallel-universe effigy of my father, and I was mad at Larry almost always and desperate to impress him.

One day he said I had good hands, and that little compliment was everything—I glowed, I crowed, I told my friends, my folks. I stared at my hands late at night in bars, stared at them for hours, entranced. And my hands got callused, grotesquely calloused, were always covered in cuts and scratches and dings and scabs that I hardly felt. Your knuckles never healed. And Larry mostly worked *hot*, meaning with the power on, because it saved time. I got shocks and blew holes in screwdrivers. I hit my head on rafters and slammed my thumb with hammers and fell off ladders and sliced my fingers (daily) and once even poked a screwdriver hard into my eye. (The blade didn't penetrate the eyeball but rolled past it and into the socket so that old Larry had to pull it out ... and we kept on working.) I drove the truck sometimes, sweet-talked the customers, ate in diners, worked squinting with a Lucky Strike in my mouth. I put in panel boxes and wired 200-amp services and installed a thousand outlets and a million switches. I drilled holes for cable, sawed rafters, snaked wire through walls. I wriggled into crawl spaces, sweated in attics, dug trenches.

I got tired of it. All that *body* work. Like every college-track kid in America, I'd been taught that someone else would do the rough stuff if I'd just use my mind. I went back to Ithaca, pleasing my parents enormously. Suddenly I was a good student—all *A*s, excellent attendance, papers handed in on time—fully engaged in a tough fight against the possibility of being a tradesman, the possibility of taking Woods II for *life*.

But after the college track had run its course, I needed to make money. I failed tests for newspaper jobs (*twenty minutes: neatly type a 500-word story around the following facts ...*), gagged at the thought of ad agencies, moved around the country for a long time, worked with cattle, bartended (which left your hands clean, at least), then landed in New York, where I got the bright idea to put up posters around the Village and SoHo and be a handyman. Independence! I did every sort of odd job for every sort of odd person, moving over the months and years to larger home repairs, leaving town to restore that Berkshires inn, coming back to sub myself out to contractors. I graduated finally to a specialization in kitchen remodels and new bathrooms, getting more and more deeply into it, hiring helpers, wearing suits to estimates, taking ads in fancy magazines, cracking the codes for admittance to the wholesale supply houses, getting good at all of it, twelve years in all, Woods II, until one day I woke up and realized I was about to take out a bank loan to buy a truck and some very expensive tools, about to start looking for a storefront, about to start paying my employees *on the books*. I headed straight to graduate school.

❀

My wife and I spent lots of our free time last summer looking for a house to buy up here in rural Maine (where I teach college), our first, an old farmhouse, we hoped. I kept telling myself that I had an advantage, which was my haphazard twenty-year fund of construction knowledge and restoration experience. I looked up at the beams and poked at the foundations and lifted the vinyl siding and pulled away carpets. I wiggled toilets and pulled on feeds and pushed on all the walls and ceilings. I got in crawl spaces and pried open hatch doors, inspected wiring, eyeballed plumbing, made the real-estate folks nervous.

And sometimes, in light of this commitment, this buying a house on a wee piece of our little planet, I thought about what would happen if the legislature shut down my branch of the University of Maine or what would happen if I didn't get tenure or what would happen if I just couldn't take the bureaucracy anymore and quit. Education presidents come and go, but people always need a plumber or someone to fix the roof, replace rotten sills, plaster the stairway wall. I could build furniture. Or renovate inns. I could take my clean college hands and plunge them into work, open all the old scars, stop being mincy and fastidious, once more revel in goo and slime, get into it: wrestle cable, kick at shovels, stand in the mud all day, hook my leg around ladders in the wind, lay tile, lift toilets and plunge my hand down that reeking fuzzy hole to pull the clog (poor Raggedy Andy one time, usually worse).

❀

My wife and I found a house, bought it, moved in. And immediately my dad, now retired, came up to visit, tools in hand. The two of us got up early the first morning he was here and headed out to the garage, a forlorn little outbuilding about to fall down and stuffed to the rafters with the owner-before-last's junk (mostly pieces of Volkswagens and cans of old bolts and misshapen gaskets and used spark plugs and odd shims and clips). My plan was to leave room to park a car, sure, but to build a wood shop, a work space from which to operate while my wife and I renovate the house (a neglected nineteenth-century quarter-cape with many additions, the newest of which is a porch built in 1953, my own year).

So for hours my dad and I worked. We cleared out and sorted all the junk, ripped down the cardboard that made the walls, stopped to stare, to think, came up with opposite plans, argued, convinced each other; then, having switched sides, we argued again. Finally we jacked up the north side of the garage, replaced the sill, dropped a corner post in cement, took the jack away, rebuilt the wall. Next we shored up the south side, then added wiring, finally installed a metal roof over the leaky old asphalt shingles. We hit our heads and cut our fingers and ripped our jackets. We peed in the woodpile. We argued, mostly about technique and a little about the Education President (who was about to go), but really, I guess, about who was in charge of the work in my garage. And even though Pop was helping me for free, even buying some of the materials, I fumed and fulminated, almost sulked: instant adolescence.

We rebuilt the barn-style sliding door and cut in a window. We ate companionably in the Farmington Diner with sawdust and plain dirt in our hair and new hammer holsters on our belts (the acerbic Down East waitress looked me over, said, "Hi, Professor," and I introduced her to my dad); we went to the dump; we gabbed at the lumber yard; we swung hammers, climbed ladders, cut wood; we gazed at our work a long time in the dark when we were done.

Pop said, "You saved that building," as if I'd done it on my own, and we went on in the house to wash up.

"THE OLIVE JAR"

"The Olive Jar" started as a single scene describing an incident from my childhood. Around this particular scene, one that explains the essay's title (I don't want to give it away), I attempted to build an essay that answered the questions: who was my grandmother, and why did she do the things she did?

As I circled around her tentatively, my lack of authority was obvious to the many editors who rejected the essay. Some saw potential, sent me notes encouraging "focused tightening" and "more of the adult narrator." They were on to something. My elusive mosaic structure asked my readers to do too much work, work I myself wasn't up to doing. And I *had* been avoiding an adult "I" narrator, happy to simply rollick in my childhood persona. I needed to find out what the essay said about the adult me. Why did I want to tell it, and why now? I really had no clue. So I lovingly polished the existing essay as if it were a junked car on my front lawn.

Then one day, mid buff, I noticed something. The essay had a long scene about shopping for my first fur coat with my mother and grandmother. The scene was solid. It was beautiful. I had grown very attached to it. And it needed to go. (The scene belongs, perhaps, in an essay about shopping.) It wasn't until I cut that scene entirely that I began to make real progress, allowing the essay to unfold in more productive directions. I had another family-themed essay I'd completed, and I soon realized that I needed to steal two major chunks out of it and donate them to "The Olive Jar." I was resistant—I didn't want to dismantle one essay for the sake of another, but I went through with the transplant. Afterwards, "The Olive Jar" was a bit improved (and, the donor essay, kaput) but it still wasn't finished, not by a long shot. I was stumped.

So I put the essay out of mind, stashed it in a drawer, and worked on other projects. Every few months, I would visit it (to make sure it was still there!) and see it from a new angle. In the meantime, life went on. My sister had a serious car accident. My husband and I divorced. And my mother and I continued to have more conversations about Grandma. My family, especially my mother and sister, have been very supportive every step of the way. My mother has enjoyed the various drafts of the piece simply because she is my mother. Her biggest concern is always which actress will play her in the motion picture adaptation. (She's decided she would like to play herself.)

After dismantling and rearranging the essay countless times over a four-year period, I finally had a draft I was mildly satisfied with. I asked my fiction writer friend, Amos Magliocco, to give it a read. He said that he wanted to physically "see" Grandma earlier than page seven. This insight spurred one of my most comprehensive revisions and resulted in the version that found a home in *Ecotone* magazine. It took a fiction writer to remind me that essays have characters, too, ones we need to not only circle around, but show. I moved the description up several pages, which caused major structural mayhem (and led to major structural revisions). The resulting narrative finally felt more logical, coherent. It's the difference between a mosaic whose tiles display random bits of sea, fin, tail, seaweed, and a mosaic in which, I hope, the reader can detect the clear likeness of a dolphin—or the "what" the essay is about—swimming through the exposition and scenes of the overall piece. Who knows? Maybe in another five years, the essay will demand a new direction. And if it does, I will be happy to hear its grievances. But for now, here it is:

—Kristen Keckler

THE OLIVE JAR, BY KRISTEN KECKLER

I'm squatting in an olive grove in Montelepre, Sicily, searching the ground for caterpillars. It is quiet except for whistles of Redwings, the clip-clop of horseshoes. Some workers climb up and down ladders shaped like tepees, the letter

A, while others haul baskets on their shoulders. My great-grandfather, Niccolo Riccobono, and his brother Giuseppe survey their trees, discussing the rain. They pause to examine the fruit: unripe green among mottled purple. As Niccolo strokes the silver underside of a leaf, he cocks his head. He glances over his shoulder, sees shadows big as clouds. Three Mafiosi swoop by on horseback, overtaking him. They aim their guns. They shoot Giuseppe, then Great Grandpa, three bullets each, their legs and backs and necks.

I gasp, covering my eyes. The workers scatter, shouting words I don't understand. And as he lies wounded, his blood pooling like *pumudamuri*, sauce, my great-grandfather whispers to his brother: "Are you okay?"

But Giuseppe is dead. When the Mafiosi hear Niccolo, they shoot him once more, through the head.

You see, Niccolo has refused the Mafia's offer of protection. He hasn't paid them off.

My grandmother, as always, ends the story with the sweep of her hand and a cruel, if not practical, lesson. "My father, he shoulda kept his big mouth shut."

Decades later, when my sister loses her keys in the Atlantic Ocean, Grandma wades in to retrieve them. She pushes through the water, her arms like five-pound Arthur Avenue salamis. Kara calls out to her, but Grandma doesn't answer, perhaps because she can't hear over the breaking surf.

Or perhaps because Grandma is dead.

I'm in Texas, sitting on my front porch, listening to my sister's dream. On the edge of my yard, the mimosa tree wears its blossoms like a big pink boa. Kara (Grandma's favorite *picciotta*, little girl) is in Westchester, New York, where we both grew up. We haven't lived in the same place for more than a few months since she was thirteen. I'm five years older. Though we don't look alike (she's blonde, blue-eyed, curvy; I'm brunette, brown-eyed, wispy), I'm always struck by how similar our voices sound, especially over the phone.

"So that's kinda weird, right? I mean, what does it mean?" she asks.

"I guess I'd be worried if Grandma was doing, like, some normal grandmotherly thing. Knitting freaking booties or something."

My sister laughs. We both know it's totally in character for Grandma to be fending off jellyfish and sharks in search of a tangible symbol of freedom.

So I tell Kara my theories. Using the canvas of a dream, Grandma is relaying another one of her stories. We both know that it's got to do with the accident, Kara hit head-on by a school bus: car flattened, jaws of life summoned,

EMT shocked to find her alive. Though she would have several shoulder and knee surgeries, her pretty face was unmarred.

I tell her that ocean waves point to something tumultuous, could be the accident. Grandma is sending her a message, perhaps that she was looking out for her the day of the accident.

"Maybe she's trying to recover something you've lost. I mean, literally, your car, but maybe also something abstract, like courage?"

My sister listens intently, interjecting an occasional supportive "Uh-huh." She's a classic younger sibling, assumes I know more simply because I'm older. An approaching freight train bellows like two notes on the organ played at a giant's funeral. It shakes my porch and briefly drowns our conversation. We pause until it passes.

I usually don't care about other people's dreams, but there's something about my grandmother wandering through my sister's psyche. I can't help but feel spurned, ignored.

When it's quiet, I ask: "Why doesn't Grandma visit me?"

"I dunno," Kara says. "But you're gonna tell me, right?"

"Maybe it's that you're the dreamer," I say, "and I'm just the translator, looking for the answers in our genes."

"Answers to what?" says Kara.

Something the body remembers.

❋

After she sold her dress factory and retired, our grandmother became a compulsive gambler. Every week she boarded a bus full of senior citizens and rode four hours to Atlantic City, New Jersey, hoping to turn her social security check into a jackpot. Her specialty was blackjack, though she also played the slots.

One Friday when I was eight, Grandma called collect precisely at 6 P.M. I accepted the charges.

"Tell your mother I missed the bus," she said. I could hear coins clinking, machines whirring, and she hung up before I could answer. We both knew she didn't miss the bus; she was winning.

The following afternoon, my mother and I fetched Grandma at the bus stop in front of the Yonkers' Nathan's, a hot dog chain on the Central Avenue strip crowded with clothing outlets, furniture stores, supermarkets. Among the throngs of old people, she was unmistakable: a stout woman with a big bosom, 5'7" in heels, wearing a black dress with bright red, yellow, and purple tulips (she always wore dresses, never slacks), plus coral lipstick and too much rouge. She'd been watching for us and hurried to the car with purpose, scattering a flock of pigeons squabbling over a paper cup of french fries.

Grandma had survived a case of spinal meningitis when she was my age, eight. Everyone thought she'd die except her father, who remained by her bedside. Though she recovered, the doctors said she would never be quite right afterwards. Then, when she was eleven, and the Mafia killed her father, she, her mother, and four sisters boarded a boat from Sicily to Ellis Island. She never returned to school, working in textile factories as a teenager. She boasted that she was the only one in her or her husband's family—male or female—to work during the Great Depression. Eventually, she owned a small dress factory in the Bronx, which she named after my mother, "Bobbie's."

Yet, despite her knack for survival, my mother worried, didn't want her wandering around Atlantic City in the middle of the night.

"You could have gotten a room," Mom said as Grandma made a show of settling into the passenger seat, wedging her cane between the armrests.

"Ah, room! I play, then I rest in the lobby."

"Someday, someone's going to rob you, and I don't wanna hear about it!"

"What, rob me! I hit them with my cane!"

Mom and Grandma had similar Roman noses; as their nostrils flared, I imagined steam filling the space between them.

"Gum?" requested four-year-old Kara, beside me in the backseat. Grandma passed us a ten-pack of Juicy Fruit.

"Did you win?" I asked. Grandma peered over the headrest, moving her finger to her lips, her dome of hair dented like grass after field day.

When we got home, she unloaded her white leather pocketbook onto the kitchen table. She could fit a whole meal in there. In aluminum foil, half a turkey club, the lettuce wilted and shiny. A leg of fried chicken. A smooshed piece of carrot cake. And to top it off, a whole dill pickle in a wax paper pocket. All from the "boo-fay" at the casino.

"*Mangia!*" she said, motioning to the spread. But I knew the food had sat around in her purse for over a day, and I was picky in that way, a milk sniffer. She snatched up the leg and bit right in. "Ah, delicious. Outta this world."

Well, I did love pickles (and vinegar in general; I drank it out of little teacups, playing wine). But it was warm and sour, had lost its crunch.

"Good?" she asked, and just to make her happy, I nodded, knowing that just beneath the crumbling food lay rolls and rolls of shiny quarters, and that one roll, ten bucks, had my name on it.

In the months to come, I realized that Grandma stowed more than food and quarters in her purse. My grandmother was a *klepto*. In the huge Rock-bottom pharmacy in Yonkers, my mother hissed, "Watch her!" as Grandma disappeared toward the medicines. I suddenly understood the cache of un-used make-up in her bathroom. The endless packs of Juicy Fruit. And the pocketbook full of trinkets she said she bought on the Atlantic City board-walk: jelly bracelets, T-shirts with beaded fringes, rabbit's feet key chains, rainbow shoelaces. They, like my favorite earrings, gold streamers with fake garnets at the ends, were, well, *hot*. I knew my Ten Commandments, and that by accepting the gifts I was complicit and might go to hell if I died in my sleep. Hell! Yet, refusing the gifts would hurt Grandma's feelings, and I figured that God wouldn't punish me for her sins. Plus, having stuff like lacy Madonna headbands gave me status among the girls at school, and I needed all the help I could get.

Mom later told me that when Grandma was a girl in Sicily, her family was poor, and that she and her siblings stole from the vendors in the city. Yet why, sixty years later, would she take stuff she didn't need? It was the thrill. It was the power. But most of all, I think she felt she had a *right* to things.

❋

I was intimately aware of Grandma's quirks and routines because she lived with us. In 1979, when I was five, my parents bought a two-story extended ranch in Hartsdale, and Grandma and Grandpa moved in upstairs. While tour-ing the shabby eight-bedroom, four-bath house with the real estate agent, we lost Grandma almost instantly. As she called "Bob-bie!" from somewhere above us, Mom turned to the agent, joking: "It's perfect. We'll take it."

One Friday that January, there was no one to meet me at the bus stop. I skipped up the block past dirty mounds of snow, excited when I spotted a black Lincoln in our driveway. Mom's brother, Nick, and his wife, Aunt Al-ice, were probably in the kitchen, drinking coffee and eating crumb cake. Though the door was open, I found everyone upstairs. They looked surprised to see me. Grandma was firing Sicilian into the phone, and my mother paced the hallway, saying, "I'm going back to the hospital." My father, who was never home during the day, grabbed Mom by the shoulders, told her, "Hun, it's too late."

Then Mom pulled me into Grandma's bedroom and held me tightly. Her tears dampened my hair. "Grandpa died today," she sobbed.

I cried too because I had never seen my mother so sad. I thought about how much I loved my own daddy and immediately understood: my mother's *daddy* was gone, and was never coming back. Later, I plucked the words "heart attack" from the adult conversations floating around me. I didn't know what that meant, just knew that the night before, at dinner, Grandpa had sat beside me, munching happily on the green, stringy broccoli rabe that looked like seaweed. I figured it must have been all that broccoli rabe. It had strangled his heart.

Grandma moped around the house for months, often raising her fists to the ceiling, shouting: "Dominic, you sonuvabitch! Why did you leave me?" I was frightened and fascinated by her grief. Sometimes it reminded me of the dramatic feuds on the daytime soaps Grandma and I watched. Other times it reminded me of Lent, walking the Stations of the Cross, the agony in the garden, Jesus' crown of thorns. And of those filmstrips we watched, Mary Magdalene weeping beside an open grave.

After a few months, Aunt Alice and Uncle Nick treated Grandma to a vacation in Atlantic City, hoping to get her out of the house, to cheer her up. And in the casinos that lined the strip—Tropicana, Bally's, and The Taj Mahal—Grandma finally found relief.

❋

Something about the casinos must have reminded Grandma of her dress factory: the noise, the action, the people, the excitement. Grandma found order in disorder. A meticulous pack rat, her upstairs apartment was cluttered with what my ex-Marine father called "gah-bage." When my father roamed the house with oversized trash bags on a cleanliness mission, Grandma defended her turf, and he often retreated. She kept a closet full of Grandpa's clothes and shoes, as if he were due back shortly. She had huge barrels of fabric, hatboxes full of buttons, snaps, seam binding. Because in Grandma's mind, everything was useful, and there was nothing she couldn't fix.

Like the red corduroy dress Mom bought me one winter. Mom said I swam in it, which meant it was way too big.

"Why your *sceminedu* mother buys this piece-of-shit dress?" Grandma asked, and I shrugged, gazing down at the crimson sea of fabric shrouding my body. Maybe my mother *was* an idiot. I was in her sewing room, standing on a folding chair, as she clucked at a fist full of hem. Grandma's sewing machines were ready and humming. They looked like miniature pewter locomotives built into wood tables. My bedroom was directly beneath them, and I would lounge on my bed after dinner, listening to the ebb and surge of the motors, fantasizing that the tracks of stitches led to Disney World.

Her hands deftly measured and folded, and she kept a supply of straight pins clamped between her lips. As she ordered, "Ah, stay still!" I watched the pins dance, dangerously shift. I worried that she would swallow them, that they would poke holes in her guts, and so I held my body stiff, arms out like a cross. Outside the little windows above the machines, I saw the fig tree Grandpa had planted when we moved in. Grandma had bundled it for the winter with blankets and string.

With the dress pinned snugly around me, Grandma surveyed me. "*Chi bella.* Beautiful girl," she said. I knew better: brown and plain, I faded into the background like a walnut on Thanksgiving. But Grandma believed that one day soon, I would grow into my beauty. She often told me, "When I was a young woman, I was so beautiful, the birds used to drop dead from the trees." I imagined crows perched on the branches of some fluffy tree keeling over and spiraling to the ground like fat, black, kamikaze snowflakes. Beauty could kill!

Grandma carefully pulled the booby-trapped dress over my head. At moments like these, her love felt gentle. I caught a breeze and shivered, half-naked in my Strawberry Shortcake underwear.

Much later, when I was in college, I was less appreciative of Grandma's ability to mend things. I dyed my hair various shades of fuchsia, painted my fingernails black, and allowed my drunken friends to pierce my ears. I wore my favorite Levis until they frayed at the hems, grew grungy holes in the knees. When an especially seasoned pair once wound up in her ironing pile, Grandma not only ironed them, but also trimmed off the fringes and closed the jagged tears.

"Look what you did!" I accused, shaking the jeans. "The holes, that's the style!"

Grandma narrowed her black eyes at me. "But, I didn't know," she said, adding, as I stormed away, "*Coccciutu pazzu!*" You're crazy stubborn.

She couldn't take a needle and thread to my Uncle Joe's heart, or steal him a new one. That she left to God, but not without thinking that she might sway Him. During my uncle's bypass surgery, Grandma lit tall red votives around her apartment. Afraid she would burn the house down, my father made her put them in her bathtub. She said she didn't mind—every time she used the toilet, it reminded her to pray.

Uncle Joe, the oldest brother, was overweight, smoked cigarettes and had made a fortune on aerosol sprays. Behind his back, my mother called him the Big Cheese, or simply, The King. Mom took all of Grandma's shit, while when Uncle Joe breezed through from time to time, usually with a toaster oven, it was like the Second Coming. He was married to Aunt Margaret, whose shaky voice reminded me of jingling keys. I didn't know if I loved him, because I honestly didn't know if he loved me, and I was like that—cautious, guarded. But I certainly didn't want him to die. Mom said that would be the end of Grandma, and I believed her.

Grandma refused to leave the house and her candles except to visit the hospital. "Jo-ey, Jo-ey, Jo-ey," she'd murmur from her armchair, gazing at the sad-eyed Jesus Christ above the TV, last year's Easter palms secured under the frame. She spoke to the miniature Saint Anthony on the table, and to the two-foot tall Virgin Mary, who, with pretty folded hands, guarded the back staircase. She was by no means a devout woman. She was the best liar I had ever met. But she knew how to ask for help. She believed.

I, too, had my rituals of faith. Every night, even if I was too tired, I prayed. I assumed that if I didn't, something tragic might happen. I asked God to make me pretty like my classmate, Sara Clausen, with her long, sunny locks and creamy cheeks, and to grant me perfect scores on all my tests so that Mom wouldn't have to ask what Sara got. I prayed that my father would not die driving home from the bar. (He had had one accident already, twenty-four stitches in his head.) And moved by a *60 Minutes*–type special on starving children in Africa—their bloated bellies and broomstick limbs, the flies flocking around their crusty eyes and lips—I prayed for Africa. Sometimes the salty streams that collected in the corners of my mouth surprised me. At the very least, I hoped that remembering those children would help balance out my more selfish requests.

But Grandma viewed the scale holding her petitions with her eye for business. "St. Anthony, I do for you, you do for me," she said, wagging her finger at the statue, and promptly, as promised, sent a hundred dollar check to his namesake orphanage in Sicily. When St. Anthony came through, and Uncle Joe recovered, Grandma kissed the saint's porcelain feet. She rose early on a Sunday morning to cook an elaborate feast: chicken, roast beef, lasagna, sausage and peppers, rabbit stew. *Melanzane,* or eggplant parm, potatoes with onions, mushrooms, *insalati*, and the *antipasti* (meats, cheeses, olives). And finally, she returned to Atlantic City, and sprinkled holy water over the slot machines.

❀

One summer I begged off the certain hell called day camp. I had just finished fourth grade. I always got stuck in the early morning swim group, the water unbearably cold, and anyway, I knew how to swim, and quite proficiently. I was sick of dumb games, like Capture the Flag and Telephone, of grass stains on my white jean shorts. Plus, the public-school kids who populated the local camp were hard and mean, touched, I thought, by a certain evil. I told my mother my time would be better spent at home, reading. I could also keep Grandma company, I reasoned out loud. I even enlisted Grandma's support; she always took my side, or as she said, "my part," against my mother. My mother, as usual, caved in.

Mornings, I woke to a pleasingly quiet house. I lounged around in my pjs, ate my cereal while watching my favorite game shows (*Tic-Tac-Dough, The $10,000 Pyramid, The Price Is Right*). Often, when I was hungry again, Grandma would cook me a delicious *frittata* for lunch.

In the afternoons, the fragrant old woman and I would sit on the front porch in the big white Adirondack chairs. I would read my latest Nancy Drew mystery while Grandma, in her flowered housedress, light as a nightgown, would read the supermarket sales flyers, fanning herself periodically, complaining *figghiu 'e puttana*—sonuvabitch heat. We watched the Monarch butterflies circle among the impatiens, and sometimes Grandma heaved out of her seat, gracefully plucking one from a flower. As she held it, its tiny legs would bicycle for a while then cease.

"Where's your, *comu si chiama*, how do you call it? Your special book?" Grandma would ask, and I'd get the photo album I collected stickers in. (Mom bought me a sticker—scratch 'n' sniff, glittery hearts, rainbows, lips—for every book I read. Sixty and counting!) Grandma would carefully press the butterfly into one of the back pages where I kept the others and cover it with the plastic sheet. It reminded me of displays in the Natural History Museum, and I imagined that there was a secret code written in the patterns of its wings. Then, Grandma would brush the fine powder from her fingers, and I'd help her shuck corn or snap the stems off green beans.

✹

By the time I was ten, I had started snooping through Grandma's stuff while she gambled in Atlantic City. A barrel of fabric samples could inspire hours of fashion projects. One day, I found myself rooting around her bedroom. I didn't know what I was looking for; I was simply fascinated by things that didn't belong to me. I wanted to understand the adult world, especially Grandma's world.

By then, I was also a seasoned eavesdropper. Like a mosquito I'd hover in corners as they talked on the phone: Grandma upstairs, Mom downstairs, both complaining about each other. My mother said she couldn't breathe. That she "worked day and night like a dog," and when she got home, Grandma nagged, endlessly, "Where the hell have you been?"

With her sisters, Grandma often slipped into Sicilian, but I could guess the topics through her inflections, peppered with some English. My mother gave her *acitu,* heartburn. "*Chistu ca*, this one, she treats me like a dog. I sit here all day and look at the trees."

Though I also resented the fact that Mom worked all the time, I tended to take Mom's side. She *had* to work, to help pay for the house that we all lived in. She taught around the clock: at a local Catholic college and at a place she called EOC (a continuing education program in South Yonkers ghetto). Besides, Grandma had a car; she wasn't a prisoner. Like my mother, I had felt the intensity of Grandma's neediness and knew she only heard what she wanted to hear. Occasionally, Grandma gave me the silent treatment, often when she decided I had been "fresh." Matched in stubbornness, we could keep it going for days. But the silence, while initially liberating, eventually blistered inside of me. I always broke first, knowing all I needed to do was give her a kiss and say I was sorry, and she'd open her arms, call me her *gioia mia*, her sweetheart, and let me back in.

So, one Friday, while Grandma was pressing her luck in the casinos, I opened her shellacked dresser and inhaled the scent of powder, sweat, and lilies. I dug through girdles, slips, and bras the color of Ace bandages. I examined stacks of postcards with their faded foreign words. I lifted glittering costume jewelry from plastic trays, and pinched gaudy clip-on earrings to my lobes, just to feel their weight.

Then, suddenly, I struck treasure, a glass jar hidden among balls of panty-hose. It had a red lid, like olive jars did, and inside it was something indistinct, like a brownish insect, three inches, or maybe a dried, curled leaf. I turned the jar around in my hand, conjuring tadpoles. I studied it, detecting little hands and feet. A tiny belly button hole. A head. I shivered, vaguely recalling the illustrations in a book Mom had read to me when she was pregnant with Kara. It was like finding your own tooth floating on your mashed potatoes: odd yet familiar.

When Mom got home from work, I dragged her upstairs and fished the jar from its underwear sea.

Her black eyebrows dipped toward her nose like wings. "Oh," she said. "She still has it."

Her brief explanation of a miscarriage confirmed my suspicions and offered me new terminology: the word *fetus*. But were people supposed to keep them in jars? In dressers?

"Your grandmother is not normal," Mom sighed. She, too, turned the jar around in her hand. (Years later, she told me that before the formaldehyde evaporated, the fetus was plump as a peppercini).

I wanted to know how much older than Mom this sibling would have been. I was obsessed with ages, even charted the Brady Bunch children in my notebook, liking the math of them, their ages equally spaced like inches on a ruler.

Mom squinted as if reading an invisible sell-by date on a carton of milk. Ten years older, she figured. Ten years! Kara and I were only five years apart, and five years often seemed like an eternity.

For weeks after my discovery I was overwhelmed with the truth: you could die before you were even born. I couldn't fathom the scope of unrealized possibility, the cousins I might have had, the additional stacks of Christmas presents under the tress. The fetus flew through my dreams with papery angel wings. It was better than any science project I could think up, more interesting than anything I had ever seen.

But there was more to it, much more. Grandma had been playing tug of war with God.

I forget about the olive jar for nearly twenty years. I don't know what brings it back. Maybe, half-sloshed, I'm contemplating the speared olives in my third happy-hour Bloody Mary. Or perhaps I'm digging through my dresser drawer, searching for the argyle sock I haven't seen in months. Or maybe I'm consoling a friend who can't seem to get pregnant. Maybe my recent divorce has got me thinking about the big issues. Maybe the olive jar is just about doubt: what if beyond the physical, we are nothing?

So I ask my mother: "Whatever happened to the baby in the jar?" Barbara, my mom, is in cold, dreary New York, while I'm in hot, buggy Texas. In the background, I hear her Cockapoo's manic barking. Though we are talking on the phone, we could be sitting across the same kitchen table. There is something about physical distance that makes me a better friend and lover, sister and daughter, something that makes me softer.

We're mulling over the particulars, brainstorming. "Didn't Grandma have three miscarriages and a stillbirth?" I ask.

"Four miscarriages, no stillbirth," Mom recalls, "but I can't be sure." After all, she was born last, when Grandma was almost forty.

I insist because I remember the word, *stillbirth*, recall asking Grandma what that meant, and her candid reply, "It's when the baby comes out white. *Mortu*. Dead." I remember picturing a dead baby, white as a snow angel, mysteriously emerging from Grandma's belly on its way to heaven.

But now, on the phone, I revert to science, logic. A stillbirth is miscarried after twenty weeks. I estimate that Grandma's fetus when fully hydrated was probably between six and nine inches, weighed between half pound and a pound, consistent with a pregnancy of twenty plus weeks. One of the four miscarriages *had* been a stillbirth. "He was the one in the drawer," I conclude.

But my mother corrects me: "She."

She?

Mom bases her gender theory on another of Grandma's oral legends: Grandma claimed that after one of her miscarriages, *Momadon* (grandma's mother) told her, "I'm sorry you lost your baby girl." Grandma had gone ballistic.

Mom tells me that unlike women of her time and culture, career-oriented Grandma wanted only two children: a boy first, then, a girl. Among Sicilians, a daughter's legacy is to take care of her parents in their old age. When her second child, Nick, was a boy, Grandma had said, "Throw him out the window!"

Only when Momadon appealed to her vanity, saying, "But he's dark and beautiful and looks just like you," did Grandma relent, accept him. In Grandma's world, one spoke what one felt. She repeated these dark tales not only for their theatrical value, but because for her they held some convoluted moral.

"I assumed the baby in the jar was the girl she had always wanted," Mom says. Her doorbell chimes, some neighbor, and I listen as she coaxes her manic Cockapoo away from the door with a biscuit.

After we hang up, I'm left wondering: why have I assumed the fetus was a boy? I don't recall whether or not I detected a penis, or if a penis would have even been detectable. When I try to picture it, to zoom in on its privates, I come up blank. Memory is like trying to reconstruct a dandelion from the fuzzy orb of its seeds; the more you try, the more they gather wind and scatter. It is more likely that the fetus being a boy was simply my assumption. Grandma, like many Italian mothers, privileged her sons, placed them on an altar glowing with candles. Mix this with Catholic education: Jesus was a boy; God was the Father.

Sons were worth saving.

※

As a semi-responsible woman, one who lies awake at night worrying about the Dalai Lama, and as a born-again tree hugger, a reigning Shanghai Rummy champion, as a daughter, a sister, a lover, a friend, I want to say I don't steal, hoard, lie, obsess. But that wouldn't be true. When there is a table of free books, I'll take them all, even if I know I'll never read them. At Kroger, when the cashier forgets to check under my cart, I waltz out with a case of soda, no guilt. My closet is filled with clothes that don't fit and I never wear, and when I finally give a bag or two to Goodwill, I feel both euphoric and dejected. I lie in hundreds of small ways. An A minus becomes an A. Four beers evaporate to three. A $20 pair of shoes really cost me almost $30. And as Grandma predicted, I've grown into my beauty, and have been known to, here and there, bed as many admirers as I could. Lies are simply fractals of truth. Grandma knew that.

Once, I stole a pair of Victoria's Secret thong underwear from Kara's Christmas stocking. Much later, she spotted them in my laundry pile, held them up, saying, "I wondered where these went." I was embarrassed. Yet even when caught red-handed, my first impulse was to deny everything. It's not that I want to steal from my own sister. There's a difference between the act and the intention. Maybe I'm just impulsive or feel entitled to take what I want. Or maybe, like my grandmother, I'm a scavenger, a memory junkie. But there's no use putting an icicle in the freezer, thinking you can hold onto winter. Or trying to get to the other side before it's your time.

❁

Whenever Grandma brought up the subject of her own death, it was usually to tell us how sorry we would be when she was gone, how we would finally appreciate her, but that it would be too late. Besides this, she had two simple requests for her burial arrangements. One, she did not want to be put in the ground. (Easy enough, she and Grandpa had purchased a wall vault at the Gate of Heaven Cemetery.) And two, she wanted to be buried with the jar, with her child. Grandma was kind of like an armadillo: tough on the outside, timid on the inside. I think she was simply afraid of being alone.

Okay. In 1994, at age eighty-nine, Grandma suffered a minor heart attack. During her month in the hospital, she seemed tired and frail, sometimes only spoke Sicilian as if she had altogether forgotten English. A week before being discharged to a nursing home (she always hated nursing homes—said they were filled with *pazzi*, old crazies), she decided to check herself out—permanently.

Uncle Joe refused to give the fetus to the funeral home. Perhaps he was just being the archetypical control freak, or maybe he was embarrassed by his mother's half-cocked superstitious rituals. Mom recalls that she held the jar out to him and said: "Think of it as our chance to give her a child to keep her company. If we don't, Joe, which one of us do you think she'll come looking for next?"

Hers was my first open-casket wake. I was twenty. I remember the darkened room overflowing with gladiolas and lilies, carnation wreaths, mum-covered crosses. From the remaining old guard Sicilians (Grandma's three sisters among them) came the occasional wail or pantomime of fainting. Even my father was misty-eyed.

Mom was freaking out about Grandma's lipstick. "That's not the color I gave you!" she barked, backing the funeral director into a table of Mass cards. I understood my mother's reaction to the lipstick as I knelt by the casket, looking in. Instead of her Grandma's trademark salmon, her lips were painted like Ronald McDonald's. Worse, I knew that Grandma would have called the color *russa puttana*—slut red.

I focused on her hands, molded to clasp a string of rosary beads, found comfort in the familiar age spots, which had always reminded me of the freckles on a banana. I kissed my fingers then touched them to her hand. Her fingers were cold and rubbery like a bowl full of wax. For a moment, swept by vertigo, I couldn't breathe. Grandma's gold wedding band twinkled in the low lights aimed at the casket. Little did I know that tucked into the satin folds, inside a jar with a red lid, was someone for her to take care of.

"ON APPRENTICESHIP"

I wrote "On Apprenticeship" in 1994, a time when I was just learning about some of the disappointments of the literary life—my first book had come out, for one example, published by Houghton Mifflin, and my life hadn't changed much at all, none of the heavenly trumpets I'd expected, merely more work ahead of me. I detect some of that in the tone of this piece as I reread it today, a bit of a chip on the shoulder, a feeling that the world should appreciate more what I was trying to do. With middle age comes wisdom: that the greater world doesn't much care is a given, no longer a surprise.

But I do have readers: "On Apprenticeship" has been reprinted dozens of times since its first appearance in *Maine in Print* (the newsletter of the Maine Writers and Publishers Association), in magazines, journals, newsletters large and small. I think the message is still important, these days when so many conversations with aspiring writers are part of my life and so many people want to talk about careers rather than sentences, paragraphs, drafts.

Also, I've been amused over the years to see the central anecdote of the piece, about the brain surgeon, become something of a writer's urban myth. I've heard several speakers use it since, and have had several published essays or op-ed pieces or interviews sent to me because a friend recognized the borrowed story, sometimes barely disguised, always claimed by the writer. I even had the story told to me in Australia, where my host said he'd heard it from another visiting American writer, one, no doubt, with a subscription to *Maine in Print*. Well, I'm happy to be part of the cultural collective. And now I offer the anecdote to you—go ahead and tell about the time you met a doctor at a party and got talking about writing. Just for the record, though, let's get it straight: I'm the one it really happened to.

—Bill Roorbach

ON APPRENTICESHIP, BY BILL ROORBACH

Every time I run a workshop at a writing conference and every time I make small talk at gatherings of professors or family or old acquaintances or friends I'm reminded how little our culture appreciates artistic apprenticeship, how little we writers (members, after all, of an unappreciated culture) admire our own apprenticeships, how much, even, we hate them.

At a Christmas gathering back home in the flatlands of Connecticut, I got stuck at a house party talking to a real-estate lady and her banker husband. Nice folks. She had read my book, a memoir called *Summers With Juliet*, which chronicles eight summers spent traveling with my now wife, the painter Juliet Karelsen. He had not read the book, even grinned and admitting he hadn't actually read a whole book since college. Maybe not even in college, ha ha.

And she said, "We could have written that book."

"Yes!" he cried, "All the adventures we've had!"

"And the long courtship, too," she said.

I liked her. Who wouldn't? Lovely, intelligent, active, charming, successful.

He said, "Always wanted to take off a month and write the darn thing!" He really said this. A pleasant banker who hadn't read a book maybe *ever*.

"This is before we settled down," she said.

"Rent a little cabin, write the darn thing," he said, dreamily. Some of his rough edges, most of the possibility of personality, had been rubbed off by banking, but not all. There was enough of a man left there to take him seriously.

I smiled, said nothing. I'm not entirely churlish sometimes, and I know people say dumb things sometimes. I do have a sense of humor. And I have had such conversations before:

Graduate student in English: "When I finish my dissertation I'm going to write just such a book! I've got a whole summer before I'm off to Oxford."

Zoology professor: "So you see, my story is just as interesting as yours: I'll get it written when I finish my treatise on color distribution in weasels."

Nearly everyone: "If I only had time like you!"

Folks don't quite see the difference between the story and the work of its telling. People don't quite see the enormous price of all that seeming free time.

A physician at a conference I won't name in Montana (and a doctor at Stonecoast and a doctor at Steamboat Springs and a doctor at every conference I've ever braved teaching—doctors are famous offenders) strode up to me during cocktails and announced that—now that she was established as a surgeon (in fact, perhaps a little bored with it by now, the glamour having worn off)—yes, now that she had control of her time, she was going to take six months off and write her story. Mine had inspired her, she said.

I said I was pleased to be her inspiration. I wished her luck. Then there was a pause. The rattling of ice cubes. I knew how smart it would be to keep silent, but I gulped my drink and said, "You know, you've inspired *me*! I'm going to take six months off and become a surgeon like you, since I admire you, and since neurology seems most up my alley—after all, I work with my brain practically every day! Yes! That's it! Now that I'm an established writer, I think I'll just take six months off and heal a few brain wounds!"

She didn't get the joke. Didn't even smile. "You can't become a doctor in six months time," she said.

I just looked amazed at her and watched her walk away.

❉

But even among the enlightened, among the best students I've ever had, among the best new writers I have ever talked to (and certainly within my younger self), contempt for the many years of apprenticeship (fully equal to the years required for an M.D., usually twice again more) seems a devastating undercurrent. We've all of us internalized our parents' question, our dentists' question, the competitive question at conferences: "Oh, you say you're a writer." Wry face. Then: "What have you published?"

And no matter if you've published two feeble stories in the *Wrinkly Elbow Review* or ten spectacular books: "Why, no, I haven't heard of that one."

The next question (we don't ask doctors this!): "Huh. How much do they pay you?"

And bless you if you haven't published at all. The smirk, the little anecdote about the aunt who thought herself a writer (before her suicide, poor thing), about the strange brother who wrote stories no one could make the least sense of. The anecdote about that spy-writer guy who made ten million on his first book. *Why don't you write about spies*?

So it's no wonder that the first question many a new writer asks of her (usually struggling) teachers is: "How do I sell this thing?"

Consider the apprentice of a glassblower. No one condemns her. No one says she should be blowing spy figurines. She's paying to learn, hoping to reach the point where she can earn wages as journeyperson so that after a prescribed number of years she'll be a master at her craft and able to make a real living. If you ask her what she's sold, she'll look puzzled, tell you (with aplomb and a little pity at your ignorance): "Sold? I'm an apprentice. Sold? I'm proud to be able to sweep up around here. *Sold*? I know I'll be able at length to blow the perfect lamps the masters blow now. Oh, god, let me show you the lumpy vase I've made before I smash it to make shards to melt for the next try! I'm working on necks, now; I'm working on making my vase necks perfectly graceful."

Imagine the glass apprentice taking vase-marketing courses before she's learned to make the glass. Imagine an entire Book-of-the-Minute club devoted entirely to books aimed at glass apprentices and titled "Selling Your First Weak Attempts at Glasswork." First—and any apprentice to any master can tell you this—*learn the craft*. (And where does one find a master when it comes to writing? In the library, for starters.)

We've heard that writing is a talent, that one is born to it, that it can't be learned. Malarkey! Imagine the glass apprentice's parents saying, "Glassblowing? Glassblowing takes *talent*! You can't learn glassblowing." Or the medical student's: "If you can't do a heart transplant when you're in high school, you'll never do one." Every apprentice in any endeavor arrives with certain talents, certain facilities, all intermixed with flaws. One hopes to hang onto talents while correcting deficits. Perhaps our glassblower is lucky enough to be naturally good at goblet stems (goblet stems are hard!). Should she quit because she's bad at vase necks?

No. She goes to work; she learns. And when she fails, she smashes the faulty lamp or pitcher, musters all she's learned, and tries again. No one suggests she keep working on the flawed apprentice work, just as no one suggests that a medical student continue to work on her assigned cadaver until it comes to life. (Or worse, that she try to sell the bestitched and bloodless thing, or send it a bill.)

Here is the only rule I'm willing to make about writing: Honor your apprenticeship. Call yourself a learner. When your goblets are good they will sell (first at yard sales, then in better and better boutiques, then to the fine museums). Before that time, smash them and use what you've learned to make the next. One day, people will clamor for what you do. But first you must—we all must—learn to write. When some well-meaning banker asks what you've published, look shocked. Say, "But I'm an apprentice!" Be proud of this, be glad of it. Buy yourself a beer. Write yourself an acceptance letter. Cultivate patience. Quote Shunryu Suzuki: "In the beginner's mind there are many possibilities, but in the expert's mind there are few."

❋

At a Maine Writers & Publishers Alliance (MWPA) autumn retreat at Lincolnville, Maine, an older woman stopped to ask me a question, manuscript in hand. She didn't ask for my agent's phone number, didn't ask about "markets," didn't want to know if her story was publishable. She wasn't all bruised and cowering from periodical rejection, wasn't sure she'd been misread by the editors of *The New Yorker*. She simply (and cheerfully) showed me a section of dialogue—one page in the middle of the story—even gave me time to read it aloud.

She said, "How do I make this better?"

We got down to work.

APPENDIX D

Suggested Readings in Creative Nonfiction

These are books and collections and anthologies I've enjoyed and learned from over the years (or have been impressively irritated by), united simply by their places on the shelf of creative nonfiction. Remember that the books on the shelf represent a broad continuum from memoir to the personal essay to literary journalism, all with an *I* at the center, all made with reverent attention to language, and either a strong core of storytelling or a lyrical sense of ideas and associations (often both). Most of the titles here could be listed in any of a number of our categories, but I've decided for simplicity's sake to list each book only once. I've also generally listed only a few books per author, when many have several or more good books for you to crack open. And I know I've missed a good many wonderful books—let these be your own discoveries. (My apologies to writers I've left out, among them many friends, no doubt.)

Don't be daunted by the length of the list—just know that there are lots of good books out there that might inform whatever project you are working on. A good place to start would be in one of the anthologies listed at the end of this appendix (*anthos* is the ancient Greek word for flowers; an anthology is a gathering of flowers, a bouquet). In the anthologies, you'll find introductions by smart editors who announce subgenres and define forms and include shorter samples from a huge array of writers, some of whom you'll surely want to follow up on. Another good place to start is simply at the library or book store, browsing for literary soul mates.

Reading is writing!

MEMOIR

Achebe, Chinua. *No Longer at Ease*
Adams, Henry. *The Education of Henry Adams*
Akey, Stephen. *College: A Memoir*
Alberts, Laurie. *Fault Line*
Allison, Dorothy. *Two or Three Things I Know for Sure*
Anderson, Mark Curtis. *Jesus Sound Explosion*
Angelou, Maya. *I Know Why the Caged Bird Sings*
Ansay, A. Manette. *Limbo: A Memoir*
Apple, Max. *I Love Gootie: My Grandmother's Story*
—. *Roommates: My Grandfather's Story*
Asher, Don. *Notes From a Battered Grand: A Memoir*
Ashton-Warner, Sylvia. *Teacher*
Auster, Paul. *The Invention of Solitude*
Austin, Mary Hunter. *Earth Horizon: Autobiography*
—. *The Land of Little Rain*
Baker, Russell. *Growing Up*
Balakian, Peter. *Black Dog of Fate: A Memoir*
Baldwin, James. *Notes of a Native Son*
Barber, Phyllis. *How I Got Cultured: A Nevada Memoir*
Bateson, Mary Catherine. *With a Daughter's Eye:*
    A Memoir of Margaret Mead and Gregory Bateson
Beard, Jo Ann. *The Boys of My Youth*
Beauvoir, Simone de. *Memoirs of a Dutiful Daughter*
Benchley, Robert. *Benchley Beside Himself*
Bernhard, Thomas. *Gathering Evidence: A Memoir*
Bernstein, Jane. *Loving Rachel: A Family's Journey From Grief*
—. *Rachel in the World: A Memoir*
Blew, Mary Clearman. *All But the Waltz: A Memoir of*
    Five Generations in the Life of a Montana Family
Bogan, Louise. *Journey Around My Room:*
    The Autobiography of Louise Bogan: A Mosaic

Bourdain, Anthony. *Kitchen Confidential:*
  Adventures in the Culinary Underbelly
Bourke-White, Margaret. *Portrait of Myself*
Brodkey, Harold. *This Wild Darkness: The Story of My Death*
Broyard, Anatole. *Kafka Was the Rage: A Greenwich Village Memoir*
—. *Intoxicated By My Illness : And Other Writings on Life and Death*
Buechner, Frederick. *Now and Then*
—. *The Sacred Journey: A Memoir of Early Days*
Burn, June. *Living High: An Unconventional Autobiography*
Burroughs, Augusten. *Dry*
—. *Running With Scissors*
Cantwell, Mary. *American Girl: Scenes From a Small-Town Childhood*
Carkeet, David. *Campus Sexpot: A Memoir*
Charyn, Jerome. *The Dark Lady From Belorusse: A Memoir*
Chesnut, Mary Boykin. *A Diary From Dixie*
Coetzee, J.M. *Boyhood: Scenes From Provincial Life*
Cofer, Judith Ortiz. *Silent Dancing: A Partial*
  Remembrance of a Puerto Rican Childhood
Cohen, Leah Hager. *Train Go Sorry: Inside a Deaf World.*
Colebrook, Joan. *A House of Trees*
Conover, Ted. *Newjack: Guarding Sing Sing*
Conrad, Joseph. *The Mirror of the Sea*
Conroy, Frank. *Stop-Time*
Conroy, Pat. *The Water Is Wide*
Conway, Jill Ker. *The Road From Coorain*
Cooper, Bernard. *The Bill From My Father: A Memoir*
—. *Truth Serum: Memoirs*
Cournos, Francine. *City of One: A Memoir*
Cowser, Bob. *Dream Season: A Professor Joins*
  America's Oldest Semi-Pro Football Team
Crews, Harry. *A Childhood: The Biography of a Place*
Dahlberg, Edward. *Because I Was Flesh:*
  The Autobiography of Edward Dahlberg
Dana, Richard Henry. *Two Years Before the Mast*
Daniel, John. *Looking After: A Son's Memoir*
Dann, Patty. *The Baby Boat: A Memoir of Adoption*
Davison, Peter. *Half Remembered: A Personal History*

Day, Clarence. *Life With Father*

Day, Dorothy. *The Long Loneliness: The Autobiography of Dorothy Day*

deBuys, William and Alex Harris. *River of Traps: A New Mexico Mountain Life*

Delaney, Sarah and A. Elizabeth Delaney with Amy Hill Hearth.
   Having Our Say: The Delany Sisters' First 100 Years

Delbanco, Nicholas. *Running in Place: Scenes From the South of France*

Didion, Joan. *The Year of Magical Thinking*

Digges, Deborah. *Fugitive Spring: A Memoir*

Dillard, Annie. *An American Childhood*

Dinesen, Isak. *Out of Africa*

Doig, Ivan. *Heart Earth*

—. *This House of Sky: Landscapes of a Western Mind*

Doty, Mark. *Firebird: A Memoir*

—. *Heaven's Coast: A Memoir*

Douglass, Frederick. *Narrative of the Life of Frederick Douglass*

Dubus, Andre. *Broken Vessels*

Dudman, Martha Tod. *Augusta, Gone: A True Story*

Dunham, Katherine. *A Touch of Innocence*

Durrell, Lawrence. *Bitter Lemons*

Earley, Pete. *Crazy: A Father's Search Through America's Mental Health Madness*

Eastman, Charles Alexander. *Indian Boyhood*

Edelman, Hope. *Motherless Daughters: The Legacy of Loss*

Eggers, Dave. *A Heartbreaking Work of Staggering Genius*

Eighner, Lars. *Travels With Lizbeth*

Eiseley, Loren. *All the Strange Hours: The Excavation of a Life*

Eisenberg, Nora. *The War at Home: A Memoir-Novel*

Ellroy, James. *My Dark Places: An L.A. Crime Memoir*

Ernaux, Annie. *A Man's Place*

—. *A Woman's Story*

Facey, A.B. *Fortunate Life*

Fairey, Wendy W. *One of the Family*

Finneran, Kathleen. *The Tender Land: A Family Love Story*

Fishman, Steve. *A Bomb in the Brain: A Heroic Tale
   of Science, Surgery, and Survival*

Fitzgerald, Robert. *The Third Kind of Knowledge: Memoirs &
   Selected Writings*

Flynn, Nick. *Another Bullshit Night in Suck City: A Memoir*

Ford, Ford Madox. *Your Mirror to My Times: The Selected*
Autobiographies and Impressions of Ford Madox Ford

Foster, Patricia. *All the Lost Girls: Confessions of a Southern Daughter*

Fox, Suzanne. *Home Life: A Journey Through Rooms and Recollections*

Franklin, Benjamin. *The Autobiography of Benjamin Franklin*

Fries, Kenny. *Body, Remember: A Memoir*

Fuller, Alexandra. *Don't Let's Go to the Dogs Tonight: An African Childhood*

Gallagher, Dorothy. *How I Came Into My Inheritance*

Garland, Hamlin. *A Son of the Middle Border*

Ghosh, Amitav. *Dancing in Cambodia, At Large in Burma*

Gilberg, Gail Hosking. *Snake's Daughter: The Roads In and Out of War*

Gilmore, Mikal. *Shot in the Heart*

Glasgow, Ellen Anderson Gholson. *The Woman Within*

Goldbarth, Albert. *A Sympathy of Souls: Essays*

Golden, Marita. *Migrations of the Heart*

Gonzalez, Ray. *Memory Fever: A Journey Beyond El Paso Del Norte*

Gordon, Emily Fox. *Are You Happy?: A Childhood Remembered*

—. *Mockingbird Years: A Life In and Out of Therapy*

Gordon, Mary. *The Shadow Man*

Gorky, Maxim. *My Apprenticeship*

—. *My Childhood*

—. *My Universities*

Gornick, Vivian. *Fierce Attachments: A Memoir*

Grandin, Temple. *Thinking in Pictures:*
And Other Reports From My Life With Autism

Grant, Ulysses S. *Personal Memoirs of U.S. Grant*

Graves, John. *Goodbye to a River, a Narrative*

Graves, Robert. *Good-Bye to All That*

Gray, Spalding. *Sex and Death to the Age 14*

Grealy, Lucy. *Autobiography of a Face*

Green, Henry. *Pack My Bag: A Self-Portrait*

Greene, Graham. *A Sort of Life*

—. *Ways of Escape*

Griffin, Gail B. *Calling: Essays on Teaching in the Mother Tongue*

Grumbach, Doris. *Coming Into the End Zone: A Memoir*

—. *Extra Innings: A Memoir*

Guinness, Alec. *Blessings in Disguise*

Hall, Donald. *Life Work*

—. *String Too Short to Be Saved*

Hall, Edward Twitchell. *An Anthropology of Everyday Life: An Autobiography*

Hamper, Ben. *Rivethead: Tales From the Assembly Line*

Hampl, Patricia. *A Romantic Education*

—. *Virgin Time*

Handler, Evan. *Time on Fire: My Comedy of Terrors*

Harnack, Curtis. *The Attic: A Memoir*

—. *We Have All Gone Away*

Harrison, Kathryn. *The Kiss*

Hart, Moss. *Act One: An Autobiography*

Hecht, Ben. *A Child of the Century*

Heilman, Samuel C. *The Gate Behind the Wall: A Pilgrimage to Jerusalem*

Hellman, Lillian. *Pentimento*

—. *Scoundrel Time*

—. *An Unfinished Woman: A Memoir*

Hemingway, Ernest. *Green Hills of Africa*

—. *A Moveable Feast*

Hendra, Tony. *Father Joe: The Man Who Saved My Soul*

Herr, Michael. *Dispatches*

Hochschild, Adam. *Half the Way Home: A Memoir of Father and Son*

Hoffman, Eva. *Lost in Translation: A Life in a New Language*

Hoffman, Richard. *Half the House*

Hood, Ann. *Do Not Go Gentle: My Search for Miracles in a Cynical Time*

Horgan, Paul. *Tracings: A Book of Partial Portraits*

Howard, Maureen. *Facts of Life*

Hudson, W.H. *Far Away and Long Ago: A History of My Early Life*

—. *The Purple Land*

Hughes, Langston. *The Big Sea: An Autobiography*

Hull, John M. *Touching the Rock: An Experience of Blindness*

Hurston, Zora Neale. *Dust Tracks on a Road*

—. *Mules and Men*

Huxley, Elspeth. *The Flame Trees of Thika: Memories of an African Childhood*

Jacobs, Harriet. *Incidents in the Life of a Slave Girl*

Jacoby, Susan. *Half-Jew: A Daughter's Search for Her Family's Buried Past*

Jamison, Kay R. *An Unquiet Mind*

Johnson, Fenton. *Geography of the Heart: A Memoir*

Johnson, James Weldon. *Along This Way:*
The Autobiography of James Weldon Johnson

Johnson, Joyce. *Minor Characters*

Jordan, June. *Soldier: A Poet's Childhood*

Jordan, Teresa. *Riding the White Horse Home: A Western Family Album*

Kamenetz, Rodger. *Terra Infirma*

Kaplan, Alice. *French Lessons: A Memoir*

Karr, Mary. *The Liars' Club: A Memoir*

Kaysen, Susanna. *Girl, Interrupted*

Kazantzakis, Nikos. *Report to Greco*

Kazin, Alfred. *A Walker in the City*

Keillor, Garrison. *Lake Wobegon Days*

Keller, Helen. *The Story of My Life*

Kilgo, James. *Deep Enough for Ivorybills*

Kincaid, Jamaica. *My Brother*

—. *A Small Place*

Kingston, Maxine Hong. *The Woman Warrior:*
Memoirs of a Girlhood Among Ghosts

Kittredge, William. *Hole in the Sky: A Memoir*

Knapp, Caroline. *Drinking: A Love Story*

Knopp, Lisa. *Flight Dreams: A Life in the Midwestern Landscape*

Kusz, Natalie. *Road Song*

Land, Brad. *Goat: A Memoir*

Lavender, David Sievert. *One Man's West*

Lawrence, T.E. *Seven Pillars of Wisdom: A Triumph*

Levi, Primo. *The Reawakening*

—. *Survival in Auschwitz: The Nazi Assault on Humanity*

Levin, Harry. *Memories of the Moderns*

Lévi-Strauss, Claude. *Tristes Tropiques*

Lewis, C.S. *Surprised By Joy: The Shape of My Early Life*

Lewis, Mindy. *Life Inside: A Memoir*

Lorde, Audre. *The Cancer Journals*

—. *Zami: A New Spelling of My Name*

Lott, Bret. *Fathers, Sons, and Brothers: The Men in My Family*

Lusseyran, Jacques. *And There Was Light: The Autobiography*
of a Blind Hero of the French Resistance

Mackall, Joe. *The Last Street Before Cleveland: An Accidental Pilgrimage*

MacNeil, Robert. *Wordstruck: A Memoir*

Mairs, Nancy. *Carnal Acts: Essays*

—. *Waist-High in the World: A Life Among the Nondisabled*

Mason, Robert. *Chickenhawk*

Masters, Hilary. *Last Stands: Notes From Memory*

Mathabane, Mark. *Kaffir Boy: The True Story of a Black Youth's Coming of Age in Apartheid South Africa*

Maxwell, Gavin. *Ring of Bright Water*

Maxwell, William. *Ancestors: A Family History*

McCarthy, Mary. *How I Grew*

—. *Memories of a Catholic Girlhood*

McClanahan, Rebecca. *The Riddle Song and Other Rememberings*

McConkey, James. *Court of Memory*

McCourt, Frank. *Angela's Ashes: A Memoir*

McElmurray, Karen Salyer. *Surrendered Child: A Birth Mother's Journey*

McKain, David W. *Spellbound: Growing Up in God's Country*

McKay, Jean. *Gone to Grass*

McKenna, Rollie. *A Life in Photography*

McLaurin, Tim. *Keeper of the Moon: A Southern Boyhood*

Mead, Margaret. *Blackberry Winter: My Earlier Years*

Mehta, Ved. *Daddyji*

—. *Face to Face*

—. *Mamaji*

—. *Up at Oxford*

—. *Vedi*

Merrill, James. *A Different Person: A Memoir*

Merton, Thomas. *The Seven Story Mountain*

Miller, Henry. *Big Sur and the Oranges of Hieronymus Bosch*

—. *The Books in My Life*

—. *Remember to Remember*

Miner, Valerie. *The Low Road: A Scottish Family Memoir*

Mitchell, John Hanson. *Living at the End of Time*

Mitchell, Joseph. *McSorley's Wonderful Saloon*

Momaday, N. Scott. *The Names: A Memoir*

—. *The Way to Rainy Mountain*

Monette, Paul. *Becoming a Man: Half a Life Story*

Moodie, Susanna. *Roughing It in the Bush, or, Life in Canada*

Moody, Anne. *Coming of Age in Mississippi*

Moore, Dinty W. *The Accidental Buddhist:*
    Mindfulness, Englightenment, and Sitting Still

Morris, Wright. *A Cloak of Light: Writing My Life*

—. *Solo: An American Dreamer in Europe, 1933–1934*

—. *Will's Boy: A Memoir*

Muir, Edwin. *An Autobiography*

Muir, John. *My First Summer in the Sierra*

—. *The Story of My Boyhood and Youth*

Munro, Eleanor C. *Memoir of a Modernist's Daughter*

Murray, Pauli. *Proud Shoes: The Story of an American Family*

—. *Song in a Weary Throat: An American Pilgrimage*

Nabokov, Vladimir. *Speak, Memory*

Naipaul, V.S. *The Enigma of Arrival: A Novel*

—. *Finding the Center: Two Narratives*

Nelson, Richard K. *The Island Within*

Neville, Susan. *Iconography: A Writer's Meditation*

Newby, Eric. *Love and War in the Apennines*

Noël, Christopher. *In the Unlikely Event of*
    a Water Landing: A Geography of Grief

Norris, Kathleen. *The Cloister Walk*

O'Faolain, Nuala. *Almost There: The Onward Journey of a Dublin Woman*

—. *Are You Somebody?: The Accidental Memoir of a Dublin Woman*

Offutt, Chris. *The Same River Twice: A Memoir*

Ofri, Danielle. *Singular Intimacies: Becoming a Doctor at Bellevue*

Olmstead, Robert. *Stay Here With Me: A Memoir*

Ondaatje, Michael. *Running in the Family*

Owens, William A. *This Stubborn Soil: A Frontier Boyhood*

Patchett, Ann. *Truth & Beauty*

Peacock, Molly. *Paradise, Piece By Piece*

Pemberton, Gayle. *The Hottest Water in Chicago: Notes of a Native Daughter*

Perelman, S.J. *Most of the Most of S.J. Perelman*

Phibbs, Brendan. *The Other Side of Time: A Combat Surgeon in World War II*

Ponce, Mary Helen. *Hoyt Street: An Autobiography*

Price, Reynolds. *A Whole New Life: An Illness and a Healing*

Puleston, Dennis. *Blue Water Vagabond*

Rafkin, Louise. *Other People's Dirt: A Housecleaner's Curious Adventures*

Rapp, Emily. *Poster Child: A Memoir*

Rawlings, Marjorie Kinnan. *Cross Creek*

Reichl, Ruth. *Tender at the Bone: Growing Up at the Table*

Rhodes, Richard. *A Hole in the World: An American Boyhood*

Ríos, Alberto. *Capirotada: A Nogales Memoir*

Rodriguez, Richard. *Days of Obligation: An Argument With My Mexican Father*

—. *The Hunger of Memory: The Education of Richard Rodriguez: An Autobiography*

Rogers, Annie G. *A Shining Affliction: A Story of Harm and Healing in Psychotherapy*

Roorbach, Bill. *Summers With Juliet*

Roth, Philip. *Patrimony: A True Story*

Sacks, Oliver W. *The Man Who Mistook His Wife for a Hat*

Saint-Exupéry, Antoine de. *Wind, Sand and Stars*

Sandoz, Mari. *Old Jules*

Sarraute, Nathalie. *Childhood*

Sartre, Jean-Paul. *The Words*

Scofield, Sandra. *Occasions of Sin: A Memoir*

Scott, Evelyn. *Escapade*

Sedaris, David. *Me Talk Pretty One Day*

—. *Naked*

Segal, Lore Groszman. *Other People's Houses*

Selzer, Richard. *Confessions of a Knife*

—. *Down From Troy: A Doctor Comes of Age*

—. *Mortal Lessons: Notes on the Art of Surgery*

—. *Raising the Dead*

Shammas, Anton. *Arabesques*

Shapiro, Dani. *Slow Motion*

Sheed, Wilfrid. *Frank and Maisie: A Memoir With Parents*

—. *In Love With Daylight: A Memoir of Recovery*

—. *My Life As a Fan*

—. *People Will Always Be Kind*

Shen, Congwen. *Recollections of West Hunan*

Shulman, Alix Kates. *Drinking the Rain*

Silverman, Sue William. *Because I Remember Terror, Father, I Remember You*

—. *Love Sick: One Woman's Journey Through Sexual Addiction*

Simon, Clea. *Mad House*

Simon, Kate. *Bronx Primitive: Portraits in a Childhood*

—. *Etchings in an Hourglass*

—. *A Wider World: Portraits in an Adolescence*

Simpson, Eileen. *Poets in Their Youth: A Memoir*

Slater, Lauren. *Welcome to My Country*

Smith, Alison. *Name All the Animals: A Memoir*

Smith, Annick. *Homestead*

Smith, Lillian Eugenia. *Killers of the Dream*

Smith, William Jay. *Army Brat: A Memoir*

Snyder, Don J. *The Cliff Walk: A Memoir of a Job Lost and a Life Found*

Soyinka, Wole. *Aké : The Years of Childhood*

Spark, Muriel. *Curriculum Vitae: Autobiography*

Spiegelman, Art. *Maus*

Stacey, Patricia. *The Boy Who Loved Windows: Opening the Heart and Mind of a Child Threatened With Autism*

Staples, Brent. *Parallel Time: Growing Up in Black and White*

Stavans, Ilan. *On Borrowed Words: A Memoir of Language*

Stegner, Wallace. *Wolf Willow: A History, a Story, and a Memory of the Last Plains Frontier*

Stein, Gertrude. *The Autobiography of Alice B. Toklas*

Stratton-Porter, Gene. *Moths of the Limberlost*

Styron, William. *Darkness Visible: A Memoir of Madness*

Suleri, Sara. *Meatless Days*

Talayesva, Don C. *Sun Chief: The Autobiography of a Hopi Indian*

Thomas, Dylan. *Portrait of the Artist As a Young Dog*

Thomas, Lewis. *The Youngest Science: Notes of a Medicine-Watcher*

Thompson, Flora. *Lark Rise to Candleford: A Trilogy*

Thurber, James. *My Life and Hard Times*

—. *The Thurber Carnival*

Toner, Jim. *Serendib*

Toth, Susan Allen. *Blooming: A Small-Town Girlhood*

—. *Ivy Days: Making My Way Out East*

Trevelyan, Katherine. *Through Mine Own Eyes: The Autobiography of a Natural Mystic*

Trevor, William. *Excursions in the Real World: Memoirs*

Trillin, Calvin. *Remembering Denny*

Trilling, Diana. *The Beginning of the Journey:*
The Marriage of Diana and Lionel Trilling

Trollope, Anthony. *An Autobiography*

Twain, Mark. *Life on the Mississippi*

Updike, John. *Self-Consciousness: Memoirs*

Vertosick, Frank T. *Why We Hurt: The Natural History of Pain*

Wade-Gayles, Gloria. *Pushed Back to Strength:*
A Black Woman's Journey Home

Walls, Jeannette. *The Glass Castle: A Memoir*

Washington, Booker T. *Up From Slavery*

Waters, Ethel with Charles Samuels. *His Eye Is on the Sparrow: An Autobiography*

Weigl, Bruce. *The Circle of Hanh: A Memoir*

Welty, Eudora. *One Writer's Beginnings*

West, Paul. *Words for a Deaf Daughter*

Wharton, Edith. *A Backward Glance*

Wideman, John Edgar. *Brothers and Keepers*

Williams, William Carlos. *The Autobiography of William Carlos Williams*

Wilson, Edward O. *Naturalist*

Wolff, Geoffrey. *The Duke of Deception: Memories of My Father*

Wolff, Tobias. *In Pharaoh's Army: Memories of the Lost War*

—. *This Boy's Life: A Memoir*

Wozencraft, Kim. *Notes From the Country Club*

Wright, Richard. *Black Boy*

X, Malcolm and Alex Haley. *The Autobiography of Malcolm X*

Yourcenar, Marguerite. *Dear Departed*

Zachter, Mort. *Dough: A Memoir*

Zailckas, Koren. *Smashed: Story of a Drunken Girlhood*

PERSONAL ESSAY AND BOOK-LENGTH ESSAY

Ackerman, Diane. *A Natural History of Love*

—. *A Natural History of the Senses*

Auster, Paul. *The Art of Hunger: Essays, Prefaces, Interviews*

Baker, Nicholson. *The Size of Thoughts: Essays and Other Lumber*

—. *U and I: A True Story*

Ballantine, Poe. *Things I Like About America: Personal Narratives*

Baudrillard, Jean. *The System of Objects*

—. *The Transparency of Evil: Essays on Extreme Phenomena*

Berry, Wendell. *Another Turn of the Crank: Essays*

—. *What Are People For?: Essays*

Blount, Roy, Jr. *Crackers*

—. *One Fell Soup, or, I'm Just a Bug on the Windshield of Life*

Burroughs, Augusten. *Magical Thinking: True Stories*

Burroughs, Franklin. *Billy Watson's Croker Sack: Essays*

Burroway, Janet. *Embalming Mom: Essays in Life*

Butler, Hubert. *Independent Spirit: Essays*

Buzzi, Aldo. *Journey to the Land of the Flies and Other Travels*

Codrescu, Andrei. *The Dog With the Chip in His
    Neck: Essays From NPR and Elsewhere*

Cohn, Nik. *The Heart of the World*

Cooper, Bernard. *Maps to Anywhere*

Crouch, Stanley. *Notes of a Hanging Judge: Essays and Reviews, 1979-1989*

D'Agata, John. *Halls of Fame: Essays*

D'Ambrosio, Charles. *Orphans*

Daniel, John. *The Trail Home: Essays*

Derricotte, Toi. *The Black Notebooks: An Interior Journey*

Didion, Joan. *Slouching Towards Bethlehem*

—. *The White Album*

Dunn, Stephen. *Walking Light: Essays and Memoirs*

Ehrlich, Gretel. *A Match to the Heart*

—. *The Solace of Open Spaces*

Eiseley, Loren C. *The Immense Journey*

—. *The Night Country*

—. *The Unexpected Universe*

Elkin, Stanley. *Pieces of Soap*

Elkins, James. *The Object Stares Back: On the Nature of Seeing*

Ellison, Ralph. *Going to the Territory*

—. *Shadow and Act*

Epstein, Joseph. *A Line Out for a Walk: Familiar Essays*

Fisher, M.F.K. *Among Friends*

Fitzgerald, F. Scott. *The Crack-Up*

Foster, Patricia. *Just Beneath My Skin: Autobiography and Self-Discovery*

Frazier, Ian. *Family*

—. *Great Plains*

—. *On the Rez*

Gass, William. *On Being Blue: A Philosphical Inquiry*

Gates, Henry Louis, Jr. *Colored People: A Memoir*

Goldbarth, Albert. *Many Circles: New and Selected Essays*

Gonzalez-Crussi, F. *Notes of an Anatomist*

Gornick, Vivian. *Approaching Eye Level*

Gutkind, Lee. *Forever Fat: Essays By the Godfather*

—. *Stuck in Time: The Tragedy of Childhood Mental Illness*

Hall, Donald. *Here at Eagle Pond*

Harvey, Steven. *Bound for Shady Grove*

Hearne, Vicki. *Adam's Task: Calling Animals By Name*

—. *Bandit: Dossier of a Dangerous Dog*

Heilman, Robert Leo. *Overstory: Zero: Real Life in Timber Country*

Hemley, Robin. *Nola: A Memoir of Faith, Art, and Madness*

Hiestand, Emily. *Angela the Upside-Down Girl and Other Domestic Travels*

Hoagland, Edward. *Balancing Acts: Essays*

—. *The Tugman's Passage*

—. *Walking the Dead Diamond River*

Kingsolver, Barbara. *High Tide in Tucson: Essays From Now or Never*

Kitchen, Judith. *Distance and Direction*

Kittredge, William. *Owning It All: Essays*

Lamott, Anne. *Traveling Mercies: Some Thoughts on Faith*

Levi, Primo. *The Periodic Table*

Lopate, Phillip. *Against Joie de Vivre: Personal Essays*

—. *Bachelorhood: Tales of the Metropolis*

—. *Portrait of My Body*

Lopez, Barry. *Crossing Open Ground*

Lynch, Thomas. *The Undertaking: Life Studies From the Dismal Trade*

Mairs, Nancy. *Voice Lessons: On Becoming a (Woman) Writer*

Malcolm, Janet. *The Silent Woman: Sylvia Plath and Ted Hughes*

McMurtry, Larry. *Walter Benjamin at the Dairy Queen: Reflections at Sixty and Beyond*

McNair, Wesley. *Mapping the Heart: Reflections on Place and Poetry*

Miller, Brenda. *Season of the Body: Essays*

Montaigne, Michel de. *Essais*

Nye, Naomi Shihab. *Never in a Hurry: Essays on People and Places*

Oliver, Mary. *Blue Pastures*

Ozick, Cynthia. *Art & Ardor: Essays*

—. *Fame & Folly: Essays*

—. *Metaphor & Memory: Essays*

—. *Quarrel & Quandary: Essays*

Pollitt, Katha. *Reasonable Creatures: Essays on Women and Feminism*

Sanders, Scott Russell. *The Paradise of Bombs*

—. *Staying Put: Making a Home in a Restless World*

Sandor, Marjorie. *The Night Gardener*

Sante, Luc. *The Factory of Facts*

Schor, Mira. *Wet: On Painting, Feminism, and Art Culture*

Schwartz, Lynne Sharon. *Ruined By Reading: A Life in Books*

Schwartz, Mimi. *Thoughts From a Queen-Sized Bed*

Sedaris, David. *Barrel Fever: Stories and Essays*

Seneca. *Letters From a Stoic*

Shacochis, Bob. *Domesticity: A Gastronomic Interpretation of Love*

Shields, David. *Remote: Reflections on Life in the Shadow of Celebrity*

Simic, Charles. *The Unemployed Fortune-Teller: Essays and Memoirs*

Sontag, Susan. *Illness As Metaphor*

—. *Under the Sign of Saturn*

Steinberg, Michael. *Still Pitching: A Memoir*

Stern, Gerald. *What I Can't Bear Losing: Notes From a Life*

Thomas, Abigail. *Safekeeping: Some True Stories From a Life*

Thomas, Elizabeth Marshall. *The Hidden Life of Dogs*

Vidal, Gore. *Matters of Fact and of Fiction: Essays 1973–1976*

Vivian, Robert. *Cold Snap As Yearning*

Weschler, Lawrence. *Vermeer in Bosnia: A Reader*

White, Bailey. *Mama Makes Up Her Mind: And Other Dangers of Southern Living*

White, E.B. *Essays of E.B. White*

—. *One Man's Meat*

—. *The Second Tree From the Corner*

White, Edmund. *The Burning Library: Essays*

White, Katharine S. *Onward and Upward in the Garden*

Winterson, Jeanette. *Art Objects: Essays on Ecstasy and Effrontery*

Wolff, Geoffrey. *A Day at the Beach: Recollections*

Woolf, Virginia. *The Death of the Moth and Other Essays*

—. *Moments of Being: Unpublished Autobiographical Writings*

—. *A Room of One's Own*

Journals, Letters, and Diaries

Adiele, Faith. *Meeting Faith: The Forest Journals of a Black Buddhist Nun*
Bass, Rick. *Oil Notes*
Bukowski, Charles. *Notes of a Dirty Old Man*
Cheever, John. *The Journals of John Cheever*
Dennison, George. *Temple*
Ellis, Edward Robb. *A Diary of the Century: Tales From America's Greatest Diarist*
Frank, Anne. *The Diary of a Young Girl*
Gauguin, Paul. *Noa Noa*
Hubbell, Sue. *A Country Year: Living the Questions*
Jurgensen, Geneviève. *The Disappearance: A Primer of Loss*
Klaus, Carl H. *My Vegetable Love: A Journal of a Growing Season*
Pepys, Samuel. *The Diary of Samuel Pepys*
Rhys, Jean. *The Letters of Jean Rhys*
Rilke, Rainer Maria. *Letters on Cézanne*
—. *Letters to a Young Poet*
Sarton, May. *The House By the Sea: A Journal*
—. *Journal of a Solitude*
—. *At Seventy: A Journal*
Silko, Leslie Marmon and James Wright. *The Delicacy and Strength of Lace: Letters Between Leslie Marmon Silko and James Wright*
Truitt, Anne. *Prospect: The Journal of an Artist*

Nature and Place

Abbey, Edward. *Desert Solitaire: A Season in the Wilderness*
Barnes, Kim. *Hungry for the World: A Memoir*
—. *In the Wilderness: Coming of Age in Unknown Country*
Bass, Rick. *Winter: Notes from Montana*
Brox, Jane. *Here and Nowhere Else: Late Seasons of a Farm and Its Family*
Burger, Joanna. *The Parrot Who Owns Me: The Story of a Relationship*
Carson, Rachel. *Silent Spring*
—. *Under the Sea Wind*
Coke, Allison Adelle Hedge. *Rock, Ghost, Willow, Deer: A Story of Survival*
Dillard, Annie. *Pilgrim at Tinker Creek*
—. *Teaching a Stone to Talk: Expeditions and Encounters*
Dorfman, Ariel. *Heading South, Looking North: A Bilingual Journey*

Emerson, Ralph Waldo. *Nature*

Fabre, Jean-Henri. *Social Life in the Insect World*

Galvin, James. *The Meadow*

Gould, Stephen Jay. *Ever Since Darwin: Reflections in Natural History*

—. *The Flamingo's Smile: Reflections in Natural History*

—. *Hen's Teeth and Horse's Toes*

—. *The Panda's Thumb: More Reflections in Natural History*

—. *An Urchin in the Storm: Essays About Books and Ideas*

Hauser, Susan Carol. *Full Moon: Reflections on Turning Fifty*

—. *Sugartime: The Hidden Pleasures of Making Maple Syrup
        With a Primer for the Novice Sugarer*

Heat-Moon, William Least. *PrairyErth (A Deep Map)*

Hersey, John. *Blues*

Hoagland, Edward. *The Courage of Turtles*

Hölldobler, Bert and Edward O. Wilson. *Journey to the Ants:
        A Story of Scientific Exploration*

Hongo, Garrett. *Volcano: A Memoir of Hawai'i*

Houle, Marcy. *The Prairie Keepers: Secrets of the Grasslands*

Hubbell, Sue. *A Book of Bees: And How to Keep Them*

Huntington, Cynthia. *The Salt House: A Summer on the Dunes of Cape Cod*

Kimber, Robert. *Living Wild and Domestic: The Education of a Hunter-Gardener*

Klinkenborg, Verlyn. *The Last Fine Time*

Kooser, Ted. *Local Wonders: Seasons in the Bohemian Alps*

Lazar, David. *The Body of Brooklyn*

Lea, Sydney. *Hunting the Whole Way Home*

Leopold, Aldo. *A Sand County Almanac, and Sketches Here and There*

Lopez, Barry. *Arctic Dreams: Imagination and Desire in a Northern Landscape*

—. *Of Wolves and Men*

Lord, Nancy. *Beluga Days: Tales of an Endangered White Whale*

Maclean, Norman. *A River Runs Through It*

Martone, Michael. *The Flatness and Other Landscapes: Essays*

Mayle, Peter. *A Year in Provence*

McPhee, John. *Coming Into the Country*

Middleton, Harry. *The Bright Country: A Fisherman's Return
        to Trout, Wild Water, and Himself*

—. *The Earth Is Enough: Growing Up in a World of Flyfishing, Trout & Old Men*

—. *On the Spine of Time: An Angler's Love of the Smokies*

Mowat, Farley. *The Siberians*

Norris, Kathleen. *Dakota: A Spiritual Geography*

Philip, Leila. *A Family Place: A Hudson Valley Farm,*
    Three Centuries, Five Wars, One Family

Price, John. *Not Just Any Land: A Personal and Literary Journey*
    Into the American Grasslands

Rekdal, Paisley. *The Night My Mother Met Bruce Lee:*
    Observations on Not Fitting In

Roorbach, Bill. *Into Woods: Essays*

—. *Temple Stream: A Rural Odyssey*

Roorbach, Bill (with Wesley McNair and Robert Kimber). *A Place on Water*

Sachs, Dana. *The House on Dream Street: Memoir of*
    an American Woman in Vietnam

Spragg, Mark. *Where Rivers Change Direction*

Stepto, Robert B. *Blue As the Lake: A Personal Geography*

Thaxter, Celia. *An Island Garden*

Thomas, Lewis. *The Lives of a Cell: Notes of a Biology Watcher*

—. *The Medusa and the Snail: More Notes of a Biology Watcher*

Thoreau, Henry David. *Cape Cod*

—. *The Maine Woods*

—. *Walden*

Williams, Terry Tempest. *Refuge: An Unnatural History of Family and Place*

Wormser, Baron. *The Road Washes Out in Spring: A Poet's Memoir*
    of Living Off the Grid

TRAVEL WRITING

Bryson, Bill. *Neither Here Nor There: Travels in Europe*

Chatwin, Bruce. *In Patagonia*

Chatwin, Bruce and Paul Theroux. *Patagonia Revisited*

Gutkind, Lee. *Bike Fever*

Heat-Moon, William Least. *Blue Highways: A Journey Into America*

Iyer, Pico. *Falling Off the Map: Some Lonely Places of the World*

—. *Sun After Dark: Flights Into the Foreign*

—. *The Global Soul: Jet Lag, Shopping Malls, and the Search for Home*

Muir, John. *Travels in Alaska*

O'Hanlon, Redmond. *Into the Heart of Borneo*

—. *In Trouble Again: A Journey Between the Orinoco and the Amazon*

—. *No Mercy: A Journey to the Heart of the Congo*

Orlean, Susan. *My Kind of Place:*
    Travel Stories From a Woman Who's Been Everywhere

Stauver, Hank. *Off-Ramp: Adventures and Heartache in the American Elsewhere*

Theroux, Paul. *The Great Railway Bazaar: By Train Through Asia*

—. *The Pillars of Hercules: A Grand Tour of the Mediterranean*

New Journalism/Literary Journalism

Ainslie, Ricardo C. *Long Dark Road: Bill King and Murder in Jasper, Texas*

Almond, Steve. *Candyfreak: A Journey Through the*
    Chocolate Underbelly of America

Armour-Hileman, Victoria. *Singing to the Dead: A Missioner's Life*
    Among Refugees From Burma

Ayers, Bill. *Fugitive Days: A Memoir*

Borich, Barrie Jean. *My Lesbian Husband: Landscapes of a Marriage*

Borton, Lady. *Sensing the Enemy*

Bryan, C.D.B. *Friendly Fire*

Capote, Truman. *In Cold Blood: A True Account of*
    a Multiple Murder and Its Consequences

—. *Music for Chameleons: New Writing*

Conover, Ted. *Coyotes: A Journey Through the Secret World*
    of America's Illegal Aliens

—. *Rolling Nowhere*

—. *Whiteout: Lost in Aspen*

Conley, Dalton. *Honky*

Daniell, Rosemary. *Confessions of a (Female) Chauvinist*

Didion, Joan. *Salvador*

Donofrio, Beverly. *Looking for Mary, or, The Blessed Mother and Me*

Ehrlich, Gretel. *Questions of Heaven:*
    The Chinese Journey of an American Buddhist

Frey, Darcy. *The Last Shot: City Streets, Basketball Dreams*

Galeano, Eduardo. *Soccer in Sun and Shadow*

Greene, Melissa Fay. *Praying for Sheetrock: A Work of Nonfiction*

Gutkind, Lee. *Many Sleepless Nights: The World of Organ Trasplantation*

Haffner, Sebastian. *Defying Hitler: A Memoir*

Harrison, Jim. *Off to the Side: A Memoir*

Hayden, Tom. *Irish on the Inside: In Search of the Soul of Irish America*

Hemley, Robin. *Invented Eden: The Elusive, Disputed History of the Tasaday*

Hendrickson, Paul. *Sons of Mississippi: A Story of Race and Its Legacy*

Hersey, John. *Hiroshima*

Hochschild, Adam. *King Leopold's Ghost: A Story of
    Greed, Terror, and Heroism in Colonial Africa*

Hoffman, Eva. *After Such Knowledge:
    Memory, History, and the Legacy of the Holocaust*

Johnson, Joyce. *What Lisa Knew: The Truths and Lies of the Steinberg Case*

Junger, Sebastian. *The Perfect Storm: A True Story of Men Against the Sea*

Keneally, Thomas. *Schindler's List*

Kidder, Tracy. *Among Schoolchildren*

Kotlowitz, Alex. *There Are No Children Here:
    The Story of Two Boys Growing Up in the Other America*

Krakauer, Jon. *Into the Wild*

—. *Into Thin Air: A Personal Account of the Mount Everest Disaster*

—. *Under the Banner of Heaven: A Story of Violent Faith*

Kuramoto, Kazuko. *Manchurian Legacy: Memoirs of a Japanese Colonist*

Lamont, Anne. *Traveling Mercies: Some Thoughts on Faith*

Larson, Erik. *The Devil in the White City: Murder, Magic,
    and Madness at the Fair That Changed America*

Lavergne, Gary M. *Bad Boy From Rosebud: The Murderous Life
    of Kenneth Allen McDuff*

Lefkowitz, Bernard. *Our Guys: The Glen Ridge Rape and the Secret Life
    of the Perfect Suburb*

Lowry, Beverly. *Crossed Over: A Murder, A Memoir*

Mailer, Norman. *The Armies of the Night: History As a Novel, the Novel As History*

—. *The Executioner's Song*

Mairs, Nancy. *Ordinary Time: Cycles in Marriage, Faith, and Renewal*

Malcolm, Janet. *The Journalist and the Murderer*

McPhee, John. *Assembling California*

—. *Coming Into the Country*

—. *The Control of Nature*

—. *Encounters With the Archdruid*

—. *Irons in the Fire*

—. *Looking for a Ship*

—. *Oranges*

—. *The Pine Barrens*

—. *Rising From the Plains*

Olsen, Tillie. *Silences*

O'Reilley, Mary Rose. *Barn at the End of the World:*
    The Apprenticeship of a Quaker, Buddhist Shepherd

Orlean, Susan. *The Orchid Thief*

—. *Saturday Night*

Phillips, Caryl. *The Atlantic Sound*

Powers, Ron. *Far From Home: Life and Loss in Two American Towns*

Roach, Mary. *Stiff: The Curious Lives of Human Cadavers*

Shilts, Randy. *And the Band Played On: Politics, People,*
    and the AIDS Epidemic

Sides, Hampton. *Americana: Dispatches From the New Frontier*

—. *Blood and Thunder: An Epic of the American West*

—. *Ghost Soldiers: The Epic Account of World War II's Greatest Rescue Mission*

Singer, Natalia Rachel. *Scraping By in the Big Eighties*

Sontag, Susan. *Regarding the Pain of Others*

Talese, Gay. *The Bridge: The Building of the Verrazano-Narrows Bridge*

—. *Thy Neighbor's Wife*

—. *Unto the Sons*

Terkel, Studs. *Working: People Talk About What They Do All Day*
    and How They Feel About What They Do

Thompson, Hunter S. *Fear and Loathing in Las Vegas*

Tiberghien, Susan. *Circling to the Center:*
    One Woman's Encounter With Silent Prayer

Wells, Ken. *Travels With Barley: A Journey Through Beer Culture in America*

Wolfe, Tom. *The Electric Kool-Aid Acid Test*

—. *From Bauhaus to Our House*

—. *The Right Stuff*

Wright, Lawrence. *The Looming Tower: Al-Qaeda and the Road to 9/11*

ANTHOLOGIES

The Anchor Essay Annual, Phillip Lopate, editor

The Art of the Personal Essay: An Anthology From
    the Classical Era to the Present, Phillip Lopate, editor

The Best American Essays, annual anthology, Houghton Mifflin

Contemporary Creative Nonfiction: The Art of Truth, Bill Roorbach, editor

Essays on the Essay: Redefining the Genre, Alexander J. Butrym, editor

The Granta Book of the Family, Bill Buford, editor

Imagining Ourselves: Classics of Canadian Non-Fiction, Daniel Francis, editor

In Short: A Collection of Brief Creative Nonfiction,
    Judith Kitchen and Mary Paumier Jones, editors

*In the Middle of the Middle West: Literary Nonfiction From
    the Heartland*, Becky Bradway, editor

The Literary Journalists, Norman Sims, editor

Modern American Memoirs, Annie Dillard and Cort Conley, editors

*The Muse That Sings: Composers Speak About
    the Creative Process*, Ann McCutchan, editor

The Norton Book of Nature Writing, Robert Finch and John Elder, editors

The Private I: Privacy in a Public World, Molly Peacock, editor

Scoot Over Skinny: The Fat Nonfiction Anthology, Donna Jarrell
    and Ira Sukrungruang, editors

Sisters of the Earth: Women's Prose and Poetry About Nature,
    Lorraine Anderson, editor

Staring Back: The Disability Experience From the Inside Out, Kenny Fries, editor

The Truth of the Matter: Art and Craft in Creative Nonfiction,
    Dinty W. Moore, editor

Turning Toward Home: Reflections on the Family From Harper's
    Magazine, Katharine Whittemore and Ilena Silverman, editors

Uncommon Ground: Toward Reinventing Nature, William Cronon, editor

Unrooted Childhoods: Memoirs of Growing Up Global,
    Faith Eidse and Nina Sichel, editors

Wanting a Child, Jill Bialosky and Helen Schulman, editors

Writing Creative Nonfiction: The Literature of Reality,
    Gay Talese and Barbara Lounsberry, editors

*Writing Women's Lives: An Anthology of Autobiographical Narratives
    By Twentieth-Century American Women Writers*, Susan Cahill, editor

INDEX

Drama, 115-116
and relationships, 105
Dry, 15, 107, 122-123

E

Editing, cutting length,
   223-225
Editors, finding, 234-235
Ellison, Ralph, 46-49
Emotion
   presented as scene, 46
   in voice, 131-132
Essay
   experiencing other writer's
      I, 159
   I in, 68-69
   lyric, 207
   "On," 70, 72-73, 75, 77-82
   origin of term, 69
   translating ideas into,
      66-67
   true nature of, 74
   See also Personal essay
Ethics, in presenting characters, 95
Etymology, and metaphor,
   166-167
Excursions in the Real World, 30
Exercises
   adumbration, 174-175
   "Against" essay, 131
   analyzing scene, 82
   angry voice, 131-132, 133
   apologizing to reader, 60
   arbitrary structure, 204-05
   automatic writing, 67-68
   bumper sticker slogans, 80
   characters and telling de-
      tails, 116-117
   characters as traits, 104
   classical structure, 214
   composite characters,
      102-103
   conclusions. *See* Exercises,
      introductions and con-
      clusions
   constellations of charac-
      ters, 103-104
   creating motif, 178
   creating scene from photo,
      63-64
   creating work space, 11-13
   cutting draft in half, 224-225

cutting exposition, 58-59
day of the week, 59-60
deep thinking, 85-86
density, 192
diagramming, 211-212
dialogue, 107-108
doing nothing, 84
epistolary, 121
essay as try, 74
finding editors and agents,
   234-235
finding subjects through
   expertise, 83-84
finding ten readers, 221-222
first lines, 23-24
friendly conversation, 71
generic disclaimer, 34
getting revenge on bad
   characters, 98-99
good writing, 220
grammar, 183-186
high exposition, 78
idea notebook, 42-43
imitating voice, 133
index cards, 215-216
Internet, 145
interviews, 150-153
introductions and conclu-
   sions, 36
juxtaposition, 177
lauding positives about bad
   character, 99
letter-writing campaign,
   235-236
library research, 140, 143
living as writer, 238
mapmaking, 28-29
map story, 32
metaphor, 168-172
method writing, 132-133
monologue, 111
mosaic, 210
motion, 190
naming for details, 154-155
observation, 61-62
"On" essay, 75
outline, 211
packing away old writing, 43
poetry scramble, 170-172
precision, 197
public voice, 130
punctuation, 185-186
reading aloud, 111

reading and writing, 19-20
rejection slips, 232-233
relationships and drama, 105
research, 147-149
revisiting character, 114
rewriting from memory,
   222-223
rhythm, 195
scene, 52-53, 59
sensory, 63
sentence and paragraph
   length, 35
slang, 134
stage business, 113
story arc, 215
submitting work, 231-232
symbolic language, 177-178
talking about subject, 156
target publications, 226-227
texture, 199
time lines, 41-42
top ten secrets, 100
transcribing dialogue,
   111-112
urgency, 200-201
voice, 127-128
watching movie as scene, 60
writing about parents,
   93-94
writing circle, 21
writing schedule, 21-23
writing something awful, 83
writing truth, 61
value of, 7-9
Expectations, high, 10-11
Experimental nonfiction, 209
Expertise
   every person's, 71-74, 83-84
   in grammar, 183-185
Exposition, 92-93
   defined, 45-46, 76
   describing mother, 94
   evocative, 48
   as interruption, 51-52
   pure, 75-77
   types of, 76-77
   See also Voice-over
Exposition of opinion, defined, 77

F

Farris, Gow, 3-5, 10-11, 25-26,
   29, 32-35, 56-58, 78-79, 81,
   103, 135, 176-177, 196-197

ACKNOWLEDGMENTS

This book has a lot of makers—all the writers I've read, all the teachers I've learned from, all the students, all the editors, all the colleagues, all the friends, all the family. And speaking of family, let me start with special thanks to my dad, Jack, and to my siblings, Randy, Carol, Doug, and Janet, and of course very special thanks to my girls, Juliet and Elysia.

Thanks to my writing teachers for most of what I know (and in memory of those on this list and the lists following who have passed away): Max Apple, Harold Brodkey, Daniel Halpern, Edward Hower, Joyce Johnson, Stephen Koch, Richard Locke, Phillip Lopate, Frank McShane, Ron Powers, Susan Richards Shreve, Robert Towers.

Thanks to my writing-and-teaching colleagues for the rest: Lee K. Abbott, Andrea Barrett, Debora Black, Alice Bloom, Jennifer Boylan, David Bradley, David Citino, John Clayton, Bob Cording, Stephen Dobyns, Paul Doiron, Kathy Fagan, Melissa Falcon, David Gessner, Daniel Gunn, Peter Harris, Michelle Herman, Barbara Hope, Nicolas Howe, Robert Kimber, Georgina Kleege, Sebastian Knowles, Anthony Libby, Liesel Litzenburger, Peter Lourie, Daniel Lusk, Wesley McNair, Jeredith Merrin, Pat O'Donnell, Pamela Painter, Vince Passaro, Leila Philip, Sandra Prior, Kenneth Rosen, Richard Russo, Lore Segal, Deborah Sobeloff, Debra Spark, Edward Tayler, Melanie Rae Thon, Tom Wicker.

Thanks to my editors and agents, past and present, for many lessons learned: Darlyn Brewer, Bill Buford, Stephen Dubner, Lee Gutkind, Barbara Hanrahan,

Sloan Harris, Colin Harrison, Jay Heinrichs, Susan Kamil, Lewis Lapham, Betsy Lerner, Speer Morgan, Laurie Muchnick, Jack Schwartz, Dawn Seferian, Abigail Seymour, John Sterling, Peter Stine, Jean Tolle, Amanda Urban.

And of course, thanks to Jack Heffron, Amy Jeynes, and Lois Rosenthal of Story Press, for their smart help and sure sense of direction and clear vision with the original edition of this book, and to Lauren Mosko of Writer's Digest Books and Sarah Domet for their dedicated work on the new.

Thanks to the English Departments, administrations, and libraries at the University of Maine at Farmington, the Ohio State University, Colby College, the University of North Texas, and the College of the Holy Cross.

Thanks to the generous early readers for this project: Jennifer Cognard-Black, Lisa Dush, Kristina Emick, Beth Lindsmith, Tom Moss. Special thanks to Maureen Stanton, who helped compile the reading list at the end of the original edition.

Thanks to my brave students whose work is included herein: Jacki Bell, "Janet Bellweather," "Mindy Mallow-Dalmation," "Gow Farris," Wendy Guida, Nancy Kuhl, Jane Renshaw, Tim Rushford, Vicki Schwab, and "Chuck."

And most of all, thanks to Kristen Keckler for her quietly brilliant and inspired help on the new edition, and thanks to her folks, Barbara and Richie, and her sister, Kara, for making her so smart.